WILD HEART

WILD HEART

A TRUE STORY OF HIPPIES, HEALERS, AND HARLEYS

STACEY MARIE KERR, MD

GIRL FRIDAY BOOKS

 GIRL FRIDAY BOOKS

Published by Girl Friday Books™, Seattle
www.girlfridaybooks.com

Produced by Girl Friday Productions

Cover design: Joanna Price
Production editorial: Bethany Fred
Project management: Kristin Duran

Image credits: cover © Shutterstock/Ravshan M

ISBN (paperback): 978-1-959411-30-7
ISBN (ebook): 978-1-959411-31-4

Library of Congress Control Number: 2023900377

To Barbara, who only ever wanted to be a mother and a housewife, but let me be so much more.

Must ride to the coast
Where too hot turns to too cold.
Plum jam can just wait.

Astride Magdalena Pearl, feet firmly on the footboards, I gain speed as I roar up the on-ramp to the freeway, shifting through gears and riding the vibrations. Magdalena is my second Harley, a 2009 Softail Deluxe with almost 1600 cc of power. She replaced my little Sportster three years into riding, when I was ready to graduate to a bigger bike. Magdalena Pearl is a true workhorse. She simply wants to move in willing response to my demands, and I love her. She takes good care of me. Sometimes I stroke her fuel tank to show my love. But this is the best part—accelerating up to 70 mph. The on-ramp is only a block from my garage, but in that block, I have already become one with the bike again, getting over the what-the-fuck-do-you-think-you-are-doings and remembering I know how to ride this beast.

I ride with over one hundred horses between my legs, responding to the twist of my right hand on the handlebar throttle. My other hovers over the left handlebar and the clutch, and I am grateful for the hydraulic retrofit that accommodates my small hand. Inside my helmet, I think of where I might want to ride today, but my eyes are busy scanning the highway and all the surrounding traffic. I anticipate drivers even *thinking* about changing lanes. I avoid riding in anyone's blind spot. And I zip past bad drivers as quickly as possible. *Should I ride some beautiful roads that wind through vineyards and redwoods here in Northern California? Should I do a short ride to buy veggies at the farmstand out on Highway 116? Maybe a trip out to the coast and a ride up the Pacific Coast Highway for a bit before coming back in along River Road. I don't care. I just want to ride. And any day I ride is a very good day.*

Often while cruising, my helmet thoughts turn to writing haiku that I will memorize and later jot down in my journal—word images that capture moments on two wheels.

Men say they ride for freedom. I consider this as I ride out to the coast on a machine capable of well over 2500 rpm. Why do I ride? It's not for freedom, because I don't feel free from fear. I feel tightly bound to my hypervigilance, to the controls that keep the bike upright, to the integrity of two tires keeping me off the asphalt. I try not to think about these things too much, because fear does not make me smarter. I also don't look down at the hard road blurring under my wheels or imagine landing on that unforgiving surface.

Today, I realize that what I feel is similar to what I used to feel in the operating room with a scalpel in my hand, something I truly miss since I retired my scrubs: that huge responsibility to make every single move exactly right, knowing I have the skill but counting on vigilance and a good bit of luck to make it all work. It's what I felt delivering a difficult baby, knowing I could do this only if I gave it my full focused attention every single moment. I'm in my zone when I'm doing what I love to do and doing what I do well. I am in a position of skill and danger, and for just a while, I am daring and confident too. Riding Magdalena Pearl means riding the edge, which makes me feel completely alive.

On Magdalena Pearl, I am also seen! I am powerful again! Now that I am older, I often feel I've become invisible. People talk over me or simply don't see me. Sometimes I don't mind because this lets me get away with stuff no one ever notices. Easier to be incognito when I want to be discreet. But what I do mind is that my muscle strength is less than it was when I was twenty years old . . . or forty . . . or even fifty, for that matter. And when I'm not being seen *and* feeling that I have limited strength, I become frustrated. I just want to yell out, *Hey! Look here! I am a person and I have something to say! And why the fuck can't I open this jar of pickles?* When I am on Magdalena, I have tremendous force under my command, and I ride for power and strength.

CHAPTER 1

SUMMER IN SONOMA COUNTY

Warm sun, winter green
Magdalena Pearl and me
Great ride. Blessed be!

My life changed years ago when I tripped and fell while wearing some really cute sandals—fancy backless platform sandals with thin leather straps. At the time, I was active in community theater, and three of us were about to perform as a single character in Susan Miller's award-winning play *My Left Breast*. I was focused on memorizing some of my lines. "Is the structure of everything dissolving? I can't count on whatever it was that held me up, supported my notions, my exertions. Osteoporosis. It's hard to say the word . . . It's an old person's disease. It's the antifeminine. It's the crone."

I struggled because this particular section kept eluding my efforts to get it right. Lennie, my perceptive acting coach, reminded me that when this happens, it is often because the troublesome lines hold something personal, something that I subconsciously want to avoid. I was fifty-five years old, and by then there were probably many of those subconscious holes I could fall into. I didn't want to believe I might inherit osteoporosis from my mom, yet I couldn't help but think of her and that last day when she fell and hit her head. We wondered if her bones had simply given way and could no longer support her.

I had parked in the empty field next to the theater. Still muttering lines to myself, I got out of the car and headed to the back hatch to get a few things that I needed to take with me to rehearsal. The field had gopher holes scattered throughout, and distracted by my thoughts, I must've stepped into one of them just as I reached for the hatch latch. My ankle gave way, my foot twisted, and I felt a sharp pain as I fell to the ground. True to form, my first response was to yell "Fuck! Fuck! Fuck a Duck!" and grab my stubbed toe. Except it wasn't a stubbed toe. Picking my left foot up in both hands to assess the damage and gently remove the sandal, I felt the foot sag into my hands like a loose bag of marbles. Was I imagining this? I felt again. Nope—marbles. *Shit.*

The thin leather strap had snapped all four long toes right down the middle of my foot, and I could readily feel each break. As a practicing physician in emergency rooms, I had seen plenty of fractures, and I knew I was going to go into shock within minutes—shock that would leave me shaking and dysfunctional with pain—so I used years of trauma training to move into action. *Got to get back into the front seat of the car before I can't move again. Got to call for help. Need an X-ray. Move while you can. Get help now.*

I crawled on my hands and knees around the side of the car, and using my arms and one good leg, I pulled myself up into the passenger's seat. Grabbing my phone, I called my friend, who lived about five minutes away, and told her

I needed help. Like, *now*. Once I knew she was on her way, I called the play's director.

"I'm out in the parking field and can't be at rehearsal today—I fell and have to go to the ER."

Within minutes the whole cast was surrounding my car, peering in the windows, commiserating about my situation, and making me the star of an unscripted show, but I put on a brave smile and assured everyone I'd be just fine.

"You all just go on without me, and I'll be at rehearsal as soon as I'm fixed. Might have to move the opening date back a bit though." I laughed through the pain that had started to hit with a vengeance.

It took surgery to repair the damage done to my fragile bones by a simple thong sandal strap. By then, it was pretty clear I had inherited Mom's osteoporosis, along with her eyes, her face, and her love of theater. The diagnosis pissed me off. I wasn't ready to be old. I wasn't ready to be frail. I wasn't ready to be a crone!

I started medication to protect what bone integrity I had left. I considered my lifestyle options. Should I get super careful? Wrap myself in Bubble Wrap, get flat-soled shoes, make sure there were no rugs to trip over in my home? I resisted. I was only in my midfifties and had plenty of life ahead of me. Wrapping myself up for safety's sake was simply not going to happen.

Instead, a year later, after two surgeries and several months of physical therapy, I signed up for a motorcycle training course over at the Sonoma County Fairgrounds. My muscles were not fragile, and as long as I didn't fall, my bones would be just fine. I had ridden a motorcycle years ago when I was in college, but after mistaking first gear for fourth, and doing a wheelie that totaled the bike, I had not tried again. Now I was ready. After years of working as a mother, a teacher, and a family physician, I had finally reached a time in my life when I could pursue interests simply for the sake of the joy they bring, and riding on two powerful wheels was my definition of pure joy. And while being on the back of someone else's motorcycle was exhilarating, I wanted the freedom of riding my own. I wanted fun without filters.

A two-day course of riding around in circles in the county fairgrounds parking lot, weaving among an array of orange cones under close supervision, taught me the basics of switching gears, braking, taking turns, and managing emergency stops. After a couple of lectures about the rules of the road for motorcycles, I was ready to take the test. I passed the written test and then the riding test on a borrowed highway Honda, which was the closest bike they had to the Harley I wanted. The grinning instructor congratulated me.

"Great, Stace! Now you're ready to ride in any parking lot in California!"

I agreed. Parking lots only. The thought of riding a motorcycle out on the streets and highways was still terrifying. But that was the point: facing my fear, refusing to accept you-can't-be-too-careful-now-that-you-are-fragile, and living life as fully as I ever had.

Two of my former patients, Tim and his wife, Mary, had become good friends, and Tim was a Harley dude who rode, built, and loved his motorcycles. He was a big, burly, tattooed man with a kind sense of humor that just never stopped. I'd loved riding on the back of his bike; he was my enthusiastic motorcycle hero. So I decided to call him.

"Hey! I'm going to buy a Harley! Will you help me?"

"Yes—now?" I could hear him set some kind of heavy tool down and envisioned him in his garage, where he had probably been working on his own bike.

"Definitely! Like . . . *right* now!"

"Okay then. I'll just finish this tune-up here and be right over to pick you up."

We went together to the Harley dealer, me riding on the back of his bike, free to stretch my arms out wide and pretend I was flying all the way to the next town. Once there, I eagerly entered the showroom, where my eyes caught sight of a gorgeous cobalt-blue Harley Sportster 883. It wasn't as big as Tim's Fat Boy, so it wasn't that intimidating. I took it for a test ride and didn't freak out after riding my very first Harley. In fact, I fell in love. I fell in love the way a young girl does when someone loves her back, when she just can't believe her good luck. I signed the papers. I gave them my credit card and made a financing deal. And then I named her Boudica, after a badass ancient warrior queen.

I followed Tim back home again. He had reminded me to use my swivel-head to keep an eye out for road hazards and traffic, but on that first ride, it was all I could do to hold on tight and keep the back of Tim's bike in my sights. I was terrified, riding my very own motorcycle out on public roads. But I was also fueled by the thrill. When we got home, he encouraged me and kept telling me that all I needed was miles. Miles of experience. Miles in the saddle. Just miles.

So I rode. All that summer I put the miles on Boudi. Tim and his friends had a riding club called Wind & Fire, a group of mostly retired firefighters who all rode Harleys. He would call and say, "We're coming to get you—be there in half an hour! Let's ride!" and I would gear up. I didn't care where we rode. I just needed those miles. And slowly but surely, I got comfortable. I learned to pay attention to the 360-degree-surrounding hazards like rapid lane changers, debris in the road, potholes, vehicles behind me that didn't see me, and sudden traffic stops. I learned the cultural expectations of riding in a group, like riding in staggered formation, signaling the riders behind me when there were hazards in the road, and riding with the flow so the herd of motorcycles could cruise smoothly in formation down highways. I was accepted by the other riders in Tim's group and taken care of like any newbie should be.

Once, he took me to ride with the local chapter of the Hells Angels. They welcomed any friend of Tim's, and that made me feel really cool, but I was terrified I'd do something stupid or accidentally ram into one of their bikes. The thought of damaging a Hells Angel motorcycle was horrifying. I couldn't even park my bike when we stopped along the way at a dive bar because backing up safely in between all those other bikes, and looking over my shoulder without getting off balance, was way too challenging. But then there was Tim, facing me, straddling my front wheel and steadying my handlebars to guide me back. I was only too aware of all the other riders watching us while I was nervously wondering, *Why am I not going anywhere?*

Then Tim leaned forward until his face was right in front of mine, inches from my face shield. He looked me in the eyes and calmly said, "Now, Stacey, it'd help if you took that death grip off the brake."

I survived that ride with the club but never rode with them again. Too much stress and not my style.

Another time, I told Tim I was afraid of riding River Road, a bucolic, two-lane winding road that follows the course of the Russian River from inland vineyards all the way to the Pacific Ocean.

"Why's that?" he asked.

"Because there was a fatal motorcycle wreck there a couple of weeks ago . . ."

"Then that's where we ride today!" he replied. He would do that. He would take me safely where I was afraid to go. When I rode, I forgot about being fragile. I forgot about being afraid of crashing and ending up forever disabled. I felt strong and capable and brave. One day I would be brave even when Tim wasn't there to support me. I would be brave enough to ride alone.

One afternoon, coming home from a ride with Wind & Fire through the vineyards of Sonoma County, I was at the back end of the ride, riding sweep. As the group rode into town and came to a busy four-way intersection, I found it a bit jarring to be in so much traffic after riding in the quiet countryside for those few hours. But this was part of the deal—handling whatever the road served up. The others made the light and rode on ahead, but I got stopped when it turned red. Tired and not as focused as earlier in the day, I unconsciously handled Boudi as if she were a bicycle, not a huge Harley. I casually leaned her over onto my left leg as I stood there waiting for my turn to go. But Boudi was not a bicycle. At almost six hundred pounds, she was a super-heavy machine that, when leaned even a little, wanted to fall right over on her side. Which is what she did. So suddenly there I was, the light now green, with my Harley on the ground completely blocking an ever-growing line of cars behind me. I was creating a traffic jam on one of the busiest intersections that side of town.

Panicked, I started going through the motions of ergonomically picking her up off the asphalt. *Blast it!* The YouTube video I'd watched had said that *anyone* could pick up a bike if they did it right. And I tried. I really did. I turned my back to the side of the bike, bent my knees into a squat, and grabbed the front handlebar and the rear foot peg. Keeping my back straight, I tried to walk backward on my heels, hoping I would feel the bike lift up just like it had in the video. I used all my strength to try to lift that sucker. But my heels were taking me nowhere, and Boudica wouldn't budge. Hiding inside my helmet, I was thankful for the privacy because I could feel my face burning in embarrassment and shame. I imagined I could hear everyone at that crowded intersection watching me and commenting. *Girls. Shouldn't ride if they can't handle a big bike.* Or, *Isn't she cute, trying to be strong.* Or, *Glad I'm not her . . . wonder how she's gonna get out of this mess!* My riding buddies were miles down the road by then, and I was scrambling in panic mode.

Suddenly, there was a voice behind me. I turned and looked over my right shoulder.

"It's okay," the man said. "My first one was a Softail." And then he easily got my six-hundred-pound Sportster upright on two wheels again.

This was one of many motorcycle lessons I would learn: there are angels out there on the road. And I was lucky enough to find one that day.

As I got back astride the bike and prepared to take off again, Tim came roaring up from the other direction. He had noticed that I was no longer with the pack and had come back to get me. Two angels. Saved.

A few years later, I would be in the office of an osteoporosis specialist, discussing the results of a year of bone-building medicine I had injected into myself. His words were music to my ears.

"Stacey, if you fall off the Harley and break, it won't be because you have osteoporosis. It will be because you fell off a motorcycle." Now that was a risk I was willing to take. With joy.

. . .

I learned early on that riding with friends was more fun, and my friend Nancy and I became a motorcycle gang of two in Sonoma County: two women newbies to the sport, embracing the road and finding strength in each other. *What the fuck were we thinking?* Middle-aged, but still young in our hearts and souls, we handled our big Harley-Davidson bikes with cautious bravery.

We called our motorcycle club Los Locks, named after Goldilocks, because we only rode when it was Just Right. Not too hot, not too cold, not too weekend busy, not too unfocused or stressed. Just Right. Otherwise, we would meet for lunch, like normal women do. Our logo was a bright pink skull with pigtails. For our hand signal, we would form two Ls with our open palms and outstretched thumbs to signify our sisterhood. We remained a gang of two until Nancy sold her bike to pay for her divorce, and she never bought another one.

But before that happened, she and I went to an annual Thanksgiving event created by the Sea Ranch Girls, a group of women whose core had formed during residency training in family medicine. Over the years, we continued to bond through life-and-death doctor lessons, the addition of new partners and like-minded friends, and regular gatherings at Sea Ranch—a planned community that hugs the rugged California Pacific coast just south of the Mendocino County line. We have met up there every summer and again every fall, where we rent a large house, drink wine, prepare and devour amazing food, take long walks along the bluffs to catch up with one another, and give thanks for the community and love we have nurtured for decades.

That Thanksgiving, I found myself at a table with two women I hadn't seen in a year or two. Joan and Kristin had both trained in the same family medicine residency as the rest of us and were now working for the Indian Health Service in Arizona. While Nancy and I shared some of Los Locks' latest adventures on bikes, the others at our table were hanging on our every word, excited that two of us were stepping out in such an unconventional way. After all, most of these women were doctors who had worked the emergency room and had seen what motorcycles could do to a person. These women rode high-end bicycles, not motorcycles. They listened to us with worry they tried to hide, some judgment, and maybe even a little bit of envy.

Then, while refilling Joan's wineglass with a fine local cabernet, Kristin spoke up, perhaps reacting to the group's worry and envy. "Joansie and I have motorcycles too!"

"What?" I cried out. "You both ride?!"

With a big smile that only Kristin could pull off, she replied, "Yep. We just started riding last summer. The wide-open roads of the Southwest are perfect for motorcycles!"

And so it began. The rest of that Thanksgiving dinner was spent talking two wheels and hatching a plan for Joan, Kristin, and me to ride together, our hearts racing and our dreams taking on color as the possibilities unfolded. It was bittersweet, knowing that Nancy would not be able to join us. Through both Tim and Nancy, I had learned that riding motorcycles is best when done in a flock of riders that moves in synchronicity, communicating telepathically, all sharing the same asphalt and talking about it later over fine food and good wine. I would miss Nancy, but I was thrilled that Boudica and I had found our new flock. Three women, three bikes, and thousands of miles ahead of us.

CHAPTER 2

RED ROCK ROAR, 2007

What I tell myself
when riding with my posse
Note: Ride your own ride.

The first reality check came when Joan said I should pack a rainsuit. *Rainsuit?* I had never considered wet riding as part of the deal, just idyllic runs through gorgeous landscapes in perfect weather, Los Locks–style. But when you are out on a road trip and have to get somewhere to eat and sleep that night, you just might have to ride through 40 mph cross-winds and driving thunderstorms. Going on long motorcycle trips is a combination of backpacking and road-tripping. This was not Los Locks fairyland. This was the Great Unknown. Anything could happen.

I did not want to ride solo, alone on a motorcycle for hours and hours down endless highways, so I was getting ready to haul Boudica on a trailer all the way from Northern California to Tuba City, Arizona, where Joan and Kristin worked and lived on a Navajo Nation reservation. Standing in my garage, in that area I came to call the Bat Cave because it was where I would magically turn into a motorcycle girl, I looked at the piles of gear that took up all the available open space, and I thought, for the umpteenth time, *What the fuck am I doing? Am I being foolish here? I hope I don't kill myself.* And then I took a deep breath and forged ahead. That was the only option at this point: go forward. This is the cardinal rule of riding a motorcycle: As long as I'm moving and as long as I have forward momentum, I will not fall down. Stopping is the problem.

So I moved forward. Boudica, even though she was only one year old, had been serviced and was ready to go. Now it was time to pack. Leathers, including chaps. Cool gloves. Warm gloves. Silk liners. Socks, underwear, riding clothes and lounge clothes. Bluetooth speaker, phone charger, camera, first aid kit, and my journal. Hiking shoes, earplugs, tire gauge, water bottle. Rainsuit. Courage. Rechargeable courage.

Preparations had actually started weeks before the packing with many emails back and forth between Arizona and California. I do like to have plans; they make me feel held, which is comforting, and Joan and Kristin felt the same way. This was a good sign—already we were in alignment. I hadn't really known or spent time with Joan and Kristin when we'd all lived in the same town, because they were still in medical training while I was already out running my own practice as a family physician. Then they'd gotten married, and although their wedding was right near my home in wine country, it was just a year after I got divorced, and I wasn't going to any weddings. I was still busy climbing out of divorce depression and flying solo for the first time in twenty years, and I couldn't take all those big, happy gatherings celebrating life partners' commitments; they were my version of hell at the time. I heard it was the best wedding ever, and I believed it, and now I could feel their energy. I could see the respect and integrity they carried for each other. And I was willing to join them on the road. Would I feel like a third wheel? Would I offend them with my independent ways? We would soon see if we were a riding match.

Kristin took the lead in plotting our route based on beautiful roads, national parks, daily mileage, and excellent B&Bs within walking distance to good food each night. Her planned route would take us first to the North Rim of the Grand Canyon, then into Zion, onward to Capitol Reef, Arches, Moab, Needles, and finally back home to their place in Tuba City. I felt safer with all the reservations made ahead of time, taking the *Where shall we stop and sleep?* concerns off the table. There would be plenty of other unexpected worries along the way without that one looming.

It would take a couple of days to haul my trailer to them, and I'd never done this before. Riding a motorcycle is one thing, but loading, hauling, and unloading the bike is another. I'd had a hitch installed on my SUV, and that ball hitch looked both promising and threatening at the same time. I still had to rent a trailer—but not just any trailer. A motorcycle trailer, one low enough to the ground to load a bike. And this is where I got overwhelmed. I could not imagine pulling all this together. *Have I bitten off more than I can chew?* I called Tim.

"Hey, Tim . . . I think I need help here. I have to load Boudica onto a trailer and haul her to Arizona and I don't know if I can do that."

"Aw, Stace! We can do *any*thing! Don't you worry—we'll get it done."

"Yeah, but I've never hauled a trailer before, and I don't know if I can even get this bike up onto one. Do I need a special license to do this?"

"You can pull a trailer," he said with a laugh. "You tellin' me that you can save a life but you can't drive a car with a trailer hitched to it? And no, you don't need a special license. You're funny!"

"It's different!" I argued. "This is out on the road, with traffic, for hundreds of miles going 70 mph with my precious cargo out there in the elements. And I'm going it alone, Tim."

"It's okay, Stace," he replied. "I'll help you."

With Tim's assurance in my back pocket, I drove over to the local U-Haul to rent a motorcycle trailer. When I joined the salesman in the yard to see what they had available, I came up with some yang energy that made me swagger a bit like I had this all under control. *Aha. Hmmm. A trailer. Yep. Open, no cover. That's good. Cool.*

"This will do me just fine," I said, as if I knew exactly what I needed. It was all a show, partly for him but mostly for my own insecurities. I really had little idea because this was the very first time I'd looked at a trailer at all. Tie-down anchors—four points—ramp for loading. *What's the pitch of that ramp? Is it so steep that my low-riding Sportster 883 will catch on that top edge on the way up?* I hid all my fear by remembering Tim's words—*we'll get it done*—and put down the cash deposit to reserve the trailer. But the reservation did not calm me; it simply upped the ante. I was committed now. I had no room to be overwhelmed.

Once I finished packing, it was time to load Boudica onto the trailer. I'd be leaving at 5:00 a.m. the next morning to get in a good long first day on the road, so I called Tim and asked him to meet me at the house to load the night before. But first came the challenge of bringing the trailer home. The U-Haul dude taught me how to hook it up to my brand-new ball hitch, and together we checked the brake lights and turn indicators. All systems were go, so I jumped in the driver's seat and slowly . . . very slowly . . . eased forward out of the parking lot and onto the Santa Rosa city streets. I was looking in the rearview and side mirrors as much as out the windshield, making sure the trailer was still back there and not trusting any of this new rig system yet. Yep, it was still following me like a baby duck behind its mother. It wasn't falling off the hitch. Going everywhere I went. Just like it should.

By the time I got home, I'd had a full fifteen minutes of experience hauling a trailer. I was an old hand now . . . until I realized I had to back it into my driveway so we could load the bike. Tim was already there, waiting for me and ready to assist. I was intimidated—backing up a trailer with precision on a residential two-lane street with steady traffic coming from both directions. My neighbors came out to watch, which only increased my performance anxiety. I really wanted to do this smoothly; I needed to be proficient for my audience. I tried to recall the technique I'd been told. *Turn the steering wheel in the opposite direction you want the trailer to go?* I'd always been directionally challenged, and anyone who's traveled with me knows that if I say, "Turn right," you'd probably be better off turning left.

It took me at least seven tries. Cars and trucks stopped as I blocked the street. They watched my attempts, some drivers stone-faced tolerant, some grinning at my efforts, and some even cheering me on. In between failed attempts, I would pull back out onto the street and over to the curb so everyone was able to pass on by before I went at it again, and eventually, I got that sucker straight onto the driveway where it needed to go. I was sweating bullets, Tim was cheering, and the drivers I'd most recently blocked were giving me a smiling thumbs-up. I felt like I'd just finished a marathon, but the race had just begun.

Tim agreed to ride the bike up onto the trailer and to teach me about tie-downs. "But if I ride it up, Stace, how are you going to get it off at the other end?"

"Kristin is tall and strong and brave," I said. "She loads and unloads their bikes all the time and promised she'd do it for me."

Riding the motorcycle felt safe to me by now; a bike wants to stay upright, and as long as it's moving forward at a good speed, it will do so. But whenever I had to go super slow, and try to control the weight with my own balance and strength, that bike would suddenly feel much bigger and stronger than I was. I had no confidence in my ability to handle Boudica without forward momentum, which meant I had no interest in attempting to load or unload that bike on my own. I knew my limits, and I wouldn't hesitate to ask for help on this maneuver. Together, Tim and Kristin would have me covered.

Tim mounted Boudica and gently rode her up the ramp of the trailer. He easily took his weight off the bike as he reached the top of the ramp so she didn't scrape the trailer bed, and I knew I would not have been able to do that. I would've been stuck at the apex with no way out other than a sideways drop. When he stopped the bike at just the right place in the middle of the trailer bed, I was in awe. I would've probably gunned the engine so hard to get up that ramp that I'd have ridden right off the front edge and into the back of my SUV. My decision to call him had been wise. It would be several years before I would be up to the task of doing this on my own, and even then I would need a spotter.

My steep learning curve was even more evident once he started teaching me about tie-downs. I had purchased four extra-large ratchet straps for this, and Tim showed me how to attach them to the most stable parts of my motorcycle, hook them onto the trailer tie-downs, and then ratchet them so tight the bike would be frozen in place. He told me to stop after I'd been on the highway for an hour or so to check my riggings and tighten them down again, because they might loosen as I drove. He told me to also check the riggings every single time I stopped, for gas, for pee, for food, for air—check the riggings! Make sure the bike is still frozen tight. And for God's sake, turn off the security system so the bike doesn't flash its lights for hundreds of miles thinking it's being stolen. All these tricks that came so naturally to him were absolutely foreign to me. I was so grateful I could cry. But I didn't. Motorcycle girls don't cry at this shit.

Finally, all my gear was packed inside the SUV, which was locked up in the driveway. Boudica was loaded on the trailer, ratcheted down tight, and stored in the garage; and although the garage door would only shut down to the level of the hitch, I was confident no one was going to crawl through the eighteen inches left open at the bottom to steal my stuff. All was secure for one more night at home and ready to head out at dawn the next morning.

Those first few miles the next day were nerve-racking, even though pulling a trailer with a precious motorcycle is really easy. I had to get used to the rattles and bangs and the weight of the loaded trailer, including the influence that the added weight had on my braking distance. All this kept me anxious and busy for the first hour or two on the road. Then I adapted. Then it felt normal. Then I actually needed to remember to be extra cautious because it became easy to forget I was hauling anything at all.

Whenever I glanced in the rearview mirror, I'd think, *Hey! Quit tailgating! Get off my ass!* Then I'd realize it was my own motorcycle on my own rig and I really did want it there—that close—that in my face. This was surreal.

I had already developed a set of rules to help ensure things continued to go well:

> *Rule #1 of hauling a trailer when you are me*: Never set up a situation where you have to back up your rig. Always find a pull-through.
>
> *Rule #2 of hauling a trailer when you are me*: Always park at motels where you can see your rig from the window of your room. You will sleep better.
>
> *Rule #3 of hauling a trailer when you are me*: Remember to respect the rig and do not get so comfortable being a badass motorcycle hauler that you forget you are pulling something precious. Do not get casual.

Following all my own rules of hauling a trailer, I pulled up to my friends' home on the reservation in Tuba City the next afternoon. I had texted when I was close, so I was not surprised to see them waiting for me out in front of their house. There stood Kristin, tall and lean, her dark hair swept back and cut just above her shoulders, her Italian coloring making her huge smile shine white against a natural tan. Joan, also a brunette with a generous smile as big as her wife's, was shorter and delightfully rounder, with a solid presence that felt trustworthy and grounded. When they laughed together, they harmonized, and I was so glad to be there, feeling their emotions deeply and knowing that, in the presence of these two women, I was safe.

After big hugs and the first round of many laughs, we all set to work to release the tie-downs and unload Boudica. Kristin climbed up onto the trailer. In a glorious display of competence, strength, and courage, she gently backed my bike off the trailer, onto the road, and then over to where their two bikes were parked in their driveway, ready to go. I knew she was terrified of hurting my precious motorcycle, because she told me so, but she sure didn't show it. She was good.

Finally, our three bikes were all together for the first time, my cobalt-blue Harley Sportster 883, Boudica; Joan's two-tone red-and-silver Yamaha V Star 650, which she'd named Thelma; and Kristin's Kawasaki Vulcan 800, charcoal gray with black trim, which of course she called Louise. These three beautiful machines would be our best friends for the next ten days.

We had agreed on a name for the run—Red Rock Roar—and I'd designed a logo to go with it. I had also printed T-shirts for the ride and temporary tattoos that would reflect our attitude without permanent labeling. We knew we were being silly, but hey—three girl doctors on big bikes was weird enough already. And we knew that the trappings could make a difference in how we felt; the shirts and tats were akin to the white coats and stethoscopes we wore as doctors. Just a couple of days later those tattoos would begin to peel off as the sweat of riding through red rock country caused our slick skin to shed.

We ceremoniously applied the tats in their kitchen that

night and finished packing for an early morning start. I slept fitfully, anxious for the next day to begin, for our ride to begin, and for the challenges of navigating unfamiliar roads on two wheels. Riding motorcycles with others is not something to be taken lightly. Riding with assholes, space cadets, or inexperienced hotshots can get you killed. Fortunately, Kristin and Joan were none of that. But the three of us *were* inexperienced, even if we were focused, and we hid our insecurities as doctors are trained to do—appearing full of calm bravado and bravery but sometimes quaking inside. I was reminded of back when I had been a newly graduated doctor and was called to assist on an appendectomy; still unsure of operating room etiquette, I would act the part while still learning protocol.

Our morning ride out of Tuba City started early. I will never forget the first moment when we all started our engines, looked each other in the eyes, nodded our heavily helmeted heads, slapped down our face guards, and pulled away from home base, with fear and courage mixed together in generous amounts. We were on our way, ready to face together whatever the road had to dish out. The day would be short on miles but long on bonding.

We had to develop our own style of riding together, and we quickly agreed on a system of signals to communicate. A bent elbow with a fist raised up and down meant "jumping up and down for joy." Riding the bike in a tight swerve pattern meant "happy dog wagging her tail" and was soon followed by the other two wagging along in synchronicity. A hand raised with one finger sticking up meant "I have to go pee." We much preferred these signals and telepathy over any radio-controlled communication system and would develop more as we found the need.

It was thrilling to be out there together. Kristin took the lead since this was her home territory, and she fell easily into a leadership position. I started out the trip in the middle on Boudica, flanked in front by Kristin on Louise and Joan riding sweep behind me on Thelma. I felt safe surrounded. The Arizona highway was two lanes, wide open with very little traffic, and perfect for three newbies. High-desert sagebrush stretched as far as our eyes could see in all directions, giving me the impression that there was nothing out there to get in our way. First stop, the famous GAP Trading Post in the Navajo Nation in Cameron. Check the gear, check in with each other, get something to slake our thirst, take a picture, then back on the bikes.

Riding in formation, staggered so sudden stops would leave enough room to maneuver around each other, we began to get more comfortable. The sight of Arizona asphalt slipping away under my tires at 60 mph no longer scared me as I got used to being out there on two wheels with nothing protecting me from the elements. Soon we were all pumping our fists, jumping up and down for joy. I drank in the beauty of the mesas on either side of the highway while the endless blue sky made me feel small perched on top of my Harley. Exposed on the bike as I was, I found myself grateful for the helmet that protected my face and served as a private space suitable for screams of frustration and cries of joy.

In some stretches, the wind whipping across the mesa was so strong it felt like it could push me right over in spite of Boudica's powerful engine. Looking in my mirrors to see if Joan was doing all right handling the gusts, I noticed her leaning over her fuel tank to decrease her wind profile, so taking the cue, I bent over—keeping both hands on the controls and peering low through my windshield as I hugged the bike. It did make a difference, and it felt risky, but it was a risk I was willing to take because those sudden, severe off-balance moments, as I corrected for the buffeting wind, were scarier than going 60 mph while lying down on the bike's tank. I'd never imagined riding through winds like those on the high-desert mesas, but I was so busy handling the bike that I had no time to give in to fear. Must keep moving forward. Must stay upright. *I will not let the wind have control over me!* Inside my helmet, I wondered what Tim would think of me now and could hear him laughing with pride, cheering me on.

Even with the challenges of high winds on the mesa, I loved the feeling of being on the edge. Pushing boundaries, stretching myself beyond where I thought my limits lay. I had limits—no wish to rappel down steep cliffs, no desire to sail across the Atlantic Ocean. But embracing and living life to the fullest, and following my own imagination and passions, was the path I had chosen many years earlier when I left my parents' home.

It was 1969: anti-war protests, free speech, civil unrest, and exciting times of change. I was a young, immature twenty-year-old, and college courses were easy enough for me, which meant plenty of time to learn other valuable life skills. Like how to drink alcohol without throwing up. How to fuck, even if I wasn't very good at it. How to sit in a nightclub smoking cigarettes and listening to jazz. Skills that led me to explore marijuana, psilocybin, LSD, and mescaline.

I was also reading Carlos Castaneda's book *The Teachings of Don Juan*, and what he wrote fit right in with my personal view of the Universe, which was that there is magic out there if only one is able to see or feel it. I had known this was true since I was very young, and I was always looking for those signs of magic, which I often found in the quiet creeks and woods near every new place my family had lived: tadpoles morphing into frogs, hard-shelled eggs hatching soft baby birds, and caterpillars turning into butterflies. I saw magic as evidence of God, and I knew there was more if I could only find it. So far, I'd found nature to be fertile territory, but humans, not so much.

Doing drugs simply for jollies was not appealing to me, but using plant medicine to open doors of perception was. I was on a mission—one that would let me grow into a full human being with all my potential realized. Even so, I probably did my share of lying around slobbering as I found my way through the counterculture of sex, drugs, and rock and roll. I loved downers and the total relaxation they brought, but not the waste of time. I hated anything related to speed; it made me dizzy, uptight, and sick. I gravitated toward powerful, mind-altering plant medicine, with some LSD and mescaline thrown into the mix.

I was a quiet tripper, often spending my psychedelic time outside in nature with just a few trusted friends. I once experienced an outdoor acid trip with a group of friends where someone hung a cocoon hammock between two trees. I crawled into that hammock, zipped it shut, and for hours watched my friends from the safety of isolation. I was hidden inside the screen, right in the center of all the action, and completely enjoyed my time observing the antics of all the trippers who had forgotten I was even there. I have always been a watcher.

LSD tabs, mescaline caps, and psilocybin mushrooms opened the door to spirituality for me, a door that I would never close again. Raised in the Christian church, I was not much interested in organized religion and its accompanying rules; I had had enough of being told what to do, what to think, and what to believe while growing up as a navy brat. The spirituality that came with psychedelics was far more magical and introduced me to the unseen and to the energy that I believed was sacred. Whenever I tripped, I discovered how intensely vivid nature's colors were, how deeply I felt music in my core, and how I could actually *see* black streaks of energy spewing out of the mouths of liars. I also found that all my muscle tension would relax as I came on to the medicine, and my shoulders and hips would move more fluidly, as if they'd been recently oiled. It was a fantastic feeling, being on psychedelics. I never had a "bad trip" and never regretted those times of discovery. The two years I spent exploring with that medicine eventually started me on a spiritual practice that became a fundamental part of my life, a pervasive point of view, a way of being that permeated everything I did from that time forward. That perspective gave me a respect for the unseen, along with the sure knowledge that magic is simply what we are unable to perceive with our limited human senses of sight and sound. But in the beginning, during those first months of experimenting, I wasn't sure how those psychedelics would further my experience with Spirit.

I started asking around: Who else had read Castaneda? Who knew about the spiritual practice of taking mind-altering drugs? I could party with the best of them, but could I find my way into a deeper practice, into better vision, into higher consciousness? Could I learn more magic and wisdom? The Universe didn't take long to respond.

It was a crisp and colorful fall day in central Missouri. A few of us were outside on the front porch of our communal house in Columbia, sitting on the old couch we'd dragged out there, passing joints, and watching the constant stream of hippies wandering past. We were gentle people, and we all believed that we could do anything we wanted as long as we didn't hurt anyone. Personally, I took the law with a grain of salt, preferring to do whatever I wanted without hurting others and without getting caught. So far, so good.

My buddy Terrell joined me, perching on the arm of the couch. He was a tall, lanky young man who was married and getting ready to welcome his first child, who would be born in our communal home while we all watched excitedly through his bedroom windows. He turned to me.

"I heard you were wondering about psychedelics and Spirit. There's a dude in San Francisco who talks about this stuff. He talks about raising consciousness, taking acid, and telling the truth. I think that's exactly what you need to do— go to San Francisco and check out Stephen Gaskin. He has this meeting called Monday Night Class where he speaks to thousands of people down at the Family Dog—you know, that rock and roll ballroom in the city where Jefferson Airplane played? Out by the Cliff House on the Great Highway? You should go."

I was totally excited to find out there were others like me, searching for Spirit and magic. I took his words to heart and began making plans. A couple of weeks later, I was out on I-70 with a hitching-buddy, putting my thumb out, headed for San Francisco. In 1969, I wasn't afraid to hitch, especially with a man along. It was a Saturday morning, and our goal was to get from Columbia to the West Coast in time for me to get to Monday Night Class.

We got all the way to San Francisco in two rides—both cars driving us through the night directly to where we wanted to go with very little downtime. We took this as a sign: *if all*

is going smoothly, surely we are on the right track. Arriving
in the Haight mid Monday morning, we found our way to a
Christian commune where they let us sleep for a few hours
to recover from the road. That is where I separated from my
hitching-buddy—he to a men's sleep room, and me to the
women's. A few hours later, I woke up on a strange cot with
plenty of time to solo hitch a ride over to the Cliff House, and
from there I walked on down the hill to the Family Dog on
the Great Highway.

I was early, so I perched on the massive seawall across
the street from the Dog for a bit, with my backpack next to
me, gazing out at the Pacific Ocean as I waited for the night's
action to begin. The sun had just set, and the fog was rolling
in; I could see it rapidly moving in on me, coming in from the
hazy horizon and quickly enveloping me in a thick mist that
made all the streetlight illuminations spread into auras. As
darkness descended, I made my way to meet with hundreds
of other hippies gathering across the street to hear Stephen
Gaskin speak.

I recognized a few friends in the crowd and joined them,
finding spots on the floor of the old concert hall. An atmosphere of anticipation mingled with the sweetness of peace
and love. Stephen was already up on the raised stage in front,
sitting on a *zafu* meditation cushion in the lotus position, pa-
tiently waiting while we filled the space. He was a very tall
and skinny man, older than me by almost fifteen years, with
long, thin light-brown hair that matched his scraggly beard
and mustache. He looked like an older one of us. We were a
young crowd, packing ourselves in tightly, mostly a mellow
and kind group of hippies. The fragrant aroma of marijuana
filled the air, and occasionally a joint passed by. We each took

a hit and passed it along. Then, when Stephen began to speak, I absolutely knew that I had come to the right place.

"I am not a leader, so don't go putting me there," he said. "I am a teacher. If you lose your leader, you could be lost. But if you lose your teacher, maybe he has taught you enough that you can go on and teach others."

I was hungry for all he had to say and listened with rapt attention and joy. I believed everything he was saying. Here was the path I had been looking for! The Family Dog felt like a church that night, and we were all reverent. In my state of heightened spiritual consciousness, I welcomed his lessons and challenge. "Being spiritual does not mean to become as esoteric and as different as you possibly can, but to become like a solvent that can melt away the differences between people until only the essential thing is left. If we really understand what we're doing, we ought to get it on and find essential agreement with anybody."

This challenge became part of my daily practice for the rest of my life; I wanted to see and connect with the essential, that basic primal part in each of us that is the same. That place where we are all one. Where superficial differences don't get in the way of communication and caring.

Stephen also spoke to us about telling the truth, about the energy we each emit as we interact with others, and how that energy has a direct effect on everyone. We were all aware of how it feels when someone is kind and how different it felt when someone was cruel. Being constantly aware of the power of *our* words and deeds was the challenge. The trick was to be aware so we could manage the energy for the good of all. He also explained how the colors and patterns and images we had all seen while tripping were actually visible manifestations of energy. He said we needed to be responsible with our words and actions, take care of each other, and get smart. It was the only way to change the world, he said, and Lord knows, the world needed changing. Our country was busy fighting an unjust war on foreign soil while people went hungry. Other people were being abused by the rich and powerful. And lies were being spread by those in authority.

I felt like he was speaking directly to me, answering questions I'd been asking since I was a young child—questions that no one yet had been able to answer. *Is there a reality I can feel but cannot see (except on LSD)? How do I learn to connect with others on a deep heart level?* He didn't rely on old stories that happened two thousand years ago. Instead, he described true spiritual practice as a stack of hole-punched computer cards, reflective of technology back then, with each individual card representing a major religion. When the cards were piled on top of each other, the holes that were aligned and went all the way through represented our beliefs: do unto others as you would have them do unto you, tell the truth, and be kind—the basics. Stephen had tripped as I had, and he'd gone to those places of pure energy that made me want to know more.

When that Monday Night Class was over, I was high on the fragrant marijuana and the crowd's energy. I was invited to stay at a friend's place in the Castro, and since I had no other plans, I agreed. There, I hooked up with a casual boyfriend, Dan, for the night, and we spent the next day drinking peyote tea while hosting a constant stream of visitors knocking at the door and asking to join the tea party. After a day of that, I was ready to move on.

Having been greatly moved by Stephen's teachings—especially those about the power of telling the truth—I decided my next move was to go across the San Francisco Bay to my parents' house near Oakland. I was so close, and I knew I had some truths to tell. I wanted to be seen and heard as a grown-up by my parents, and this felt like the perfect time to introduce them to their adult daughter. But I was not going into that alone. Dan agreed to come with me, so together we made our way toward Berkeley, and while crossing the San Francisco Bay, I prepared him for what we were headed into.

"Dan, you might just want to keep quiet and watch as this goes down. I'd appreciate another point of view because I honestly don't think I see Mom and Dad very clearly after all these years. You know, Dad is a naval captain with a career in intelligence with the CIA at the Pentagon, and now he commands the NROTC unit at UC Berkeley. I'm embarrassed that he fully supports the Vietnam War and has gas masks installed in his office above every desk. I can't talk to him about that—those masks are too offensive to me—not only their presence, but the need to have them there at all. So there are places we cannot go. My mom is sweet, but she totally defers to Dad. I aim to tell them the truth about myself so they can know their daughter and who she is becoming. It might get a bit testy. I'm sorry if you feel uncomfortable, and I sure appreciate you coming with me."

Dan, a gentle man who easily rolled with the punches in those days, laughed. "It's all good, Stace. I can handle this—it's not *my* parents . . ."

My parents' house was tucked in among eucalyptus trees in Piedmont. I had never lived in this house; they had moved there after I left home for college, so it wasn't really a home to me. But it was where Mom and Dad lived, so it was parental home base. I prepared myself to play the Good Daughter, no matter what I happened to be thinking behind my façade.

Both parents were there to greet us, opening the door before we were even up the front steps in their eagerness to see me. I introduced them to Dan, not really caring if they were offended by his long dark hair, full beard, and hippie outfit of patched jeans and a tie-dyed T-shirt. With me dressed as casual as Dan, we were in striking contrast to my parents. Mom, a full head shorter than my father, was always well put together with coordinated outfits, salon-styled short silver-gray hair, and tasteful makeup. She was the Captain's wife and had an image to uphold. Dad was in his usual "civvies"— the clothes he wore when not in uniform, and as much as he may have tried to be casual and welcoming, his formal and self-controlled mannerisms felt as stifling as ever. Although I was used to this, I could still feel my protective armor automatically go up the minute I entered the house. That armor had been in place for years, serving to hide my true feelings from my conservative parents, and it would not be easily broken. Tonight, I would at least try to crack it.

After sharing a home-cooked meal, the four of us sat in the family room for an after-dinner chat. Dan and I sat together on the little love seat, facing my parents. They were each settled in their own easy chairs, and I could see how they must spend their evenings together here in front of the fireplace, probably watching TV. Everyone seemed comfortable enough, so now was the time to tell some truths—maybe one of the first times in my whole life. I wanted them to *see* me, and I also wanted to try to melt away our differences. I began to spew truth, unaware that I might cause pain. Or maybe I just didn't care, because for once I was going to speak freely.

"I have decided that consuming animal products is not only unnecessary killing, but not good for the planet. You can feed ten times more people off a field of soybeans than you can off a field full of cattle." I parroted Stephen's words from the previous night. "So, I no longer eat meat, or any animal products, and no longer wear any leather or use any products made from animals. I don't need to kill animals to sustain myself."

Mom seemed a bit put out by this. "So that's why you didn't eat the chicken I cooked tonight. How will I feed you? I just don't know, Stacey . . ." she tapered off vaguely.

I didn't bother to answer because I was on a roll. One truth down, I took a deep breath, glanced at Dan, and then entered dangerous territory. "I am not a virgin. I've had a few boyfriends and I've used birth control, but I think you should know that I am no longer a child." Shocking, but nothing they could do about that. Except they both immediately forbade Dan and me to share a room under their roof until we were married, which was never going to happen. Two truths down. Then I crossed the line.

"I smoke marijuana, and I feel better for it. It hasn't affected my ability to get good grades or to fully function, and it *has* helped me understand more about how to get along with others."

This is when the shit finally hit the fan. Mom, already visibly pale from the diet and sex reveals, could not accept that her precious daughter used drugs. She shifted in her chair, glanced at Dad, then froze and avoided my gaze; she would silently defer to the Captain on this one. At the same time, Dad immediately lost all attempts to be casual or friendly. He became once again the stern military officer who, after a brief and ominous pause, sat up even straighter in his easy chair and spoke with terrifyingly calm and controlled words.

"This is terrible news, Stacey. Completely unacceptable. Frankly, I am very disappointed in you." He looked disgusted, as if he had just eaten a piece of rotten meat. "You must promise your mother and me that you will quit and never smoke that drug again." Years of living under that authoritarian pressure, plus the sight of my mother's stricken face, caused me to cave.

"Okay, Dad. I promise I won't smoke anymore."

My mother, too agitated to sit still any longer during this exchange, got up and retreated to the kitchen, leaving the two of us alone with Dad. Dan remained silent, but I could feel him next to me and sensed him questioning my promise. I don't think he believed it for a second.

I stopped the night's truth telling right there, before my truth about doing LSD or mescaline or peyote tea. Before my truth about the spiritual path I was beginning to follow. Before my truth about the revolutionary anti-war ideas I supported. It was good I stopped. I was doing serious harm, giving my parents too much to worry about and too much information they couldn't understand. I had wanted to melt away differences, not burn bridges, and the lesson I learned that day was that telling the truth is important, but just as important is that the truth must be kind. I had yet to learn the art of telling compassionate truth.

With nothing left to say, Dan and I quietly retreated to separate rooms, and I found myself alone in the guest room, realizing that I had just told a lie. I *was* going to smoke marijuana again. As a matter of fact, I wanted to go outside with Dan as soon as possible and toke up while we talked about the truth-telling talk I'd just bombed. I could not let that lie stand. It sat out there, ugly as a black hole, ruining everything I had hoped to achieve. Without wasting another minute, and before I could chicken out, I returned to the family room where Mom now stood next to Dad's chair, both still reeling from my reveals.

"I came home to tell the truth. And the truth is, I will be smoking marijuana again. It is good medicine for me, I see no harm in it, and I like it. I'm not going to lie to you. I am sorry, but I do not want to lie anymore."

Dad, after a big sigh, looked first to Mom and then at me. "Then you will have to leave this house. You may return when you are no longer using drugs and when you are living a life-style that we approve of." My mother didn't say a word. The Captain had spoken, and his word was law.

Fine by me. I went off to gather my backpack and to get Dan out of the other guest room. I told him we had to go. It looked like we'd have a chance for that toke after all. As we walked down the hallway toward the front door, Mom came from the family room and reached out to me. Holding my face between her two tiny Mom-hands, she looked up at me with great pain showing on her face. "I could've *died* birthing you."

It was such a dramatic Jewish-mother moment—I almost laughed. But I was still sensitive to the grief I saw and the anguish I heard in her voice.

"I am so sorry, Mom, but I need to make my own decisions now. I love you very much, but it looks like I have to go."

Peeling away from her embrace that night, I left the house to pursue a life free of their fearful, controlling restrictions and open to magic and adventure.

I wanted a culture that was mine. I wanted to belong to some place that felt like home, a place I never found with my parents. Neither of them was very close to other family members. My mother's name had been changed from Feinstein to

Hunt—a surname much more socially acceptable back when having a Jewish name was a serious liability, and they never went to synagogue anyway. My father had left his home in Texas and never looked back, so we rarely saw any of his relatives when we road-tripped across the country with each change of duty. Our family never even lived on base, where we might have belonged to that nomadic military culture. No. Every time we moved, we entered a new community, new schools, and a new ethos. I had no say in the matter. I had no roots.

I had wanted a chance to find out who I was, what I was meant to do with my life, and who I could be. But the military didn't care about these things. The military shaped you to be what the platoon needed, a person without choice—because choices are irrelevant when you must follow orders. For us, it was the US Navy that controlled our lives, and friends were definitely a low priority. Not useful in the greater scheme of things. Not necessary, and probably a liability. I needed friends I could count on, and this denial may have ultimately created the strongest driving force of my life: my need to deeply be part of a community.

When I was ten, we were living in Japan on Kamakura Yama in a traditional Japanese house. Dad was at sea serving with the Seventh Fleet, and I was happier than I could ever remember in my short life. Sometimes, he wrote letters home, including a piece of Wrigley's Juicy Fruit gum. "Give this to Stacey," his note would say, "if she's been a good girl."

My friend Martha and her family lived near us on the Yama, and she and I spent hours playing in the rice paddies, getting good and muddy while we hunted tadpoles. She was the best friend I'd ever had, and that friendship was my lifeblood. Until her father and mine were given orders. We would be moved thousands of miles away from each other, and there was nothing we could do or say about it. Like my dad, I was considered the property of the US Navy, and my life was shaped by the military's needs for an aviator, a special weapons officer, or an intelligence officer—all roles my father ultimately played in the course of his career. Our family had to go along for the ride. There was no negotiating.

As I stood alone in the road in the middle of the Yama, I watched Martha waving at me through the back window of her car, her warm and familiar face disappearing into the distance. My heart broke for the first time in my young life. It was not just the loss of my friend; I had moved away from more friends than I could count. It was my newfound realization that I had no power, that I had no voice, and that what I felt did not matter.

In those moments, I abandoned my voice. I buried my feelings. I let my budding power fall away, faced with the futility of owning it. Letting go of my power when I was so young, I buried it deep, and I was not even aware I had lost something so essential.

While my mother grieved my exile, so many years later, I set off on a path with the intent to fill the basic needs I had lacked while growing up in my father's house: a strong community, a sense of my own self-worth, and my voice again. If cannabis was the catalyst for this change, so be it.

This was just the first of many times cannabis would shape my life. For years, I used it as a tool for personal growth and spirituality. I used it to change my perspective when needed, to relax, and to allow deeper feelings and thoughts to bubble up. With others, I used it to encourage deep conversations and creativity. As I matured, I learned to use it with clear intention, making sure I was being conscious rather than simply becoming a habitual stoner. I did not use cannabis when I was practicing medicine, firmly believing that those two states of mind are not compatible.

Even years later, on that first day of Red Rock Roar, as we headed out into the national parks of Colorado on two wheels, I had some cannabis flowers in my saddlebags. I didn't smoke when I was riding, preferring not to mix my highs, but I sure did enjoy it in the evenings when the bikes were parked and I was settling into another strange bed in another strange town. I slept deeply if I toked once or twice before bed. And I needed to sleep if I was going to handle the next day on the road.

The first time I ever tried to smoke cannabis, long before I'd made my way to San Francisco and Stephen's Monday Night Class, I was with Carolyn, an angel who helped me grow out of the feral state I was in when I'd first left home. She had no idea she would become the friend who would show me how to grow up when we met the day I moved into the dormitory my first year of college. While it took some time to become friends, we eventually bonded deeply after our early days together earning money as nude models for the life-drawing classes at the university. And although we were different in many ways, including having opposite body types—she was short and round, and I was tall and lanky—we ultimately traveled our life paths together for many years.

Before Carolyn, I never knew how to sustain a long friendship and relied on moving miles away to escape conflict. When I got to the university, I found myself getting so frustrated with other girls in the dormitory that I would pound on their doors, loud and feral. After going through

three roommates, I ended up in a room by myself because
no one else wanted to share a room with me. And that was
fine—people were strange and confusing.

My dorm room was across the hall from Carolyn's, where
she and her friends would disappear behind a closed door for
hours, finally emerging with laughter and always seeming to
have had fun together. I wanted to have fun too, but I wasn't
invited. Years later, Carolyn would tell me they all thought
I was a narc put there to bust them, but I wasn't. I was just
lonely. And yet, in my loneliness, I was safe, so I kept quiet
and didn't try to crash their party.

When I returned for my sophomore year of college, I was
once again assigned a room across the hall from Carolyn.
But we had both grown up a bit, and I was no longer suspect.
Enough nights coming in drunk, enough dates with different
boys, and all those typical college pranks seemed to add to
my credibility, so the day came when I was invited to join
Carolyn and her friends in her room. It was a mirror image
of mine—a typical dorm room with twin beds, two desks and
dressers, and a window that looked out onto the campus. She
and her roommate had decorated the room with Indian bed-
spreads, candles, and incense. On one of the desks was a tray
with rolling papers and leafy cannabis, and when I came into
the room, Carolyn was perched there rolling a joint.

"Hey there," I said as a way of introduction to the four
girls already there. I was a bit shy since this was my first time
in her room.

"Hey! Take a seat on the bed! I'm just rolling a joint here,
be ready in a minute."

I had never seen marijuana but was definitely interested.
I sat down and was impressed as I watched her expertly roll
dry leaves into a smooth fatty. Someone else put a record

on the turntable, and soon the Beatles were singing "With a Little Help from My Friends" and Carolyn was lighting the joint. Using the same match, she lit a candle that was shaped like a little black cat. They both burned steadily while the joint made its way around the room. I watched how the other girls took tokes off the joint, so when it came to me, I mimicked their moves. Nervous about the smoke, my first toke was very small, but it tasted quite good. It went down easy, no cough, and was much better than the Tareyton cigarettes I was smoking at the time. The next time the joint came around to me, I was braver and took a deeper drag, reclining on the bed as I relaxed into the scene. The record on the turntable finished, someone replaced it with another, and soon we were all listening to the Beatles taking us "Across the Universe," watching that black cat slowly melt into a shapeless blob of wax.

When the album was over, we decided to go out and get something to eat. This time I was a part of the gang that erupted out of Carolyn's room, joking and laughing with each other as we rode the elevator six floors down to the main lobby of the dorm. I was being accepted as part of a gaggle of girls, and it felt good. I never wanted to look back. I wanted to be with these friends forever. I still did not know how, but I knew it was what I wanted.

Carolyn also gently introduced me to LSD, mescaline, and peyote—medicine that would open my doors of perception, forever changing the way I saw the world. I continued to get good grades toward my degrees in elementary and special education while having plenty of time for extracurricular activities. At the end of that year, when we moved out of the college dorm, we found a little house in town to rent, and pretty soon our place became ground zero for a delightful band of peaceful hippies who forged strong friendships that would last for years. Carolyn and I made a pact in those early years: we would find each other when we were old, sit on the front porch, and brush each other's hair. She knew me before I knew how to be kind to others, she helped me grow up, and whenever I looked into her eyes, I found peace. She was family to me, but it was only years later that I would realize what I felt for Carolyn was a true sisterhood.

Decades later, I was beginning to discover another sisterhood—this one with Joan and Kristin. Together, we had made it through the first unexpected road-trip challenge of our journey with high, gusty winds on the mesa, and we had arrived late that afternoon at the North Rim of the Grand Canyon and checked into our digs at the Kaibab Lodge. As we shared food, wine, stories, and laughter, I realized how very lucky I was to have such good friends. But it wasn't all luck; I had learned how to work hard for significant, lasting, supportive comrades—creating community from a lonely childhood that not only had no roots but a lack of skills in how to be a friend.

Later, as I lay in bed, I let images float through my mind of that first day's ride—the views, the comforting sight of Kristin in front of me and Joan behind, the road with twists and turns we'd navigated. Something about hours riding Boudica had relaxed my muscles and made me feel like my whole body had been massaged, as if I'd spent the day on one of those vibrating beds that used to be popular in motels. My reflections of that day's ride slowly transitioned into thoughts of previous escapades, and I drifted into a memory of one of the most life-changing travel adventures: my arrival at The Farm in Summertown, Tennessee.

• • •

My first view of The Farm was from the driver's seat of my little five-window International Harvester school bus, which I'd named Edward. The bus was my self-built traveling home, my turtle shell. The seats had all been removed when I bought the bus with college graduation gift money, and I had set to work to make it my own with a built-in double bed/storage box, a tiny kitchen, a bookshelf, and a woodstove complete with stovepipe sticking up through the roof. After a few solo adventures that took me from Kansas City to Canada, I drove Edward from Columbia, Missouri, to Tennessee in 1971.

During the year that passed since I had hitched to San Francisco and seen Stephen Gaskin at Monday Night Class, I'd finished my college degree. In that same year, the hippies from Monday Night Class had hit the road in what would become known as The Caravan—a long string of more than fifty converted school buses traveling twelve thousand miles across the United States, following Stephen on a national speaking tour. They had passed through my college town and urged me to drop out and join them, but I was so close to finishing by then that I refused and stayed to complete my degree.

When The Caravan got back to San Francisco four months later, they realized they had become a village and a church. Babies had been born on the road, spiritual agreements had been forged, and there was no way everyone could go back to the separate lives they'd been living before. Besides, there was work to do if they were going to make a difference, and that work had to be done as a community. They knew that land in Tennessee was cheap, so everyone got back into their buses, drove to Tennessee, and pooled what money they had to buy land. There they could live and work together to fix what was wrong with the world. The seventeen hundred acres, sixty miles south of Nashville, became The Farm, and it had been settled for only a few months by the time I arrived in Edward.

The Gate was open, so I pulled through slowly and parked in front of The House, a no-frills structure with a sheltered porch that stretched across the front of the building. A couple of long-haired, bearded hippies came out to greet me, and while I didn't know either of them, they looked familiar. All long-haired hippies looked familiar to me.

"I'm Stacey, and I've come to join The Farm," I called out. I climbed out of my bus and made my way up onto the porch. "I was at Monday Night Class and had some stuff to finish, but now I'm here to join up." I fit right in—long, dark hair past my waist, unshaven legs and armpits, 501 button-fly Levi's, a T-shirt, no bra, and a big smile. No leather. No meat anywhere. The scent of marijuana in everything I owned.

"Well then, you better come on in and talk to Stephen," said one of the men, so I followed him inside. Stephen was sitting in a big chair next to the woodstove in the living room, surrounded by a roomful of young adults, holding court. He was as I remembered from San Francisco—a half-generation older than me, tall and lanky with long, straggly hair, a scraggly mustache and beard, and a piercing gaze that seemed to look right into my most secret places. His charisma was thick, and I was in awe being this close to someone so powerful. This is what I had come for, my chance to talk to Stephen directly and to join the community.

"I was at Monday Night Class but went back to finish college," I told him. "Then I got my bus together and here I am, wanting to join The Farm to help save the world. I'm ready to work hard and be part of the solution rather than remain part of the problem."

The problems were many in those days. We were still fighting in Vietnam, still working for free speech and basic women's rights. People around the planet were starving while the US was rich. I knew I was guilty—guilty of being an entitled American, guilty of having enough, guilty of being a military brat who unintentionally supported the military-industrial complex. I was guilty of being the daughter of a naval intelligence officer who supported all the unspeakable things the government was doing. I needed to work hard to atone for all my sins, and The Farm was the place to do it.

Stephen seemed to look into my soul as I stood there in front of him. We gazed at each other for a good long time while I squirmed in my vulnerability. *This is the man who could replace my father in guiding me through life.* I felt seen and exposed at the same time, and although I wanted this teacher to see me, I was also afraid of what he saw. I thought he could see me better than I could see myself, and that was scary. Finally, he turned to the others with his decision.

"I know I said I'd cut it off at two hundred, but she really gets it and really wants to be here, so I'm letting her in."

I didn't realize that I had been holding my breath until he spoke. With a deep sigh of relief, I relaxed my shoulders, and after looking around the room for acceptance and support, I turned back to Stephen. "Thank you." I was too overwhelmed to say more.

"Now take that little bus of yours down to the Head of the Roads and find a good place to park it," he said.

Happy to have survived my audience with Stephen, I went back out to Edward, climbed into the driver's seat, and started down the dirt road that led from The House to the main part of "town."

The Farm had no structures on its land at that time other than The House, an old barn, and an old flour mill. When hundreds of hippies in school buses landed on the property, they scattered into the woods, parking their bus homes in clearings wherever they could. I would soon learn that roads would need to be carved out and infrastructure would need to be developed. There were no other houses. No power. No water lines, although there was a central water tank. There were also no sewers. Not much at all besides green rolling hills, big fallow fields, a couple hundred hippies, and the critters that claimed the property long before we'd arrived.

As I drove slowly down the main road, I passed open fields on either side of me. The road stretched on for just about a mile until the fields gave way to wooded areas on either side with thick, tangled underbrush. I loved it already. I had longed to live in Nature and had never had the opportunity. Heck, I'd never even successfully camped out anywhere! But there I was, in my home on four wheels in the woods of Tennessee along with a community of like-minded hippies out to change the world. I had arrived in my version of heaven.

The main road led to a convergence called the Head of the Roads. From there, several dirt tracks branched out in different directions, leading to what would become neighborhoods in the coming years. I stopped and let my engine idle. *Which branch to take? Where to park this little bus so I can settle in? Who can help me out? Is there a plan? Are there rules?*

Sitting there with my engine idling, I saw a young man with a full head of dark hair and beard coming up to my bus. I opened the door, and he stepped in to greet me.

"Welcome! You come to join us?"

I told him that, yes, I was looking for a place to land.

"Why don't you tuck it in over in those trees while you get the lay of the land and decide where you want to be for reals."

With that vague guidance, I pulled Edward into the trees on the edge of the clearing and called it home. There were other buses tucked in near me, but plenty of woodsy room between us, so I felt private but not alone. Now to figure out how this place worked—where did the water come from and where were the bathrooms?

As I explored the landscape, I found hippies in the woods—a few I knew and many I did not—and I saw everyone working hard to make this empty land a home. That was when I also had my first rude awakening: there was no water tap or faucet to fill my water tanks. I had imagined living in the woods would be like something out of *Bambi*, but this was harsh reality. I found out we were collecting used five-gallon pickle buckets from the McDonald's in the nearest town to haul water from a central water tank, near the Head of the Roads, to our homes, just like peasants in developing countries. Later, when we were more together, a water truck would drive around, filling tanks in neighborhoods. But for now I would have to haul my own water. If you were lucky, you had a bike to sling buckets on the handlebars, allowing ten-gallon hauls at one time. I did not have a bike. I did not even have a pickle bucket, so I needed to score one. If only I'd known, I would've brought one with me.

I also discovered that some people weren't living in buses or vans. Someone had found a place to buy army surplus tents cheap—big sixteen-by-thirty-two-foot dark-green canvas structures—and those were being set up in the woods. At least ten people could live in a single tent, and that made things much more efficient for everyone. The woods were also populated with domes and other creative dwellings. The plan was to replace all of these temporary structures with real houses someday, but first we would have to create the most important facilities to stay safe and healthy.

John the Outhouse Man was a busy dude in those early days. He was famous because he worked so hard on something we needed desperately. We had nowhere to safely shit, so John was out all day long digging holes and building platforms that were positioned over the holes. Each platform had two or three openings to serve more than one person at a time, but there were no walls or partitions to enclose them. No time for that. Besides, if you couldn't shit in front of everyone waiting in line for their turn, then you had hang-ups that were totally uncool. Cool people were not tight-asses unable to shit in front of others.

I was not cool. If this shit-in-public was part of the deal, then I definitely did not fit in. Heck, I could hardly shit in private, I was so locked up! But I couldn't let others see that part of me—they would want to "work it out" with me, and I had no idea how to do that. A bunch of hippies talking to me about my inability to shit in public sounded like hell to me. *I am not ever going to let that happen.* So I adapted. Quietly. Secretly.

Getting a little shovel out of my gear, I would forge off into the woods every few days, dig a hole, take a shit, cover it up, and slink back to my bus, where I'd stash the shovel until next time. Until all those outhouses had walls and doors, I would hide alone in the woods. This independent streak would stay with me for all the years I lived on The Farm. It was not considered cool, but it was mine.

There was no use of cash in the community, and when

I joined, I signed a written vow of poverty, agreeing that all things were held in common with the other members. Each member of The Farm stated that intention. While we did have personal possessions, like our own clothes and toothbrushes, just about everything else was considered communal property. A free store was set up near the Head of the Roads in a surplus tent, and when food was available, we could go get rations from the food lady. But there wasn't always food to be had, so we learned to ration our own stores. In fact, there were times we went hungry, and months when we had nothing but soybeans and sweet potatoes to eat. Early on, a community kitchen was created where a crew of women would spend hours baking bread, rolling huge stacks of tortillas, and cooking soybeans for those working too hard to stop to cook their own food. We were young and we could do anything.

I soon found an available five-gallon bucket and learned to haul water to my bus. I then started looking around for what I could do to help build this town. I wandered The Farm, meeting people, learning the lay of the land, and looking for a way to contribute. But it seemed there was little for me to help with. So I often walked the mile back up to The House to hang out in the living room with Stephen and the others. After all, I was there to soak up his teachings, and if there was nothing for me to do down on The Farm, being with the inner circle was where I wanted to be. We would spend hours there passing joints, talking about developing our land and saving the world, creating a community that would show the world how it could be done.

Stephen also spent hours working it out with "trippers"— people who may or may not have been unstable enough to need psychiatric medication. He thought we could cure mental illness simply by being compassionate and truthful, so

The Farm attracted a lot of unstable people. People with psychotic and bipolar disorders, and even people with schizophrenia, were all encouraged to get off their medication and get "straight." It was fascinating, entertaining, and a true learning experience to watch Stephen and others talk with the endless stream of people who came to The Gate.

I had only been there a week or two when a young man named Daniel approached me. "Hey, would you be willing to move out of your bus? I mean, you're a single woman who really doesn't need privacy, and I have a new girlfriend. Marjorie and I need a place to be a couple, and you don't. Would you be willing to give us your bus?"

I didn't hesitate. I took this vow-of-poverty communal agreement seriously, and his reasoning made total sense. I would later look back amazed at how easily I had given Edward over to Daniel and Marjorie and moved into a sixteen-by-thirty-two canvas tent with four other hippies. That tent, which housed three men and two women, was aptly named The Single People's Tent. On The Farm, we believed in calling things exactly what they were—no frills, no spin. Truth.

In The Single People's Tent, I had a pallet to sleep on and a small space for my personal belongings. Our sleeping areas were scattered around the tent with no walls or privacy screens, so we truly lived in the middle of each other's world. And we were a motley crew. Arax was a man who believed that it was unhealthy to brush your teeth. Martin had been told by Stephen to meditate, so every morning before 5:00 a.m. he would sit zazen on the edge of his sleeping pallet, meditating on his special *zafu* pillow—which was fine until he would end his session with a very loud and harsh *ohmmm* that would shock everyone awake shortly after five, whether they were ready or not. No one could tell him to stop, because

Stephen had told him to meditate, and Stephen's word was gospel. The only other woman in our tent was Suzanne, who found out I still had some cash with me and quickly organized a shopping spree in town to spend my money. We brought back food for the tent and ate well for a few days on my stash. I had no regrets. This was the adventure I had come for. It felt like an endless slumber party.

Without electricity or generators, we relied on kerosene lamps for light, woodstoves for heat, and car batteries for DC current. Later, we would learn to power tiny TVs off car batteries, allowing us to watch about thirty minutes of TV each night—often the Johnny Carson monologue followed by fifteen minutes of *M*A*S*H*. But that would come much later. During that first year on the land, we lived rough.

We had no place to bathe other than the creek that ran across one part of the property. Sponge baths used little water, which was good when we were hauling every precious drop in buckets. I was okay with hiding out in the woods to shit, but the lack of a hot shower was harder to take. I was a suburban girl with dreams of living in the woods—dreams not grounded in reality. I did not like being deeply dirty, and I was in a community with two hundred other dirty people. We were ripe.

One day Judith, who took domestic care of The House and was part of the inner circle, pulled me aside. "You can't keep coming up here to The House and just hanging out. You have to get back down on The Farm and get to work—there's so much to do. You coming up here all the time is 'into the juice' and not cool at all."

Into the juice meant that I was being irresponsible by basking in the energy without contributing anything of worth. It was also a phrase used to shut people down; what can you say to that without seeming even *more* into the juice? I was getting kicked out of my comfort place. Worse, I was embarrassed that I was getting busted for being uncool, accused of wallowing in the energy without respect. *I was not welcome.*

It was late when I slunk out of The House feeling banished and shameful. The night was without a moon and cloudy, as dark as the Tennessee backcountry can be, and I had a mile-long walk back to The Single People's Tent. Fighting all those feelings of rejection and humiliation, I stepped out of the warmth of The House and turned in the direction of home, but I couldn't see even a small shadow or gleam in the road ahead of me. It was pitch-black. Without a flashlight or any other way to light my path, I shuffled my feet along what I thought might be the middle of the road, feeling the way the ground felt under my shoes to tell me if I wandered off. I was scared and stoned from hours of smoking joints—in no shape to be alone in the dark. I started to panic, but knowing that panic was not going to help me, I calmed myself by singing.

"Amazing Grace . . . how sweet the sound, that saved a wretch like me," I warbled, feeling rather wretched. "I once was lost, but now I'm found . . . was blind but now I see." As I sang those last words, I realized the edge of the road was barely, just barely, visible. Just enough to find my way home. It was probably just my eyes finally adjusting to the dark, but in that moment, it felt like a miracle. I felt angels guiding me and said a prayer of thanks for sight.

I did not last long on The Farm in 1971. I couldn't find a way to offer my skills as a teacher or even to organize things and do admin work, and building a town from scratch was not something I could help with. I longed for a real home with walls and heat and running water and hot showers. I frequently found myself hungry, and I was tired of digging holes to shit into. I also craved privacy. I had been learning the rules, learning the ropes of this new way of life, never knowing when I might do something that would cause me to get called out. I kept many thoughts to myself, treaded lightly, and tried to stay out of trouble.

This was not how I was going to save the world. Although I wanted to be part of this group, I realized I couldn't thrive on this land right now, without knowing how to fit in. I would have to leave. *Will I always have to leave because I will never fit in anywhere? Can I leave The Farm and still find community?*

Six weeks after arriving, I made my way back up to The House to talk to Stephen. I told him I needed to head back out into the Real World.

"Well, you do what you have to do," he said, pausing for a moment. "So, do you want your bus back?"

I was taken aback. *My bus that Daniel and Marjorie were still living in?* I was even a bit offended. *Hadn't I given it up without attachment? Hadn't I been a good Farmie/commune member?*

"No! I gave my all to The Farm, including my bus, and I don't want it back," I finally replied. It was nice of him to offer, though.

Leaving Edward behind, and with just a backpack on my shoulder, I hitched a ride with a visitor who was driving to Texas. There, I had relatives who could provide a hot shower, and after that I would figure out my next move. For now, I was free and on my own. The world was mine; I just had to figure out how to save it. But first I had to save myself.

• • •

Over forty years later, I woke to the present reality of Kaibab Lodge at the Grand Canyon, feeling once again the freedom of the road and the feeling of owning my world. I felt both super strong and scary vulnerable, an emotional mixture that would always be a part of riding motorcycles for me, and I was happy to be there with my friends. I wouldn't want to do this alone. I also knew that, together, we were getting smarter.

We rode into Grand Canyon National Park, keeping the same formation because it had worked so well the day before. It was there that I started my tradition of buying a patch for my saddlebags at every national park we would visit, and although that wasn't a very Harley-chick thing to do, I figured I wasn't your typical Harley chick. We changed from motorcycle boots to hiking shoes, and after exploring the rim for a while, we got back on the bikes so we could get to Zion before day's end.

Riding into Zion National Park, with its massive rocks looming above us on both sides, I found myself suddenly crying, overwhelmed by the majestic force and beauty of the cliffs that cradled the highway. These rocks asked absolutely nothing of me and gave me a deep feeling of security and comfort, emanating a power that made me feel the presence of God. I heard ancient voices, but I was not afraid. Instead, these voices resonated with my own Spirit. Without hesitation, I opened my heart to the spirit of Zion and allowed myself to be held by it. *So this is what it feels like to be held and accepted!* Opening my heart had never led to the intensity of comfort I felt that day. Years ago, I had opened my heart to a man who became my husband, when I thought marrying him was the right thing to do. I loved him. But he never made me feel like the cliffs of Zion did; no one yet had ever made me feel this safe. The contrast between that man and those rocks was stark, as was the realization that rocks could be more comforting than some human beings.

When we pulled over at a trailhead for a short hike, I pulled off my helmet.

"What's wrong, Stacey? Why are you crying?" Joan asked.

"Joy. Just pure joy." It would be the first of many helmet tears on these rides, all for the same reason.

As Red Rock Roar came to an end, we rode tight just ahead of a huge storm front and were laughing in our helmets as we pulled back into Joan and Kristin's driveway in Tuba City. We were like a flock of birds that travels as one cohesive group and had found our formation, a groove that allowed us to move smoothly in synchronicity and even be able to anticipate each other's thoughts. We had developed a friendship of equals with great respect for each other and for our differences. The exhilaration of a trip like this felt addicting, and that night, as we unpacked and shared a final glass of wine, we knew we had to start planning the next adventure: riding the redwoods of Northern California, which would be our biggest challenge yet.

CHAPTER 3

REDWOOD ROGUE RUN, 2008

The name of the game
is Rise to The Occasion.
So that's how we roll.

A short eight months after Red Rock Roar, the three of us were ready for another adventure. We would banish fear and build cautious confidence. We would gain skills as we covered more miles. We would deepen our friendship. It was late afternoon, on a warm day in May, when Joan and Kristin pulled up after trailering their bikes from Arizona to Sonoma County, California—my territory. After they unloaded Thelma and Louise, parking them safe and sound in my garage next to Boudica, we went inside to have one last homemade meal.

Kristin had mapped out a route, which we fine-tuned together. Over the next ten days, we'd ride up through Northern California Gold Country to Ashland, Oregon, to the Tu Tu' Tun Lodge on the Rogue River, to Ferndale, down through the Avenue of the Giants redwood groves, and then back down along the Pacific Coast Highway to my home. The roads would be ocean cliffside or tree-lined and winding— very different from the endless expanse we rode in red rock country. I was comfortable with the route we had planned, and with that first trip under our belts, we were all cocky. We were strong. We thought we were ready.

Over a big platter of puttanesca fragrant with garlic, tomatoes, and anchovies, Kristin made a proposition. "This is your territory, Stacey, so do you want to ride lead in the morning?"

Her suggestion made sense; the most geographically experienced should take the lead. I considered what a challenge it would be for them to ride in unfamiliar territory, having been landlocked and riding only on wide-open Arizona highways while I was used to winding, narrow roads. "Sure thing," I replied, helping myself to more salad while there were still croutons in the mix. Tomorrow would be a grand adventure for all three of us.

I had spent a good amount of time since our last ride contemplating my new, increasingly close relationship with these two women. I had seen how much they seemed to respect and take care of each other, without a whole lot of tension. They fit together so well . . . which was a situation I had rarely experienced with anyone in my life. Their marriage seemed to work the way a true loving partnership should. My own marriage had been so very different, from the beginning to the inevitable end. The contrast was striking.

It was 1970 in central Missouri when I first met Don, and I did not think he was cute at all. I was a newly converted

acres of woods with trails that led to the year-round flowing Auxvasse Creek. That creek was where we would go to bathe if thunderstorms didn't come frequently enough to grab a bar of soap, run outside, and shower in the front yard. Don was a passionate and skilled gardener, so we had huge gardens that grew enough food to keep us well stocked from season to season. Tomatoes, melons, squash, peas, eggplant, asparagus, onions, and garlic were all in abundance in his gardens. I canned and preserved food when I wasn't at my day job teaching English and math to emotionally troubled adolescents at the local hospital in town. The few families who lived on the land were content to be Mother Nature's children. Like the hippies on The Farm in Tennessee, we were part of the back-to-the-land movement—living simply, growing our own food, and shunning consumerism. We were in communal bliss.

I spent many free days in the garden with Don, weeding and picking vegetables in the nude since it was our private property, and we were not ashamed. In the early mornings we would hike out to the field and pick a ripe cantaloupe from the garden, still cold from the night air. We'd crack the melon open to eat right then and there, letting the juice drip down our chins as we devoured the perfect orange fruit. Then we'd smoke a joint and go to work weeding or picking, depending on the season and the need. When it got hot midday, Don and I would make our way down the narrow trails through the woods to the creek. Stinging nettles thickly covered the banks, so we would steel ourselves, run straight through that painful patch, and jump into the creek—cooling the burning sting with the rush of cold water. And whenever butterflies landed on my bare shoulders, I felt like a charmed character out of a Disney movie. This was the life I had dreamed of, and I was content.

Don would get up in the early morning hours to stoke the woodstove, so I would never wake up cold again. Don would grow, harvest, and cook veggies so I would never be hungry again. Don could take apart a chain saw, store all the pieces for months, and then put it all back together again so it would work better than ever. With him, I would never be without a handyman. The sex was not good, but then I had never had good sex, so I didn't know what I was missing. He was not an emotionally nurturing man, but I wasn't raised with emotional support, so how could I miss what I had never known? I thought we were best friends.

When I realized that we were going to be together for a while longer than one or two nights, I made an appointment to get an IUD for birth control. I did not like the pill and how it made me feel. Condoms weren't an option because neither one of us wanted to use them. So far, I'd avoided pregnancy by only fucking when I wasn't even close to ovulation. But that wasn't going to work with a partner who wanted sex whenever he wanted sex. I was not yet a liberated woman and wouldn't be for many years, and I did not want to deny him sex because then he might not want to be with me. And I *needed* him to want me. I'd had an IUD before without any problems, so it was my personal choice for protection. And I had to make that choice because Don was very honest and clear: "I do not want nor do I believe in marriage. And I do not ever want children."

I took his pronouncement with a grain of salt. I did want a committed relationship, and I did want to carry, give birth to, and raise children. I figured these details could be worked out later, when our connection was deep enough to change his mind. I was a very young and naïve twenty-two.

I took myself to a local clinic to get an IUD. After the

required pregnancy test, a doctor came into the exam room with a nurse. He was a kind, gray-haired, middle-aged man, portly and wearing the proverbial white coat.

"Stacey, you are pregnant. So we won't be giving you an IUD today. Do you know what you want to do about this?"

Oh shit.

I sat there on the edge of the table, undressed and vulnerable in a gown that opened in back, listening to him tell me my life as I knew it was over. *At least this explains why, for the last couple of weeks, I haven't been able to stomach breakfast in the mornings.* In my shock, I had no room for emotion. I shut down so fast I hardly heard a word he said, other than *pregnant.* But I did hear his question, and I gave him an automatic reply.

"I'll need to get an abortion. I can't have a baby."

This was central Missouri in 1972. We were living on the edge of the Bible Belt, and abortions weren't legal in Missouri. But Don didn't want a child, so, in that moment, abortion seemed to be the only way out. It was a back door out of my unwanted situation. But the doctor had a few words for me.

"Do you realize that you aren't making sense? You had sex without protection. You got pregnant. Some part of you may have wanted this to happen, but now you say you want an abortion. There is something wrong with your way of thinking. Consider your choices carefully, Stacey."

Bullshit. He doesn't know anything about me or my situation. I left his office in a daze, hardly seeing the receptionist at the front desk or any other patients in the waiting room. My head was buzzing, and my stomach was clenched with fear and anxiety. I made it to my car, and sitting alone in the driver's seat, I knew I wasn't focused enough to drive anywhere, so I didn't even put the key in the ignition. I just sat there and

started sorting through my options. First things first, go tell
Don and figure out how to get out of this mess. I had not yet,
in my short life, found myself in a situation I could not back
out of. I could back out of this one. *But is that really the right
thing to do?* I needed advice.

I would gather information, get opinions from people
who dealt with this kind of problem all the time. First, I went
to the local pastor, thinking maybe someone who talked
to God on a daily basis would have a helpful point of view,
and even though I had little respect for organized religion,
I did respect spiritual leaders enough to consult with one.
However, this was a small, central-Missouri town with one
Southern Baptist church, and I was far from being a Southern
Baptist. Sitting together in his airless office in the back of the
church, we discussed my dilemma, but he gave me little guidance. Instead, he seemed more interested in whether or not I
would extend my practice of free love to include him and his
own personal sexual needs. Grossed out by his advances, I
left that church, never to return.

Enough of spiritual leaders and their opinions. Next, I
went to a birth control counselor in the local college town to
get a referral to an abortion clinic. I wasn't tempted by back-
room abortions; the risk was too great. New York had legal-
ized abortion in 1970, and I had a girlfriend there who would
help me. I would be safe there. I was good at bullshit, so when
I met with the counselor, I made it seem like I had thought
this through and knew my own mind without question. I got
the referral, but it was only as valid a decision as my own
bullshit allowed. It was worthless.

I struggled with my conscience. I honored life. I wanted
babies. I also knew that I could not raise a child on my own—I
was not single-parent material. Oh sure, I'd try, and I'd do my

best . . . but I was an impatient, immature, still somewhat feral woman and would have raised children alone with an overload of anger and frustration. This much I knew about myself.

Finally, I could think no more. I could not do this. I could not raise a child alone, but Don was a solid *no*. I needed out. So I closed my mind, booked a flight to New York, and quit thinking about it. Every day I went to work as a teacher at the local psych hospital, and every night I came home to Don, who assumed I was not going to carry his child for the next nine months.

The night before my flight to New York, I closed up my classroom and headed home. I was running on automatic, trying hard not to think about anything at all, just doing what was in front of me and getting through the days. As I pulled up to the old farmhouse, one of our housemates, Carla, came out to greet me.

"Hey, Patricia is in there and waiting to talk with you. Thought you'd want to know before you went in."

Shit. Not Patricia! She was one of the more conservative members of our group, and I just wasn't up to her trying to talk me out of my abortion plans. I was certain that's what she wanted, and I was exhausted with soul-searching and other people's opinions. But there was no way out. I went inside.

The late afternoon sun streamed through the window over the sink, making the kitchen cozy and cheerful at the same time. There was Patricia, sitting at our old wooden kitchen table with kindhearted Roy over at the sink doing up some dishes. He was someone I trusted, with no personal agenda. *At least there will be a fair witness to this conversation.* I sat down at the table across from her. *Let's get this over with.*

Patricia surprised me. She did not lay into me with judgmental platitudes. She was calm and kind, and simply started a conversation with me about my plans. She listened to the description of my painful process and absorbed some of my angst. And then she said her piece.

"I understand exactly what you are struggling with, and I know it is perhaps the hardest decision you will ever make. I just want to make sure it's a decision that *you* want . . . not one for someone else. Because you, and only you, are the one who will live with this decision for the rest of your life. You can choose either life or not for this baby. Either way is no skin off my back, but you are the one to carry the consequences. Make sure it is *your* decision and not anyone else's. That will make it easier to live with, and that's all I have to say."

Roy had been listening over at the sink. "And if you choose to keep this baby, you will not be alone. We will all be here to help you." He meant well, but I knew raising a child was hard enough, even when it was your own family. Still, I appreciated the sentiment. It was good to know I had friends willing to offer support.

Their words rocked my world and cut through the protective barrier I had erected around me. Roy's kindness and Patricia's wisdom gave me clarity. That was the moment I realized that, whatever way I went, it would be forward. Forward raising a child. Forward carrying a chosen loss. There would be No. Back. Door.

Shit.

I made my way to our little room upstairs and lay on our mattress on the floor. Don wouldn't be home for another hour or two, so I had some time to consider my options with this new point of view. Lying there in the fetal position, I held onto myself as I shook with fear and awe. I trembled when

I realized that the decision to have an abortion was *absolutely Don's* choice. Choosing to abort was not something I wanted right now, and however hard it may turn out to be, I would have to have this baby. That was the choice I could carry. Years later, as a physician, I would support women who wanted abortions. I would support and care for them, and I would use Patricia's wisdom to counsel them; it should always be *their own* choice. And that day, I made the decision for myself that felt exactly right.

This was scary stuff. Really super scary. Now I had to tell Don.

When he came home, I told him that I would be having this child. The decision was mine to make and I had made it. He could do what he needed to do; I just asked that he please let me know so I could plan.

He agreed to stay with me until the baby was born. Then all bets were off.

My pregnancy wasn't easy. I never got over the nausea that came every morning and lasted all day. I ate very little, which was part of the problem, but I put up with the discomfort because I was fulfilling another dream of mine: to create a human being with this female body I had been given. My belly swelled and I watched it grow. I drove sixty miles south into the Ozarks to a respected physician for prenatal care, choosing to go where I could birth my baby in his birthing center instead of a hospital where they would take her away from me the minute she was born, as was the practice in those days. If all went the way Mother Nature intended, I could go have my baby where I felt safe and then come home after a couple of hours. Birthing at home was not what I wanted because I didn't yet know what kind of baby-haver I was; I just knew that I didn't want any system or protocols to mess with me.

Then something happened that changed our idyllic lives forever.

One day, Don went into town to run errands and hitch-hiked back with a man who seemed quite nice. When they arrived, he was busy telling Don a sad story about how it was his anniversary, he had no gift for his wife, and he asked Don if he could spare a joint so he could go home a hero instead of a schmuck. I didn't trust this man, but Don was friendly and generous and agreed to give him a joint. Impressed by Don's generosity, I was embarrassed by my own fearful stinginess. But then we both knew something was wrong when the man wouldn't smoke with us, and again when he insisted on paying for the joint. He pulled a coin out of his pocket. "Even just a quarter? Here! Take it!" We refused.

There were just too many red flags, and we were right to be nervous. The local sheriff showed up two hours later to arrest Don on possession and transfer, to an undercover deputy sheriff, of a controlled substance. Possession was a serious offense in Missouri in 1972. People were being sent to prison for life after getting busted for weed.

The court was surprisingly lenient with Don, and he was given only a year's probation. During that time, he would have to meet with his probation officer once a month, and I went with him. Then, a few months later, in the spring of 1973, the probation officer dropped a bombshell.

"In the state of Missouri, it is illegal to cohabitate. The two of you are living together. You are breaking the law, Don, and you have three choices: move out, get married, or go to jail."

By then I was seven months pregnant, and this was a curveball I had not expected. I was knocked up by a man who didn't want kids and who also didn't believe in marriage, and in anyone's reality, this sucked. But neither of us could let some ancient state law force us apart right before our child was born. And he was absolutely not going to jail. That left marriage.

I was good with that decision; I'd be secure, and I believed in that institution. Don agreed if it would keep him out of jail. We asked our buddy Terrell, a newly licensed Universal Life Church minister, to officiate. But on April Fools' Day in 1973, when it came time for Don to say that one phrase in the traditional wedding vows—*'til death do us part*—he couldn't do it.

"I don't know . . . that's a pretty long time. I don't know if I can cop to that."

Short silence. I stood frozen, looking down at my eight-month pregnant belly. Then, thinking quickly on his feet, Terrell said, "Well, Don, if you two break up it would be the death of the relationship and that's surely a death, right?"

"Well, I guess you are right . . . okay . . . let's finish this." And the ceremony went on anyway, the papers signed without those words of lifetime commitment ever being said.

There is a difference between being emotionally strong and being emotionally isolated. I hadn't begun to see that difference until years later, when Joan, Kristin, and I soaked in the hot tub under the stars the night before we started the Redwood Rogue Run. Kristin wondered aloud if there would be rocks on this trip that would once again make me cry. She and Joan knew little about my past—that I had lived rough as a voluntary peasant on the land, or that cannabis and the state of Missouri had shaped twenty years of my life, or that I had said yes to marrying someone who was so self-centered and unwilling to marry me.

He was a good provider. We never fought about money. We agreed on parenting styles. We laughed often, cooked meals together, and truly enjoyed each other's company. Yet there was something missing. Our marriage only worked when Don was able to do as he wished, and he resented being trapped in a forced marriage. I couldn't provide what he needed—freedom—and he couldn't provide for my needs—emotional support and intimacy. Now, I thought that perhaps in the retelling of my story, I could make some sense of it all, so I shared with Joan and Kristin a past I had rarely spoken of.

It was winter in Turlock, California, in the huge Central Valley where Don grew up. He, Sarah Kate—who was just a year old—and I were living in a two-bedroom house, paying low rent to his father while we worked and saved money. I was a substitute teacher, always on call, and Don worked construction. We were not happy together. We had moved there from Missouri because it was far away from all the other women he was fucking, and this was the solution: move to a safer place. As if there was such a thing as a safe place. But I was certain: I could not be a single mother. I knew that in my bones. I couldn't earn a living and be a lonely mom all at the same time. I needed a partner to help me, and I would rather take the risk that he would start cheating again than be single. So I stayed with him after our move and hoped to work it out. I was committed.

We were both paying for choices we had made that the other one resented. I resented his anger and frustration at being trapped in a life he never intended—that of a husband

and a father. He resented my need for his support and the fact that I was the object of the frustrations that trapped him. With that much resentment, we fought. We power-played. Often. Loudly.

Neither of us wanted a relationship like this, but we didn't know how to change it. We were both young, twenty-four years old without a clue as to how to live with each other peaceably. We didn't want to break up or divorce; that would be giving up. That would mean losing, and neither of us wanted to be a loser. We just wanted to have fun raising our daughter and having adventures together.

One day, I came home with Stephen Gaskin's book called *Hey Beatnik*, written by people on The Farm. This book described the community of hippies that went back to the land in Tennessee to live together in harmony, setting an example for the rest of the world. Handing the book to Don, I told him this was a book about the spiritual community where I used to live. I invited him to check it out.

"They're doing some pretty fun stuff, and we might think about joining them."

I figured moving to Tennessee might be our best chance of figuring out how to live together; we could learn from the others who were dedicated to peace. We could also be part of saving the world while we saved our own marriage. This could be a win-win.

He had no interest in spirituality, but he was antiestablishment, and he wanted to escape the regular world of nine-to-five jobs. In fact, completely dropping out of society appealed to him. I still had my strong need for community and a strong desire to be part of a spiritual commune, but I kept my personal agenda to myself and waited while Don digested that book.

A couple of days later I brought it up. "So. What do you think of that Tennessee Farm?"

"Let's do it. Let's go join them in the woods of Tennessee and make a difference," he said. So for two very different reasons, but with both of us wanting to make our marriage work, we agreed to move to The Farm.

Where would we live when we got there? I was sure they had made progress since I had been there a couple of years before, but we were aware that, when a thousand hippies land on an undeveloped piece of land, there would be few houses, and probably not even enough houses for everyone who was already there. We also knew it was up to us to figure that part out. Since many traveled there in converted school buses, as I had just three years before, we figured that was a good option for us as a family. Great! A project! We were good at projects!

The next day, Don headed out to find a bus suitable for conversion, and within a week there was a seven-window-long full-size Dodge school bus parked in our backyard, stripped of all its seats and ready to be turned into a snug home. Don and his grandfather Cecil, who lived next door to us, set to work on the project, finding great joy in working together to create something so unusual. And they did a beautiful job. They created a full-size bed tucked into the back corner, with storage underneath. I hand-carved and stained the wooden raised edges that kept our mattress from sliding off the platform. Along one side of the bus, they created a full kitchen with a sink, a stove, and a refrigerator running on propane. I painted and decorated the front of the cabinets with tiny flowered patterns. They installed a full-size woodstove with the stovepipe sealed tight where it exited the ceiling. We covered the ceiling with carpet sample squares, creating a colorful patchwork of warmth that also softened any echoey sounds. I hung curtains across the full length of windows, changing the fabric along the way to create different "rooms": one pattern for our bedroom area, switching to another for Sarah's nursery, and another for the kitchen.

Don and I were good at making a home together. We worked well when we had a project with clearly defined roles, and we fought less. Family and friends stopped by all the time to see our progress and comment on how beautiful it all was. This was definitely the right road! Our disagreements and power plays were set aside while we each had this project to keep us busily working in tandem.

The day finally arrived. All our essentials had been packed into the bus, into ample cabinets and into the box that was the base of our high bed. Sarah Kate's crib was bolted into place behind the driver's seat, the propane fridge was cold, and the bus felt more like our home than the house did. But before we left Turlock, I decided to change the karma around our bus. It was an old Dodge with a few letters missing from the name on the front hood, so instead of DODGE, it said DOG. I decided this was bad karma, manifesting problems for us, so I dug out a screwdriver and switched those letters to say GOD instead. Don thought I was being silly, even for me with my magical thinking, but I figured it didn't hurt to call in God instead of a dog.

Maybe changing the letters didn't help the bus, but it did help me keep a positive attitude. We ended up breaking down in every single state on our way to Tennessee, but we also met many helpful people along the way. I began to appreciate the angels among us. Finally, blowing a piston sixty miles from The Farm, we got towed the last stretch, using up the very last of our cash. We arrived at The Gate on The Farm a little worse for wear, penniless, in our broken-down bus, ready to park it in the woods and to begin learning how to be married. Or at least, how to be nice to each other when not challenged and working together on creative projects.

Once again, I found myself standing before Stephen at The House by The Gate. He had accepted me into the Farm community, which we had called our Tribe, three years earlier when I was single. Now I was back, married with a husband and a toddler, and asking permission for our family to live there.

"I'm back," I said. Given that I had been a Farmie before, I had no doubts he would accept me again.

Stephen looked at all of us. "Sure, you can settle in. You're not ready to live with others yet, but if you park your bus next to families that are cool, maybe you can learn to be cool too."

Grateful to be back in the community and encouraged by the expectation that we could learn to be good with each other, I followed Don back out to our bus with Sarah on my hip.

An energetic crew of long-haired hippies brought a Farm tow truck to The Gate, and as they hauled us a mile or two down the road, I saw how much The Farm had changed in the years since I'd left. There were several water towers, a laundromat, a motor pool, a soy dairy, a clinic, countless homes creating distinct neighborhoods, and enclosed outhouses. This was definitely an improvement over open pits! At long last, we were settled in a little clearing in the woods next to a large household of three other families. Surely they could help us learn to be nice to each other. It was our only hope.

Joan and Kristin listened to me that night with interest; they had never heard such a tale! It was an adventure story to them, and as I shared my story that evening in the hot tub,

I realized that these two were an example of what I wanted in a relationship. They were angels, becoming role models for me, and I began to take more note of the way they took care of each other. But at the same time, I was content to be free of the problems that come with relationships. I was grateful for my independence. And as much as I longed for love, I was just as fearful of giving up my power all over again for the sake of peace.

Oh so ready to hit the road, we ventured out the next morning with a plan to ride 160 miles to the small town of Colusa on the Sacramento River. Our route took us through farmland in the Alexander Valley, past vineyards in Dry Creek Valley, and over Mountain House Road into Hopland by lunchtime. I took the lead, with Kristin in the middle and Joan in her favorite spot, riding sweep. The temperature rose into the high nineties as we neared Hopland, and we got seriously overheated, so we were pathetically grateful when we walked into the air-conditioned Bluebird Café to meet Laura for lunch.

I had met Laura for the first time when I was a new medical student. At thirty-six, I was older than all my classmates, the mother of two preteen daughters, and only two years off The Farm. The fact that I was different from everyone didn't bother me; military brats get used to being different. But that didn't mean I shunned offers of help. UC Davis assigned every new medical student a Big Sib—someone in the year ahead who already knew the ropes. This person was supposed to help you through that first tough year of lectures, exams, and overwhelming expectations.

Unfortunately, my assigned Big Sib wasn't helpful. She was disorganized, confusing, and often not available. I tried to connect with her but found no help there, so I steered clear and figured I could just go it on my own.

Each week started with Monday Morning Midterms—massive exams that we would cram for all weekend and sit for each Monday morning. We'd then nervously await results that would appear in our mailboxes later that week. These tests would sometimes cover material not yet taught in lectures, and they often had ambiguous multiple-multiple choice answers. For the first time in my life, I developed test anxiety. I'd always been good at taking exams, but this was a new type of test, and I was never sure if I'd done well or bombed. I developed a coping skill, grabbing my test results out of my student mailbox, disappearing into the nearest bathroom, locking myself in a stall. Only in the safety of that private place would I look at my scores.

One day, I noticed another woman going through the same ritual. I watched her open her mailbox, grab her mail, and then disappear into the bathroom. This was interesting . . . a kindred spirit!

"Hey—are you doing what I think you're doing?" I asked her as she passed by me one Wednesday.

"What? What do you mean?" Like me, Marcia was older than the other students straight out of college, and she was obviously nervous about test scores, so I felt a kinship.

"Going to check your test score in the bathroom," I answered. "I do that too. These tests are killer! I never know . . . I mean, I know the stuff, but I never know if I can answer their stupid questions right. It's nerve-racking!"

"I know! Right?!"

Right then a friendship was born. Then, when Marcia found out who my Big Sib was, she immediately offered to share hers. Laura, a second-year student, was everything

Marcia said she was—wonderful, kind, and smart enough to be in AOA, the national medical honor society. The first time I met her, I was smitten. Here was a real role model for this phase of my life. Laura was just seven years younger than me, a stately six feet tall, and had a way of moving gracefully that embraced her height rather than hiding it. She welcomed me, and from that day on, she would be my sister-support on my path to becoming a healer-physician and beyond.

Her first task was to explain the weird exams.

"You don't actually read the questions, do you?" she asked.

"Well, of course I do! I read them over and over and try to figure out the best answers from the multiple-multiple choice answers we're given: A, A and C, B and D, C, all of the above, or none of the above . . . and I just can't see it!"

"Oh, that's your problem! Just read the answers . . . the right combination is clear there. Has nothing to do with the facts being tested," she told me. I chewed on this for a bit. *Well shit. It was all a game.* This may have lessened my respect for the tests we took, but it sure increased my respect for Laura. I never learned to see those "right combinations" she talked about; I kept studying the facts and doing my best to reason out answers, and I kept passing every exam.

"Laura is my sister-from-another-mother," I told Joan and Kristin as we parked the bikes and walked over to the café. "I followed her from UC Davis to Santa Rosa to do my residency; she was a year ahead of me, so that would make her five years ahead of you in the program, I guess. Anyway, she never judged me—even when I told her what I've told you about Don. We have always shown up for each other. I stood up for her at her wedding, and I was there when her daughter was born. She was there when I got divorced, and she seriously saved me from the dangerous depression I went through during those months. Later, I was there when she got divorced, and then I rescued her from her own deep despair. Boy, have we been through it! I don't know . . . I just love her!"

I couldn't wait for them to meet Laura, and it was easy to find her in that café. She was already sitting at a table, her brunette hair falling softly in loose curls to her shoulders as she gave us a big, crooked-tooth welcoming smile the minute she saw us clomp in with our heavy boots, helmet hair, and sweaty brows. As always, my heart swelled as I looked into her kind eyes. It meant a lot to meet up with her at the beginning of this ride and to get her bon voyage blessings.

"Where do you go from here?" she asked after we had all ordered cold drinks and light lunches.

"We're headed for Colusa on our way to the Trinity Alps, then up into Oregon to stay on the Rogue River," I replied. "We have tickets to a play in Ashland, and we're going to stay at a luxury lodge for our layover on the Rogue. Then we get to ride down the Pacific Coast Highway all the way back home."

She grinned. "I think you three are incredibly brave to be doing this. . . . I've done some risky things in my life, but this . . . well, this is something I couldn't do. Just give me a fast sports car to race instead."

We laughed at her, and I said, "You people in your cages, you miss out on so much! The wind! The smells! The feel of leaning into curves on two wheels!" We did not know then that within the next few years, Laura would turn out to be the bravest of us all.

An hour in the AC and our cores were cooled down enough to hit the road, heading east with Laura's blessing for a safe adventure ahead. We scooted around the southern edge of Clear Lake, stopping in Lower Lake for a root beer float (survival cooldown), and getting some very enthusiastic cheers from some wannabe biker chicks in the drive-through lane who thought it was the coolest thing that we were on the road together. Along the way, Joan would get the benefit of these cheers as she rode sweep. People would see three big bikes, but it would take seeing Kristin and me for them to figure out it was three *girls* riding those bikes, and then they'd start cheering us all on. Joan would high-five them back and carry the glory for all of us.

Colusa was a little central California valley town off the beaten path with lots of trees and, thankfully, shade. It felt *so* good to check into the motel, peel off the sweaty riding clothes, and jump into a cool shower . . . what a relief. I was happy to be in a room by myself, able to stretch out horizontal again after hours on Boudica. Flopped naked on the motel bed, I wondered what we would do for dinner. I wasn't hungry yet, but I knew I would be as soon as I cooled my core, and that was when I spotted Kristin out the window of my room. There she was, my strong riding buddy who had immediately swapped out her jeans for some shorts and was headed out for a three-mile run in the sweltering heat. Not me! I stayed right there in front of the AC blower in my room and turned on the TV. Quiet time. Downtime. Grateful.

I slept deeply that night after a toke of cannabis, and I again rode in the lead the next morning, as we were still in my territory. We were cautious and tried to stay off the I-5 as long as possible by riding two-lane frontage roads alongside the highway; four-lane interstates with speeding cars and huge semis still scared us. We passed fields of onions, corn, rice, beans, and walnuts, but the roads got smaller, and narrower, and rougher. Then, as I was cruising along on one of those quiet two-lane frontage roads, the interstate on my left and acres of almond orchards on my right, a huge peacock flew in low from my left side and only gained altitude as it passed in front of me, barely missing my front fender with its tail feathers.

Kristin, riding right behind me, signaled a pull-over.

"Oh my God!" Joan called out. "That was amazing! Weren't you scared?"

"I didn't have time to be scared. . . . It just happened so fast," I said. "Where'd he come from?" We peered into the almond orchard, searching for the bird, and quickly decided to bite the bullet and get over our fear of interstates. The oh-too-realistic vision of me going down in a flurry of peacock feathers was way scarier than highway traffic.

We headed north on the I-5, giving the truckers plenty to look at, until we came to the Trinity Alps, a range with granite peaks that rise over nine thousand feet above sea level. What a joy to leave the farm country and get into some real hills and curves! Climbing those curves, with snow on the peaks to the west, we passed Whiskeytown Lake, wishing we could stop and jump in. We rode down to a rest stop, where we all had to lie flat on our backs on a picnic table for a while, do some stretches, and splash ourselves with cold water. Our butts hurt, my head hurt, and our helmets were getting way too heavy and hot. When we reached the air-conditioned 49er Gold Country Inn in Weaverville and were able to cool off, we had no idea we'd seen the last of our warm weather.

Oh, but it was beautiful to be in the mountains! The next day Kristin took the lead as we rode on two-lane mountain roads past Trinity Lake and along the Trinity River. Once we were above the snow line, the road started twisting its way up to Scott Mountain Summit at fifty-four hundred feet. The curves were fun at first, but as the road got steeper, the curves grew sharper until they became gnarly switchbacks that turned back on themselves. Soon all I could see was a sheer wall of dark gray asphalt in front of my windshield, the road so steep it appeared vertical. It curved up, around, and then switched back beside me, and somehow it appeared that Kristin was riding on the side of that asphalt simultaneously ahead of and beside me, like a spider zigzagging up a wall.

I'd already downshifted into first gear, but my mind could not fathom what I was seeing. It made no sense that one can perch on a motorcycle and climb a hill that steep and still stay in touch with the earth. Luckily, there was no time to try to make sense out of it. This was a true test of *keep moving forward* to stay alive. I stayed in first gear and gave Boudica as much gas as she needed, and she took the turns like a pro—carrying me right along with her. After each successful twist, I'd quickly glance into my rearview mirrors to make sure Joan and Thelma were still back there. I was scared the whole time.

Finally, all three of us made our way safely to the summit, which felt like a graduation in motorcycle riding. If we could safely ride those curves, we could ride almost anywhere, and as shaken as I was at the challenge, I was also proud of my growth in handling a Harley. We perfected our riding formation that day as we headed toward the bustling town of Ashland, Oregon, taking care of each other in heavy traffic using our synced telepathic mode. When Kristin, now in front, would signal an intended lane change, Joan would move on over behind me into the new lane, protecting the space in front of her, and then Kristin and I would move smoothly over to fill that space. It felt like a choreographed dance.

The next day was a lesson about riding a motorcycle in Oregon during the month of May, when it can be cold and wet, and even colder because of the windchill when riding. We stopped three times at rest stops on the I-5, each time to put on more layers: leather jackets with liners, rain pants, chaps, neck wraps, heavy gloves. . . . Those layers kept piling on. We were so bundled we could hardly move, and I developed a unique technique for getting on my bike. Too bundled to be graceful, and with all my gear piled up on the back of the bike, I had to put my leg straight across the seat to get on Boudica. Not easy when wearing five layers, and while my legs are not short, the bike was just as tall as my legs were long. So I'd do a little warm-up dance, get a running start, and run straight at the side of the bike, throwing my leg out in front of me to straddle the bike with all the momentum I could muster. This was a big show that my riding buddies found hysterical.

By the time we got to the luxurious Tu Tu' Tun Lodge on the Rogue River near Gold Beach, just three miles outside the Siskiyou National Forest, we were ready for the cottage with the private hot tub we'd reserved. As we rumbled into the parking lot, I could feel the stares of all the other guests, and I could imagine what they were saying among themselves. *What do those bikers think they're doing here? Don't they know this is an upscale resort?* But when we pulled off our helmets and outed ourselves as normal-appearing, friendly women, the attitude changed to one of admiration. We strutted for them as we unloaded for a two-day layover in luxury. In spite of being tired from a full day of riding, and in spite of the heavy loads we were carrying in from our bikes, we managed to look strong and graceful for the onlookers.

During those next two days on the Rogue River, we all took some time to walk or run along the river, stretching muscles that were tired from the ride. Hot tubs, massages, and good food filled our days. The last morning, after breakfast, we gave them our credit cards, closed our eyes, signed on the dotted line, said fond farewells, and promised to return. Layered up again, certain that the worst was behind us, we rode out along the Rogue River, Kristin in the lead, taking us the long way back to the 101. We were headed south for Humboldt County.

It was cold and damp on the coast when we stopped in Trinidad, a little beach town in Humboldt, to fill our tanks. Looking at each other, we saw how frozen we each appeared, in need of a hot drink, so we fought the howling wind to get to a café across from the gas station. *Maybe they'll even let us eat our picnic lunch inside the warmth there.* We quickly discovered that the café was actually a crowded converted shack with hardly any room for tables or people inside. No matter—everyone moved over to create space. We three women, two toddlers, one really gentle hippie dad-dude, and two mastiff puppies were all squeezed in, taking shelter from the elements and drinking hot mochas and lattes. I felt at home there, with the fragrance of good Humboldt cannabis that had likely permeated the scene for years, and everyone was relaxed and in good moods. Of course we could eat our picnic there! No problem!

The weather continued to plague us as we rode past Eureka and through the first of the redwoods, headed inland, and progressed toward the Avenue of the Giants, where we'd hoped to find a spiritual experience among the ancient redwoods. But it was so foggy, drizzly, and cold that we couldn't appreciate nature's awe-inspiring grandeur as we had in Zion. Kristin signaled a pull-over.

She looked miserable. Pulling off her helmet, she let herself vent in a rare display of complaints. "My feet are frozen!

And wet! And I can't feel my hands! I don't know how much longer I can keep riding like this . . . I don't feel safe."

I hung back, a bit disconcerted at this rare display of angst from Kristin; she was usually so calm, and this was the first time I'd seen her frazzled.

Joansie looked at her wife with concern, assessing the situation pragmatically like the physician she is, but also assessing her wife and Kristin's cry for help. Kristin doesn't cry wolf; when she says she doesn't feel safe, it's just not safe.

"Let's see what we can do." Joan started rummaging through her saddlebags, and after a bit of digging, she pulled out a couple of plastic bags. "Maybe if we get you some warm, dry socks, then put these bags over those, before the boots, well . . . maybe that will make the difference." Then after a short pause, "At least for your feet, honey."

Seeing that Joan had a plan, I chimed in with support. "And if your feet can be warm and dry, then maybe there will be enough warm blood to keep your hands from going numb. I have some spare gloves that are dry if you need them." I rummaged in my pack for those gloves and a couple of hair ties to secure the plastic bags to her legs.

Kristin sat down on a rock and pulled off her boots, pouring a small rivulet of rainwater out of each one as she set them down. Then her socks—wringing them out before setting them next to the soggy boots. Joan handed her a pair of thick, dry socks, and I could see the relief in Kristin's face as she pulled them on her cold bare feet. Then came the plastic bags and hair ties to hold the bags up above the bottom edge of her jeans. And then those wet boots. She stood up and stamped around a bit to get the blood flowing and to test this new system. I kept quiet, letting them take care of Kristin's situation, watching how they worked together, and wondering how much longer *I* could safely ride. I too was cold, disappointed in the weather and wishing we had been able to enjoy the red-woods. This was not fun—it was uncomfortably hard—but it would do no good to complain. There was no warm, dry place to shelter. I had to be stoic and brave and pull out my rechargeable courage to make it to that night's lodgings. As always, nothing to do but keep going forward.

By then, a brave smile showed Kristin's willingness to continue, so we all loaded up again and started our engines. Riding with our heads down, tucked in tight against our bikes, we covered miles of penetrating damp. Like Oregon, Northern California in May hadn't offered the warm sun we had expected. We'd thought we were seasoned, and we didn't like riding in so many layers and having to pass on all our side trips. But we were resolute. And we were on track and making it happen without giving up! On the last leg of the day, cruising, we thought we had it down. I hugged Boudica's engine for all the warmth it could offer while my helmet thoughts were of cozy fires and dry clothes.

But as we headed west, up over the coastal range on our way to the Pacific Ocean and Fort Bragg, the road became even more challenging than the twists and turns earlier in the ride. I took the lead on this narrow, two-lane stretch of road that climbed through the trees, twisted, and turned as it headed up into the clouds hugging the coast. The wind and rain had littered debris all over the road, and the turns came too quickly to point out all the hazards to Kristin riding right behind me. The thought of one of our bikes hitting a redwood branch and losing control was not one I wanted to imagine.

Constantly shifting between first and second gear, we just had to make our way up, up, up, curve by curve. Again, we found ourselves negotiating hairpin curves turning back on themselves, over and over and over again, and I didn't know how Joan and Kristin were doing behind me. *I don't want to think of one of us going down . . . don't know what I could do if they did . . . why the fuck did we decide to ride this road today?* When my face shield started fogging up in the cold, the only solution was to ride with it open. Huge drops of cold water started smacking me in the face, but at least it wasn't snow or sleet. My rearview mirrors fogged, and I kept swiping them with my oversize fleece-lined gloves, but it made no difference. I couldn't tell if there were two bikes behind me or one. *The two lights there could just be me seeing double. I guess if anyone falls out, I'll hear the sound of the fall. Don't know what I can do about it though . . . Oh God, don't fall!* All we could do was to keep going . . . curve by curve, as my helmet thoughts kept on worrying. *Do we all have enough gas to do this climb, to get out of these clouds? God, I hope so, but I can't look now. Just. Keep. Going.*

Forty miles can feel like forever. When we pulled into Fort Bragg, we went right to a gas station to fill our tanks. Even before taking off our helmets, we started screaming, hollering, and stomping our feet about how gnarly, how hard, how SO hard that had been.

"Oh my gawd we need a new hand signal!" I cried out as soon as I could speak. "Something that says *gnarly!*"

Joan took her balled-up fist and pounded it repeatedly on the top of her helmet, pounding it as hard as she could. Pretty soon we were all bonking our helmets, using both fists and yelling. *"Gnarly! Hard! Effin' A!"* And just like that, we agreed: closed-fisted repeated hard bonks on the helmet meant "gnarly." We added that to our tail wagging, our I-have-to-go-pee, and our jumping-up-and-down-for-joy signals.

We were high on survival when we stumbled into the

touristy Harvest Market and went straight for the open chicken rotisserie. We stood there with our hands in the heat until we could feel our fingers again, and then wondered if we would be kicked out if we put our feet up there too . . . ignoring for a moment the fact that Kristin's footbags would've melted. Deciding not to take that chance, we wandered around the store, in a daze, trying to bring our feet back to life while checking out the wine and whiskey inventory and gourmet chocolate displays. We also picked up fresh pears, gorgonzola cheese, and an excellent sourdough bread.

We rode down to the little coastal town of Elk, where we had reservations for two nights, allowing us a full day off the road to enjoy the beach and the Pacific Ocean—something very special to my two friends who lived in the desert. Hard rides, cold damp, insecurities, and fear had all taken their toll on us, and we needed time to ourselves to recover. Spending hours on that glorious beach allowed me to sit back and reflect with appreciation on how strong I had become as I'd developed my sense of self-worth. *Anyone who can ride a Harley motorcycle through the cold, damp rain and fog, as we have for the last few days, is pretty darn badass. What would Stephen's wife, Ina May, think of me now?* I had spent so many years trying to please her.

In those early years on The Farm, I was intimidated just *talking* to Ina May. She was nine years older than me . . . and so forceful that I could hardly look at her, much less really *see* her. She was the most powerful woman on The Farm, the head of the midwife crew, and the only one who could let me learn to be a midwife. Ina May was not a beauty by any means. She was my height but seemed much taller—probably because of her high social position. Her long, mouse-brown hair was thin, and she usually wore it hanging in braids like the rest of us women on The Farm, with occasional wisps escaping around her face. Without makeup or any adornments, she was still formidable, like the female lion who is matriarch of the pride. Her teeth were large and protruding, and her voice had no softness to it. She exuded a firm, no-nonsense attitude. When she spoke, she left no room for questions or discussion. Don't even try.

The midwives were the highly respected heroines on The Farm. There were less than a dozen actual midwives, and several midwife helpers serving a community of over fifteen hundred baby-having hippies. These women held a special elite status, getting perks that the rest of us never saw. They had cars at their disposal, while the rest of us had to hoof it everywhere. They took over the single party phone line when a birth was imminent, kicking everyone else off the line no matter what sort of business was being discussed. They had childcare provided at a moment's notice anytime a woman was in labor, no questions asked. They were considered true angels—holy women who managed life-and-death transitions with skills that were not only medical, but spiritual as well. While the midwives' social position was seductive, it was their skills I craved.

More than anything, I wanted to combine a spiritual practice with science and service. I had the brains, I felt a calling to service, and I was working on my spiritual practice. This was a big reason I was on The Farm—to learn how to use spirituality in practical ways that would let me help others. The midwives knew stuff I wanted to know—stuff that looked like real magic to me. This was why I wanted to become a midwife and why I was willing to be brave enough to approach Ina May, even though my defensive low-profile and fearful persona didn't typically allow my light to shine for anyone else to see.

Although it felt like I was having an audience with the queen every time I spoke to her, and I was quaking-in-my-socks scared every time I met with her, this mattered so much to me. I simply had to overcome my fear. My heart was beating so hard in my chest that I thought for sure she could see it pounding. Even if she didn't see it, I was certain in my naivete that she *knew* I was quaking because she could see *everything.*

"Please may I learn to be a midwife?"

Looking at me for a few moments, she let me squirm. I tried to be brave, working to look the part of a woman who could be a skilled midwife, a woman with potential to care for those in need, a woman who could be a healer. I kept my head up, looking straight at her, in spite of my strong desire to turn away from those piercing, judging eyes. Finally, she replied.

"I think you need to treat your husband a bit better first. He looks like he has a tight ass, so maybe if you rub it a bit more for him."

Ina May always spoke with certainty, without emotion, and I never argued with anything she said. But this advice didn't make a bit of sense to me. True, Don and I didn't have a good sexual relationship, and we did have some power struggles, but why should that matter to the midwife crew? I felt my face freeze in blank confusion because this was far from what I'd expected. Maybe a no, hopefully a "Yes, let's try it out." *But this?* I quickly tried to hide my feelings, knowing it would seal my fate if she ever saw how insulted I was with her answer, which seemed irrelevant and invasively personal.

I did not want to rub my husband's ass because Ina May

said so, but the rules of joining the midwifery crew were mysterious and nonnegotiable, and no one ever seemed to know what they were. Swallowing my feelings, as I did so many times in those years, I went home to Don and did my best to be a good wife. I probably didn't rub his butt as much as he might've liked, but I avoided as many disagreements as possible and did all I could to take care of my family with a good attitude. I worked hard to gain a respectable reputation and bided my time. I would ask again. Perseverance furthers.

I promised myself I wouldn't give up, just like Joan, Kristin, and I were now making similar promises to ourselves on the road whenever we faced tough times together. The final destination may be unchanged, but the route to get there can take turns in unexpected ways.

Our last day of the Redwood Rogue Run brought partly clear skies along the coast, with no rain and little wind. Pelicans flew in massive formations out over the surf, the sun glinted off the water, and the air smelled clean and salty. There was a mood to the ride this day—one of both poignancy and fatigue. Recalling many common memories as we came through Point Arena, Gualala, and the Sea Ranch, we made our way down Highway 1, appreciating how these gentle switchbacks were nothing compared to what we had handled in the previous few days. When we reached the River's End Restaurant in Jenner, at the end of the Russian River where it flows into the Pacific Ocean, we stopped for one more lunch on the road. We had now ridden past many rivers: the Sacramento, the Klamath, the Rogue, the Coquille with its endless middle forks, the Eel, and finally here we were at the Russian.

This was Memorial Day Monday, and the place was

crowded with several huge motorcycles parked in front of the restaurant, barely off the shoulder of the narrow two-lane Pacific Coast Highway. Riders were loading up and getting ready to head out, so Joan and Kristin went on in to get us a table while I stayed outside to park Boudica as soon as some of the other bikes left. One of the riders, a big man with tats covering his arms and neck, stopped next to me sitting there on Boudica.

"That's a cute bike."

Cute? Boudica? Just wait a minute! My biker-chick hackles went up, and I responded, super casual like he didn't matter to me one bit.

"Yeah, we just finished twelve hundred miles on these bikes . . . did a loop up through Oregon . . . comin' back down now. Hit some real hard weather." Well. That worked. Twelve hundred miles on *that* bike? Respect. I saw it in his face. Yes.

The Redwood Rogue Run, now forever renamed the Redwood Rogue *Rain* Run, ended with a sublime ride down the Pacific Coast Highway, then along the Russian River and through the redwoods of Sonoma County. We rode those perfect curves in full sun, wagging our tails, finally getting a taste of what we had hoped for on the rest of the trip. Not burning hot like the first two days, and not cold and wet like the rest of the run. The sound of surf gave way to the silence of big trees, and the smell of the ocean shifted to the warm scent of vineyards. Perfect curves, one after the other, with sunlight filtering through the trees and dancing on the grapevines. We were in the Zone.

When we pulled up to home base, we wondered how long it would be before we were ready for another ride. We'd take some time to recover, and we'd make sure the next ride was the best one yet. It *would* be planned, but we also now knew we could never completely prepare for challenges we'd find along the way. Before we rode again, I would make some changes that would help me meet those challenges—changes that would tempt my riding buddies to part with Thelma and Louise once and for all.

I would also lose a dear friend before we rode again and would once again rely on angels to help me through the loss. You'd think we'd all get better at the changes that come with age, that we'd get stronger and tougher like old leather. But somehow, my heart just seemed to be getting more tender instead.

CHAPTER 4

TOHELLURIDE TOUR, 2011

Dolores River
First on the right then the left
Now we are centered.

—J

It had been three years since our last ride. That one in the spring weather of Northern California and Oregon was unexpectedly hard, and it took a while to get up the gumption to go at it again. Plans were made to ride the Southwest again. This time we would be riding up into Colorado, into the Rockies with all the twists and turns of mountain highways, and then down to Mesa Verde and over into New Mexico, through Jemez Springs and Santa Fe to visit Joan's mother. From there, we'd head back into Colorado and park the bikes in Telluride for a few days. The Telluride Bluegrass Festival was an excellent place for a layover.

It was again time to get a trailer, get Tim to help me load, and take my bike to Arizona, where Joan, Kristin, and I would start our next adventure. A two-day haul didn't seem like too much now that I was more experienced, even though it had been three years since our last adventure and four years since I'd pulled a trailer. But I wouldn't be trailing Boudica.

In the past three years, I'd decided that my Harley Sportster 883 wasn't big enough for the long rides I wanted to take. She was also too easy to tip over. So I had gone shopping. Up until now, bigger bikes had intimidated me. Sitting on the saddle looking down at the huge gas tank and the wide handlebars had felt overwhelmingly scary. Too much responsibility. Way too big. But I had a few thousand miles under my belt now, and I was ready to face this fear. I headed to my local Harley dealer and did a test ride on a bigger bike—a beautiful silver-and-white Softail Deluxe. She felt gigantic, with almost 1600 cc of power, but she was just a bit lower to the ground and more stable than Boudica. She felt strong and capable, and only a few minutes into that test run I knew I'd found my ride. I negotiated some custom changes: a better saddle set further back for my long legs, a hydraulic clutch for my small hand, and an upgraded tachometer with some extra bells and whistles. Done deal. I put Boudica on Craigslist without any twang of sorrow, and this new ride settled into the Bat Cave in my garage. I was looking forward to getting to know this machine.

Where Boudica had been temperamental, always wanting to tip over with the slightest lean, this bike was solid. She was grounded. She felt like a workhorse with no attitude, simply wanting to go steady and hard and always asking, "Please can we just *go*?" Taking her out on her maiden run through the vineyards of Sonoma County, I pondered what her name should be. I rode, feeling out her personality and the way she ate up the curves, the hills, the stops and starts. Her speed was at the ready, and her response to my throttle twists was immediate and without fanfare. This machine simply *went*. As we rode, I felt her taking care of me, responding to my signals, and protecting me with her strength.

The name Magdalena came into my mind as an image of a mature, nurturing, strong female presence, and to adorn that power, I added Pearl. Magdalena Pearl. I meant to shorten it to a friendly Maggie Pearl, but she did not accept that. Too folksy. No, she was my no-nonsense, powerful motorcycle. When she revved in response to my demands on the throttle, I felt powerful too.

The strong female presence may have come to me because I had lost my most significant sister-support earlier that year. Laura, my Big Sib. Laura, who had helped me get through my divorce. Laura, who had been a sister in the truest sense and who had seen us off on our Redwood Rogue Run.

Shortly after the Redwood Rogue ride, Laura had been diagnosed with metastatic breast cancer. Sharing her shock, I had firmly committed to traveling the cancer road with her so she would not be alone. It was really all I could offer; there's not much else to do with metastatic breast cancer, also known as stage IV cancer because it has spread to other parts of the body. By then my dear friend was the single mother of a teenage daughter, and her goal was to stay alive until Lily graduated from high school. Three years to fight for time.

For all those years, Laura came to Santa Rosa for her chemo sessions. Sometimes she would stay over with me so I could care for her that first evening of treatment, but more often I would drive her the eighty-five miles home after her chemo and get her comfortable in her own space before the side effects hit her. We did this for three years, but in the year leading up to this Tohelluride Tour, Laura died.

• • •

Why isn't my love enough? I often wondered. *Why do I feel so inadequate? She is my sister, teacher, confidante, role model.* I had been midwifing her sickness for three years, and now I was midwifing her death. I commuted to her home in Willits for the final ten days, steeling myself the whole way an hour and a half north and crying the whole way home, an hour and a half south. I was the one her family counted on to make the right decisions and to tell them what to do, because Laura and I were best friends and because we were both doctors— although I was the only one still practicing, because she was busy dying. As I drove, I would talk to her like I always had— with frank honesty and love, as if she were there with me. I'd say things I could not say around others.

I hate pink ribbons. I hate that permanent plastic port they inserted into your chest wall. I hate the chemo infusion center with a view, where all the dying people are lined up in recliners, their skin gray with a sick mixture of cancer and chemo. The energy there is a confusing mix of fear, resignation, cheerful encouragement, and boredom. Did you know I escaped out to the car to cry that first day you got chemo? Not because you were sick—because I didn't want to do this!

I was with you when you married Steve, divorced, and then hooked up with Malcolm. I was with you when Lily was born. You've always been the one who gives me clarity. You are my heart-sister.

But why do you have to live in Willits? Sometimes that's just too far. And dropping you off after chemo, building up the fire in the woodstove, then just . . . leaving you there . . . feels like shit. Three fucking years of this shit while you buy time to finish raising Lily.

So now your liver is shot, full of cancer. You're really going to leave. My heart breaks to see the look of surprise on your face, like you thought we'd have more time to play with that bucket list.

I'm glad your sister's here . . . glad for Lily . . . and for your boyfriend to hold you all night long. Did you know I went in your bathroom and cried when Malcolm told you that you were beautiful? You looked like a dying gross skeleton, and he said you were beautiful. I know he meant it.

But I gotta tell you: there comes a time when even I can't do it anymore. This is too hard, and it's gone on too long. You're going to die anyway—just go ahead and do it. I mean, how long does it take for someone to die? How long can I do this—this driving, this crying, this wise-woman-doctor-strong gig? I'm losing it.

Her oncologist called me. He, Laura, and I were colleagues in the medical community, so there was a kind and personal connection. He called to check up on the both of us.

"Hey, Stacey. How you holdin' up there?"

"Okay, I guess. She's definitely dying but I just don't know how long it'll be . . . I really wish I knew."

"Well. It's like when a car is running out of gas. The engine dies when the fuel is used up. It happens. It's inevitable."

I thanked him and we hung up. I knew it was inevitable. It'd been inevitable for years. I wanted an expiration date and time, and all I got was what I already knew.

One early morning, as I was driving the 101 north at 70 mph, I suddenly realized that I might throw up if I had to keep driving to Willits even one more time. If I didn't throw up, I might just pass out. I wanted to scream, but there was no one to scream to. I was a mess of emotions, exhausted, and I'd reached my limit.

I could no longer keep my spirit strong and my vision

clear. I couldn't keep driving that road for three hours round trip every single day without killing myself. If I couldn't call on her, I didn't know where the strength was going to come from. For so many years, she had been my rock. She was who I called when I was overwhelmed, unsure, and confused. She was who I called about science, about medicine, about sex, about my kids, and just about everything. *Now who can I call?*

I put on my Bluetooth earpiece, but I didn't turn it on. I just hit the call button and said, "Call. God. Mobile."

"Did you say, 'Call God Mobile'?" the overly pleasant female voice inside my head replied.

"Yes."

"Calling. God. Mobile."

I heard it ring . . . and then I heard . . . voice mail pick up. *Damn!*

Um. God? I know you are really busy . . . and I know that it's all going the way it's supposed to . . . I know it's going to be okay. But I gotta tell you that I think I'm in over my head. I mean, I'm not sure if I can keep it together, and I could use a little . . . I'm just flailing and not being as nice as I should be, and I think I need . . . So . . . I don't know . . . maybe if you get in and check your messages and if there's any way you can give me . . . a sign, or something . . . I sure would appreciate it. I mean, I don't want to bother you—just, if you get a chance . . . Well, thanks for listening anyway. Bye.

Somehow, I felt a little better after that imaginary conversation. I'd done all I could. There was nothing else to do but go forward and face another day. I turned my iPod to shuffle-play, took a deep breath, and kept driving.

I guess it was about fifteen minutes later when God apparently checked voice mail, because Beth Orton's voice, singing Leonard Cohen's classic song "Sisters of Mercy," came pouring out of the speakers, surrounding me with everything I needed. Now I was really crying, and I had to pull over. Never did I expect to get an answer to my imaginary voice mail, but this was crystal-clear communication. I suddenly felt the presence of my angels, and the music was reminding me they were there. I knew I was lonely, feeling unholy, and feeling poor-me sinful. But now I also knew I was not alone. The pure compassion that poured out of my car's speakers pierced my soul.

I arrived in Willits that day with renewed strength and a comfort in knowing I was guided and supported by the Sisters of Mercy. They gave me the grace to help and the ability to rise above my own exhaustion. I regained my awareness of that holy state where we swim in the energy of birth and death. I was once again spirit strong.

Laura's sister, Susan, was in the bedroom saying goodbye. She had scheduled a flight home that day, and although she had hoped to stay until Laura left, she was running out of time and had her bag packed by the front door. I was in the kitchen making coffee when I heard her call out to me from the bedroom.

"Stacey! Her breathing is all different now. Is this normal?"

That was the moment I had been waiting for. I knew everything was changing right now. Joining Susan in the bedroom, I heard the end-of-life breathing rate, rhythm, and flow. I recognized this; I'd attended more than one death. We were close to Laura's end.

"It's time," I called to the others. Malcolm and Lily joined us, and we all gathered around the bed where Laura lay on her back in total relaxation. She was a very tall woman, six feet, and the length of her filled the bed. Gowned but uncovered, she was spread-eagled with her long arms and legs fully outstretched in a posture of facing into the future. Her chest where her heart lay, her chest where her soul may hover, her chest with its wide-open heart chakra was leading the way. She was the figurehead on the bow of a ship, showing me and others how to sail bravely into the light. There was no guarding, no resistance, no tension, no pain. Laura was at peace in the power of full acceptance. Even to the end she was my big sister showing me the way.

We surrounded her with our love, quietly watching her transition. There were no tears; those had been shed a long time ago. Instead, we stood in respect for the passage we were observing. Then she was gone. The next breath did not come. She was beautiful.

The Sisters of Mercy supported me through the next few hours when I found myself alone in a house with a dead friend and her daughter. Malcolm and Susan had left already—Malcolm to handle his grief in private and Susan to catch her flight home—and I knew we would lose Laura the minute I called hospice to take her away. So first I gave Lily, who was just nineteen years old, the opportunity to spend a few private moments with her mother. I saw her tightly cradling her beloved cat in her arms as she went in to make her own private goodbyes.

Then it was my turn. Sitting next to my dear sister-friend, I told her everything I needed to say to her face-to-face before her body left the house. Because I could always say *anything* to Laura, I shared my pain and my heartache, holding nothing back. I laughed at my own self-pity and could hear her laughing along with me. Before I left to call hospice, I had just a few final words.

"God damn it, Laura! You sure took your time leaving, didn't you. I wasn't sure I'd be able to make it this far with you, but hey—we did it to the end. Hold a spot for me; I'll be coming someday."

Later, when Laura's body had been taken away to the mortuary, when Lily was safe with her aunt and uncle who had arrived that afternoon, and when my job for that day was done, I drove back south on the 101 heading for home. Turning on my music once again, I sang loudly along with Beth Orton, thanking the Sisters of Mercy for waiting for me. For lying down with me. For holding me with generous, life-affirming love. Just as Laura used to do.

A motorcycle cannot replace a sister-friend, but Magdalena Pearl had a presence about her that also made me feel supported. She was good for me. As long as I did my part by riding her well, she would perform, and we would not get into trouble. And to my surprise, when this bike accelerated, I felt emotions I had not expected. Frustrations and resentments came to me, rose to a crescendo along with the engine's screaming rpms, and then blew out right through those big pipes with pounding speed. Whenever I thought of Laura, gone too soon, I'd realize that grief comes with a good portion of anger, and I could feel other long-stored and ignored emotions as they were released from wherever I had stashed them. Facing the open road together, Magdalena Pearl and I let go of all that fear and frustration and replaced it with joy, filling the vacuum that came with acceleration and speed.

As I trailered my new bike to Arizona, I thought about how Joan and Kristin would react to her. I knew they were really looking forward to meeting Boudica's replacement, so when I pulled up in my rig after the two-day haul, I was proud to introduce Magdalena Pearl to them. Then, as Kristin backed my brand-new bike off its trailer, I could only imagine

when others told me things about myself that were difficult
to hear. If a housemate told me I was being manipulative, my
first thought might be *No fucking way!* But instead I would
say, "Thank you. I hear you. I'm going to pay attention to that
and see if I need to change something." This response was a
good way to get others to back off, but at the same time give
respect to their point of view. I had to admit that often these
comments were right on the money and taught me invalu-
able social skills. I learned to pay attention to how the energy between people flowed, and how to be responsible with
it. I learned to hear other points of view. How to speak truth
compassionately and how to better communicate so others
might hear what I was trying to say. How to be tolerant.

But even though these skills had value, I remained frustrated because I still needed to learn how to handle intense,
high-energy situations with competence and awareness, and
birth was the ultimate high-energy event on The Farm when
we were all young and making babies. The energy of birth
was familiar to those of us who had tripped on acid; both
experiences involved an altered state where everything was
surreal with the intensity of the moment, and it was easy to
get lost in that. It was easy to get scared when Mother Nature
took over your body and you realized you had no control. A
spiritual midwife could not only manage the medical aspects
of a normal birth, but she could also help the family manage the intensity of the situation as well, so fear and confusion didn't get in the way of a good birth. I wanted to learn
to swim in that deep psychedelic energy of birth. But I was
still not considered "cool enough" to learn those skills on
The Farm. After hearing "no" from Ina May enough times, I
was frustrated and motivated to do something about it. But
I didn't show my feelings because Stephen was teaching us

to be responsible with our energy, and expressing anger was like spewing toxic gas into the atmosphere. Irresponsible and uncool. That meant that negative emotions had to be deeply stashed inside.

So, rather than leave as Carolyn had chosen to do, I adapted. Just like my experience as a navy brat had taught me, I worked to fit into the community. Part of that fitting in, at least in those early days, was doing my time with Kid-Herd every week.

One day, I'd finally gotten seven toddlers, all under the age of four, down for their afternoon nap. It wasn't easy getting them to sleep, but without a nap they would have been miserably tired and irritable when their parents came to pick them up in the evening. Also, I didn't have patience for seven tired toddlers, even though two of them were mine. I hardly had patience for seven *not-tired*, delightful, curious, active, loveable toddlers. Kid-Herd days were the hardest, but I was willing to do this job one day a week so that I could have the other four workdays free to myself.

Now they were spread out across the living room, each one on their own little mat, as I sat in my easy chair long after the last squirm. Watching with an eagle eye, I was firm, my no-nonsense attitude stemming from my experience as a teacher.

"Josh, please leave Sarah alone. Quit poking her. Now."

"Anna, get back on your own mat, please. Do I need to move you to another space?"

Finally. Quiet. It felt so good to be quiet and still for just a few minutes.

Then, pushing some mild feelings of envy aside—envy of the easy life of a toddler on The Farm—I got up to start rolling tortillas for dinner for our relatively small household of nine. Staying busy was in keeping with Stephen's teachings. "Enlightenment is not so much making it to the never-never land through the secret passageway; it's more like getting off your tail and doing something."

Don had set up DC power in our house, running off car batteries, so I put an eight-track Bob Marley tape in the stereo system and turned on the music. I knew it wouldn't wake the kids; if anything, they'd sleep longer because of it. These kids were raised on reggae and rock and roll.

After mixing up some dough with flour, water, oil, and salt, I fired up the woodstove, grabbed a rolling pin, tied my long braids in a knot behind my neck, and started rolling. When I got the timing down right, the tortilla on the griddle was ready to flip just when the next one was rolled out. I'd hand-flip the one on the stove, pick up the next one, pat and slap it aggressively to get off all the extra flour, then hand-grab the now finished tortilla, throw it on the growing pile, slap the new one onto the griddle, and turn to roll another. It was a dance. It was a meditation. With the right music, the right beat and rhythm, and some cannabis, a stack of forty warm tortillas would be piled on a plate, loosely draped with a moist towel to keep them soft, long before the kids woke up. Something about creating this tall stack of fresh tortillas made me feel righteous. Useful. Simple and functional and appreciated. *Is this really doing anything to save the world?* I wondered about this, but at least we all had dinner, and on that day, it was plenty. In a few years, I would decide it wasn't enough, and I would have to make some big changes.

Now thirty years had passed, and I was in Mesa Verde looking forward to connecting with the woman who had been there—in college and at The Farm—at the beginning. What

changes had we both been through? Would we still want to
sit on a porch and brush each other's hair?

I was checking in at the front desk of the Far View
Lodge when I heard Carolyn's familiar voice just behind me.
Turning around, I saw her grinning up at me with that same
quirky smile and those eyes that always felt like home. Still an
outdoor enthusiast, and still a redhead, my short and curvy
friend had always been pretty much the physical opposite of
me. We hugged as only dear lifetime friends can do.

That evening Carolyn and I sat up late in my little room
at the lodge, looking out at the distant mesas and catching up
on parallel lives that had been lived separately for many years.
Between us was a bottle of wine I'd brought from Sonoma
County and a little brass pipe with some fresh herb to share.
With the familiarity of our longtime friendship, we easily
slipped into sharing stories that held nothing back. This was
as safe and full as conversation could get.

Uncorking the wine and pouring each of us a glass,
Carolyn asked about The Farm. "So hey. Why'd you guys stay
so long there in Tennessee? I never expected you to last that
long . . . not the two of you!"

"What . . . you saying we weren't good Farm people?"

"No! You were great Farmies! Better than me!" She
laughed. "But Don never bought into Stephen, and you've always gone your own way in spite of where you are. I know . . .
I know . . . you're quiet. You're sneaky about being different.
But the two of you? You sure stayed a long time . . . what, ten
years?"

"Well, yeah. And I don't regret it," I replied. I sipped
my wine as I studied her. When you know and love someone deeply, you quit seeing the physical and are more aware
of that person's essential *being*. Their energy, the way they

move and hold their body, and most importantly, what you see when you look into their eyes. Carolyn, and her essence, hadn't changed. She was still the sweet, quirky, truth-telling sister who had befriended me when I was feral.

I went on. "We didn't want to live alone in suburbia, raising kids without community. We liked being part of that commune and didn't want to be 'normal,' I guess. And it was working . . . until . . . well, until it wasn't. For the most part, it allowed me to be me . . . whoever that might have been."

Don and I first lived in our bus, and then in several different tent-houses for a few years, and it was getting old. We'd scored a sixteen-by-thirty-two army surplus canvas tent, built a frame, and put the tent over the frame. That was home—I mean, it had walls! And we cut out a few windows, added a floor, and made it work for two or three families. Those were days when it was good we were young.

By the end of the first couple of years, the community had taught me how to be passive and had taught the two of us how to live together as best friends. But we wanted a real home in a real house. At that point, we knew we wanted to stay in Tennessee, but after the arrival of Cara, our second daughter, who was born in the woods with the Farm midwives in attendance, we also knew that living in a house with real walls, plumbing, and heat was becoming essential. So we talked to Stephen, getting an agreement from him that we could earn money in California, bring it back to The Farm, and build a house that would remain ours. In a community where no one owned anything, this was a big deal. This meant that, once it was built, we couldn't be asked to move out of our nice house by the housing committee. Stephen agreed, so with this assurance we went out to make money. Don worked as a skilled handyman, and I worked in a tomato cannery as a payroll processor. We earned $10,000 and then made our way back to The Farm, where we spent the summer and fall of 1981 living deep in the woods, in backpacking tents, while building a four-bedroom house. This was where we planned to settle and raise our family.

"Why did you go back to The Farm with all its obvious challenges?" Carolyn asked. Taking a sip of wine, I leaned back and thought about my answer.

I loved being part of a community. I loved the spirituality we embraced. I loved Sunday services, those mornings when a thousand like-minded hippies would gather in the meditation meadow, facing the sun as it rose over the low hills, sitting zazen and chanting each week, the interwoven tones of our collective *ohmmm* giving us all a natural high. The sound of an ohm made in that meadow by that many people . . . I'll never forget. Stephen would speak to us after the ohm, and sometimes a couple would get married at one of these services. It was like church, but *not*. It was our own way of being spiritual. We stayed because I appreciated how I was growing by living intensely with others, getting lessons every day that helped me understand how to be honest and kind.

Also, some of the inconveniences and challenges had been remedied by the time we built our house. A local town had donated a phone system, a single party line for which each household had a different ring. We learned to ignore all the rings coming out of the phone, only perking up our ears when our own *beep-beep-bong* sound came through. Not everyone had a phone, though, so if you got a call for someone who lived down the ridge a bit, you'd set the phone down, go outside, and holler to the next house over. "Janine has a call here! Pass it along!" And maybe ten minutes later Janine would come hustling in with a kid on her hip to take the call. The phone system was also a news service; you could pick it up anytime and listen in on the conversation of the moment. Of course, when there was midwife business, everyone had to hang up immediately.

Other developments included a soy dairy, which made tofu, soy milk, tempeh, and soft-serve icebean (ice cream made from soymilk). We had medical facilities, including a clinic, a lab, and an ambulance service. We also had a book publishing company and a few other small start-ups, some of which were starting to be profitable. There was no money exchanged on The Farm; we were a true commune. And while our infrastructure was still being developed, and we still depended on outhouses and the "shitter truck" that cleaned them out, we had come a long way from that first year: the outhouses were covered and had doors for privacy.

"Didn't you go renegade with that school you started before you left?" Carolyn asked. "What was that about?"

"Ahhh. The Farm Lab School," I replied. "Yep. That was pure magic. So worth going renegade to make that happen! For one beautiful year." Taking a toke off the little brass pipe and handing it over to her, I launched into the story of our alternative school, the last year we lived on The Farm. The one that made such a huge difference in many children's lives.

The Farm had built a school for the hundreds of children being born and raised there. The teachers were mothers who volunteered, and since I had a daughter in third grade and a bachelor's degree in elementary education, it was pretty clear that the job for me at that time was to serve as a teacher. I began to teach Sarah's class, sharing the responsibility with another mother so we would each have time for the rest of what life on The Farm demanded: laundry days, Kid-Herd days, and all the other labor-intensive demands of a lifestyle off the grid. But after one year of teaching in that school, I saw plenty of room for improvement.

There was no set curriculum, so there was no way to know if a child was ready to advance to the next grade. My desire for organization and my professional take on the situation motivated me to take action. I had experience teaching regular elementary school. I had also taught special education to emotionally troubled adolescents and was certified in the Montessori Method. So I felt qualified to speak up, and I did so at the end of the school year. I proposed we spend the summer mapping a curriculum that would help all these untrained teachers focus on clear learning goals for each grade.

But because I wasn't part of the leadership team, my suggestions were ignored. This made no sense, and once again, I was frustrated—with no place to direct my pent-up energy. In full agreement about the dysfunctional politics of making changes on The Farm, Don and I talked about our options.

"Why don't we start our own school?" he asked. "We could make it be so much better than what they've got going up there."

"Oh, that would be so fun!" I agreed. "We could make it big enough for the first through fourth grades, so both our girls would be covered. And we could make it so all four grades were there together, with the older kids helping the younger ones learn, totally integrated!" We were both getting excited, something that always happened whenever we were faced with a new creative project.

We commandeered an abandoned trailer just down the road from our new house. And with the help of many of the kids who hoped to go to our school, we spent the summer cleaning and painting the trailer, building learning centers from one end of it to the other. By the time September rolled around, we had a new little schoolhouse ready to teach kids in the style of the Montessori Method. Don and I enlisted Connie, a friend who had a master's in education, and Aurora, an elderly, outspoken housemate who had escaped the Guatemalan revolution and agreed to teach Spanish to the kids one day a week. With this faculty of four, we opened the doors to twenty students on the same day the main school started classes at the other end of The Farm, a thirty-minute walk from our school.

Instead of individual desks, we had learning stations—reading, math, science, geography—and the kids could choose to go to whichever station they wanted, depending on their own interests. They just had to be accountable to spend time at each station a certain number of times each week, to make sure they were getting what they needed. We took the whole school on field trips sixty miles north to the Nashville Public Library, where they learned about libraries and about how to check out books—something pretty special to kids born and raised in the woods. After recess, I often led them all through a guided meditation, bringing them back to focus and teaching them how to use mindfulness tools for self-care, tools they could use for the rest of their lives. Our students were free to learn at their own pace, and it was gratifying to watch them find their own learning styles and thrive in a true learning environment. I felt like I was using my college degree as I had always meant to use it, making a difference in children's lives.

• • •

When I finished telling Carolyn this story of our project during our final year on The Farm, the mood was a bit somber with the awareness that our naïve hippie dreams—dreams that we could create a successful spiritual commune—had not been sustainable.

"So what was the final straw?" she asked. "I mean, what happened to make you leave that house you built and the school you made happen? It must've been something pretty big, 'cuz you were in deep."

"Yep . . . it was pretty big. It was an awakening. It was also when I finally began to claim my own power, taking it back from men I had habitually trusted for so many years."

In 1982, nine of us were living in the house we'd built: our family of four, another family of four, and Aurora, who was manipulative. She would say one thing at home and then go out on The Farm and say another, always disparaging and damning to me personally, including assertions that I abused children. I'd ask her about the rumors, which quickly made it back to me, but she would deny having said these things. I couldn't figure out why she was doing this, and I couldn't talk truth with her no matter how hard I tried, so I decided to make a rare call to Stephen to ask his advice. Calling him was always difficult and scary; it felt to me like calling on the king and hoping to get him on a kind day, on a wise day.

I imagined him at home when I called, relaxed with a few close followers, passing a joint around as they often did. Stephen had known me since I was single, and he had tried to kiss me once, but offended, I pulled away, and he never tried it again. I never knew whether my rejection tainted our relationship, but I could only see him as my teacher and had absolutely no interest in him as an intimate partner. And although my point of view sometimes differed from his over the years, I still valued his teachings—when I agreed with them. So I was calling him now for advice as my revered teacher, as a wise man who knew the answers to difficult questions.

"Stephen, I don't know what to do. Aurora is really nice to my face, but then she goes out on The Farm and says horrible things about me. She denies all of this, and I honestly don't know what to do. How can I continue to live with someone who tells lies? I'm truly stumped. Do you have any help for me here? How do I get past her lying?"

Stephen replied in his cold, ex-marine, authoritative rat-a-tat staccato speech pattern. "Stacey, you called me. This is your dime. So I'm going to tell you: You're a tripper. You've always been a tripper. And until you are willing to listen to me and what I say without questioning me, I don't want to talk to you again."

I hung up. My ears buzzed, my body felt thick and frozen. My guru. My teacher. The man I had trusted more than my own father. He was judging and rejecting me, making it intolerable to stay, just as my father had done so many years before. A *tripper* was a damning label on The Farm for anyone who did not completely agree with everything Stephen said. He had just written me off, told me I couldn't have an opinion, told me I couldn't question him. And he didn't offer any advice about Aurora, the reason I had called him in the first place. Stunned, I finally realized that Stephen had turned into a despot, and we were living in a cult.

Numb with disbelief, I stumbled out and across the dirt road to my nearest neighbor's house. Staggering into her kitchen, I told her what had happened. Jane took one look at my face and knew just what to do. She fed me cookies.

When Don came home later that day, we talked. "The Farm has become a cult. We have to leave," I said.

Don was fine with that proposal. "Sure, we can head out . . . but we have to finish out the school year. It could take us that long anyway, to get it together." No argument from him. Let's face it: Don wasn't there for Stephen or Spirit anyway.

"Looking back, there was one part of this move we could have handled differently," I told Carolyn. "Our two daughters, aged ten and seven by that point, had lived most of their short lives on The Farm. Their world was communal living and they were used to that culture: hippie kids everywhere with long hair, freedom in the woods of Tennessee, and freedom to speak their minds to the adults. While Don and I had grown up out there in normal America, they had not. What we took for granted—the social expectations of normal American society—were unknown to them. It was a rough transition for our girls, but Don and I were completely focused on the logistics of yet another move, this one without a thought of coming back to Tennessee."

The four-bedroom house we had built still lacked running hot water and needed some finishing, but it was a good solid home. It had passive solar heating with clerestory windows and a greenhouse attached to the main bedroom so we could pick fresh veggies all winter long. It was a beautiful house with potential to be even better, and we would be leaving it behind. It would become someone else's home—an asset we turned over to the community—so I called the people in charge.

"We'd like travel money in exchange for our house. We won't need much, but it makes sense to help us leave so we can free up the scene here for someone else."

The phone rang with word from the Board, a newly created group that was trying to run The Farm after years of totalitarianism. "Sorry. We aren't going to pay you anything for that house. It's not fair to others who don't have a house to bargain with. Don can go to work in Nashville, and he can keep a dollar an hour of the pay he makes . . . and in time you'll have enough for your travels."

Don's response? "Fuck them! What, I can make four dollars an hour working my ass off sixty miles away and only keep a dollar? Not gonna happen."

I was mad. No, I was furious. Between Stephen and the Board, I had had enough and wasn't going to take it anymore. Looking around at my home, the large windows looking out at the Tennessee woods, the hardwood floors, the finished sheetrock and painted walls, the art on the walls. The thought that they expected me to leave all this . . . just as I had left my little school bus years earlier . . . was more than I could swallow. I fumed as I imagined how long it would take for Don to earn enough for our escape—at a dollar an hour. They had no idea who they were up against. When the two of us pulled together, we made things happen. We came up with Plan B.

A day or two later, I called the Board, knowing they were meeting and timing my call to give them my news when they were all there to hear it. Don and I had saved tons of money by tearing down old houses in neighboring towns and reclaiming windows and hardwood flooring and other building materials, so I knew I had a viable plan.

"I understand you've made a decision about our house," I said in my calmest voice. "So I just want you to know that we are planning on taking the house apart and selling the parts to make money for our travel plans. We built it out of salvaged parts, so we will get our funding by selling the windows—they're worth $400—and the hardwood floors— worth a good thousand. And we can sell the plumbing we have for metal scraps . . ."

I meant every single word.

I didn't get any further. "Wait a minute . . . wait just a minute . . . let's discuss this further," said the voice on the other end of the phone. "How 'bout we send a car down to pick you up and you come on in to our meeting to talk about it." His folksy tone did not fool me. This was a battle.

I had their attention. I wasn't surprised. I agreed.

The car came, and both Don and I jumped in. It was June in Tennessee, a warm day that still felt a bit like spring, before the heat and humidity of the South had set in for the summer months. The dogwoods were well over their bloom, and the woods were filling in with lush green. We made that mile-long ride up to The House in silence. My stomach was in knots, and I felt like I was going to a summit, trying to negotiate a treaty to stave off unforgettable, unforgivable battles. Into the small upstairs room we walked, sitting down with no fear because either way this worked out, we had a plan. We were out of there, and no one was going to stop us.

The five members of the Board were sitting in a semicircle, leaving us the open arc to sit and present our case. This was a far cry from the friendly agreements we had made years ago when The Farm was new and dreams still held promise, when we stood before Stephen and agreed that we wanted to help change the world. Stephen was not there; he was not part of the Board. Tension was palpable. No joints or pipes were being shared. The atmosphere was all business. My, how times had changed.

The Board had discussed the situation among themselves while we were being fetched, and they had a plan. "We've decided that we can give you $2,000 for your house."

That might get us a good way to California. But I should've known there was a catch.

"But you have to give $1,000 of that back immediately, to help someone who doesn't have a house to bargain with. Otherwise it's not fair. Not everyone has a house to fund their travel plans." They weren't just going to give us the thousand dollars. No, they had to make us hurt a little by teasing us with the second thousand. They needed to teach us a lesson.

I was still angry, but then again, I was already angry at the demise of our dreams. It appeared that true communism does not work. Not everyone contributes equally, not everyone can learn how to get along when living in close quarters, and if no one owns anything, nothing matters. The community kept taking on new members and was still not adequately housing the ones already there. There were "haves" and "have-nots," those with connections and those without, and we were not going to be able to make a difference in the rest of the world if we couldn't house or feed ourselves.

It was hard to separate the sources of my sadness or my anger. And anger was not cool on The Farm, so I couldn't show my resentment; they might just cut the amount further if I did. I swallowed my feelings like I had done so many times before. We had to leave. A thousand dollars was better than nothing, and it was sure better than sending Don to work in Nashville for the next year while we waited to leave. So we took their offer, and started firming up our plans. Don's parents, who had been waiting for the day we regained our senses, helped with moving costs, and before long we landed in the backyard of generous friends in Turlock, where we set up camping tents and started over.

Standing up to Stephen and the Board was the beginning of the end of my submissiveness. It was the beginning of owning my voice. I would not go back—not to Tennessee and not to passivity. My own path was opening up before me.

For a moment, Carolyn and I both sat quietly in thought, and then she looked up at me as she remembered our pact from years ago. "Want me to brush your hair?"

On the next day's ride, Kristin rode in the lead. By then, we had found our groove riding together again and had started to gel. The valley opened up around us, and at one point an iris farm whizzed by, its whites, blues, and purples a blur as we kept cruising. When we arrived in Jemez Springs, a welcome respite in the heat, we wandered the area around the inn, making our way through an open mountain meadow to a babbling brook. There, we took seats on the rocks by the water and gazed at red rock cliffs rising above on the other side—just what we needed to release the road fatigue. After a while, feeling the need for some me-time, I went back to the inn to check out the spa, got on a waiting list for a massage, and took the most delicious shower—washing the grime out of my hair and soaking up moisture through my skin. This place made me want to sit still and, for once, be a human *being* instead of a human *doing*. So I took my book, the latest in the Three Pines series by Louise Penny, down to a convenient tree swing in the meadow and read while the sun set. Looking up occasionally, I watched the ever-changing light dance against the steep cliffs on the other side of the brook, and when it got a bit too cool, I made my way back to my room to enjoy the courtyard and fountains right outside the door. At every turn, I felt blessed to be in this amazing place.

About eight thirty that evening, the massage therapist knocked on my door and said she could do a thirty-minute massage. *Hallelujah.* The spa had windows in each room that were placed so I could see sky and the top of the cliffs in the fading light while I lay on the table, and that thirty minutes felt like an hour—one of the best massages ever. Her hands felt like they loved every muscle they touched. My right arm and shoulder, tight from constant pressure on the throttle, responded to her kneading. My left hip, tired from constant shifting, responded to the stretches. My whole body released tension I didn't even know I was holding. This was the life. This was the pampering part of the adventure I had imagined.

While I lay there on the table getting my body lovingly caressed, I thought about how important it is to have human touch. I sighed. To be touched by another human being, to be nurtured, appreciated, and *seen*, is so important. Life affirming. My mind wandered to the days when touch from Don was not pleasurable, when he used my body without regard for my needs or pleasure, and when there was no physical nurturing in my life. Those were the years when we were learning to be married, and although we became best friends, we never learned to make love.

I had accepted a long marriage that did not satisfy my need for loving touch. I wasn't used to being touched; in my family while growing up, we did not cuddle or snuggle. My mother was slender, and although she loved me and she would sometimes hug me, I mostly felt her sharp edges. My father was off-limits, both physically and emotionally. He loved me through his words of praise for good grades and through his pride in my accomplishments. He showed me love with the sticks of gum he slipped into letters written from far away. I don't even remember ever seeing my two parents deeply embrace. So when I was young and married Don, given that I had never had physical nurturing, I didn't expect it from him. But, oh, how I now longed to be cuddled, to be held, to feel safe in someone's arms!

I was born with thin skin and have always felt every tiny tickle on my body. I have often longed with all my heart and soul for the warm touch and the unconditional love of another human being. So far in my life, a professional massage was the closest thing I'd found to fill the need.

A couple of days later, we rode right into the center of Taos. Lunch there was full of heavy New Mexican food, including guacamole made fresh at our table, and a discussion about where to go next: ride the Enchanted Circle or go on a hike just suggested by a shopkeeper in the plaza. Finally deciding to stick to our original plan, we set out to ride the Circle. I rode sweep, following Joan and Kristin, first along the creek and green trees . . . then throughout the open country surrounded by mountain peaks . . . past Angel Fire . . . over Bobcat Pass, at ninety-eight hundred feet . . . all the while fighting the sleepy effects of that heavy lunch we'd eaten. If I'd been a passenger in a car, I would've missed the whole thing because I would've been snoozing away the warm afternoon with a full stomach. Riding a Harley when I was that sleepy felt as risky as any of the road challenges we had faced so far, but it was a risk that came without helpful adrenaline; I fought to stay alert and upright on two wheels. Later, Joan admitted she had been fighting the same urge to nap, which made me feel a bit better.

All three of us were ready to settle in for the night, so we circled back to Taos, found our adjoining rooms in the

Hacienda del Sol, and unloaded. Someone had to go for wine, cheese, crackers, and fruit, and it was my turn. I headed out on foot, in the late afternoon heat to Cid's—a convenience store just a few hundred feet down the highway toward town. I thought maybe a walk would reenergize me after that heavy lunch and hot ride.

Cid's did not sell wine. *Drat.* So I started hoofing it down the highway to a liquor store, sweating and trudging along on the shoulder of the road, in traffic, carrying a backpack now loaded with brie cheese and Triscuits. It was absolutely no fun. On top of the fatigue and soreness from riding, every desert day also threatened dehydration. Lips dry, throat dry, thick snot every morning. Drink, drink. Shower, shower. Altitude and dry air were so strange for this coastal girl, and it didn't help my mood. I finally found the liquor store, grabbed a bottle of Ravenswood zin, found out they didn't take credit, hit the ATM machine, and finally got the hell out of there. After hoofing it back to the Hacienda and arriving all hot and sweaty, I was unusually intolerant of the sight of Joan and Kristin laughing and relaxing in the shade on the lawn with their books, enjoying the slowly developing sunset.

I took them the wine and cheese and crackers and then went back into my room to time myself out. I was not fit for socializing in that moment and needed to smoke a little cannabis, change my attitude, and recover from the heat. I was just out of a refreshing shower when Carolyn called to continue where we'd left off with our conversation a few nights ago. We would do that: not connect for months and then, when we did finally get together, the conversation would go on and on until we were completely caught up with each other's life. Carolyn said she'd been thinking about my exodus from The Farm and realized she had no idea why I'd quit being a teacher and decided to go to medical school. "Wouldn't it have been easier just to go get a teaching job and get on with it?" she asked.

But I did not want to be a teacher anymore, and that was a story I was only too willing to share.

When I finally realized that Ina May was never going to let me train in midwifery, I decided that maybe she did me a favor. Maybe that club was not one I wanted to be a part of, as much as I wanted to learn their healing skills. I wouldn't fit into that group of chosen women anyway. Then, as Don and I headed toward California when we left The Farm, we talked about what lay ahead. Somewhere in the middle of Kansas, we agreed that it might be a good idea for me to go to medical school. I wanted to learn to heal. I wanted to learn the science of medicine. So what if I was thirty-four years old? I had a girlfriend who had gone to med school when she was in her thirties, and if she could do it, I knew I could. So why not? It sure couldn't hurt to try.

"We'd never be poor again if you became a doctor, and you'd never be bored," Don said.

That was a welcome thought, considering our current cashless situation, and with his support I agreed to go for it. I'd bypass midwifery. I'd go to school to be a physician—no, a *spiritual* physician—and take care of people cradle to grave. I was confident I'd be an excellent clinician, and after my years on The Farm, I'd also know how to pay attention to more than just the physical. Mind, body, and soul—my patients would be *seen*. As a family physician, I could deliver babies, perform surgeries, and listen to my patients with an open heart. I'd be *more* than a midwife. I'd show Ina May a thing or two!

Just two months after packing up and leaving The Farm

for the last time, I met with an academic adviser at Stanislaus State University to find out what it would take to get into medical school.

"You've been watching too much *General Hospital,*" he said. "It's just not that simple or easy."

You have no idea who I am, I thought. I had not watched TV in over four years, and even when I did have a TV, I never watched soap operas. And after what I'd learned from ten years in a hippie-commune-turned-cult, I thought premed sounded like a breeze!

But what actually came out of my mouth in his office was more reserved. "Let's just see how I do, okay? Which classes should I start with?"

It seemed he decided to load me with the most intense courses he could find, perhaps attempting to weed me out with some harsh reality. Regardless, I signed up for Embryology, Genetics, Chemistry, Molecular Biology, and Calculus. These were all courses I had avoided while earning my bachelor's degree, but all were required if I was to get into medical school. I was so eager to learn, after all those years of pent-up frustration and desire for knowledge. And as it turned out, I aced every single one of those courses and won the chemistry award that year. Two years later, I applied to medical school. I was on my path toward becoming a spiritual physician.

Carolyn listened to my story. She repeated what she had told me before: she was jealous of me. My long legs. My many college boyfriends. And now, my luck in getting into med school. This jealousy was an old habit leftover from university days, when we used to compete for the same cool guys and when we were young enough to care about superficial assets. But now it was just a standing joke, and we both laughed in that comfortable place where old friends with old jokes get to be.

The next morning, the three of us loaded up our bikes and headed for our next stop: Durango. Wide-open highways with mountains in the far distance on each side. Glorious clear air, the smell of sage and verbena strong. With Kristin in the lead, we climbed up off the Taos Plateau and onto roads with spectacular vistas: snow-capped rocky mountain peaks, big valleys, gentle sweeping curves. We let cars pass us while we rode more slowly past mountain meadows: flowers blooming, baby horses, cowboys working their ranches, birds zipping around, and unknown raptors overhead! Wagging our tails, we were once again riding tight.

After one night in Durango, we cruised the main drag on our way out of town, and as we passed all the shops, we checked out our reflections in the big-paned store windows. Three girls . . . three bikes. Yep, we all looked pretty hot. This is what you do when you ride through the center of town. At least that is what *we* did. Maybe it was a girl thing.

We were on our way to Telluride, first stopping for a cold drink in Silverton, a little mining town, where we found that old men and little boys loved our bikes. Women would walk by and smile, but the men stopped to talk, and the little boys had eyes that grew huge when they came close. We were making an impression, and it felt good.

As we rode toward Ouray, we had to navigate some tight switchbacks and gnarly curves. The vistas reminded me of a sweeping movie saga, with abundant waterfalls, mountainous peaks, and valleys, but I could only glance at the landscape because it took my full attention to do the ride: press on the inside handlebar . . . raise my head to look up and out into the curves where I want to go . . . accelerate coming out of the curves. There were cars ahead of us, behind us, and coming at us from the other direction, but we were definitely better riders than we had been on Red Rock Roar, and we took it all in stride. Helmet thoughts kept me focused and confident. *I have every right to this part of the road. Those cars can't bully me. I own these ten feet of highway. Stay calm.* We took many of those curves at our own pace in first gear, and a mile outside of Ouray, we passed the thousand-mile mark on Magdalena Pearl's new odometer.

Finally, we made our way into Telluride, looking forward to its famous bluegrass festival. We had a condo to stay in, a place belonging to friends who were kind enough to share. Finding it next to a rushing stream right in the center of town, we then started the process of figuring out Where to Park the Bikes.

This was often the biggest and most stressful sort-out of each day when we were all tired. We liked to keep the bikes close to our digs, on a hard surface so there would be no chance they'd fall over. We didn't want them at risk of getting clipped by a car or truck. We wanted to be able to access them easily, and we needed plenty of room to unload and load them again when it would be time to leave and ride on out. There was a gravel parking lot behind the condo, but we had no idea when the plumbers parked there would be moving their vans. Or whether the gravel was too deep and soft to support slow-moving motorcycles. Or if all three bikes would fit. Or whether we could safely leave them there, unattended, for the three days we'd be attending the festival.

We finally found a place on a side street next to the condo. Joan and Kristin rode their bikes over from a few blocks away, where we had temporarily left them, and Joansie backed

Thelma in easily, putting her rear tire right up next to the curb. Kristin eased in next, looking back over her left shoulder and walking backward. Suddenly Louise was tipped over on her crash guard, leaning at a forty-five-degree angle into Thelma and threatening to topple them both like a couple of dominoes if she went over all the way. This was the most out-of-control moment of the day, but Joan and I rushed in with an adrenaline surge and picked Louise up so quickly that no damage was done. We were tired, hot, and doing our best to keep it together, and to our credit, no one lost their temper or snapped with a snarky remark. We kept our cool, but the tension in our bodies was evident. We knew we were all about done with this day. *Let's just park these bikes, unload, and not even think about riding for a few days now.*

I walked back to get Magdalena, by now pretty nervous about the whole parking thing. I was so tired, and after Louise's tip-over, I was a bit scared. Kristin had never let her bike fall like that, and the thought that I might be too tired to handle the task of parking Magdalena was a real worry. But in spite of an SUV parking right on my ass, all went well, and we were soon ready to schlep everything into the condo.

A quick shower, a partial unpack, and we were transformed into Festivarians! I could've simply flaked out and slept away the rest of the day; I was really tired and oxygen deprived at the almost nine-thousand-foot altitude. But we walked through town and then to the end of the canyon to Town Park, where we would turn in our three-day passes for wristbands. The excitement was infectious, and we could already hear Steve Earle ending his set as we came through the gates. Our backpacks were checked, our wristbands were checked and double-checked, and we were suddenly in the middle of a Happening! With no chairs and no tarp, we headed over to the left side of the stage and stood there in the middle of hundreds of other Festivarians, assessing the possibilities of finding a place to land in the grass. Seeing some folks picking up their chairs, we moved in and took a great spot big enough for eight. Joan and Kristin headed off to get food and beer while I sat there to save the space and soak up the scene. A nice man sitting in front of me passed me a joint; I took a hit, passed it on, and felt like I was twenty years old again, when sharing joints with strangers at music festivals made a stranger your friend.

The rest of the night, and the next three days, were all about the music scene. Children wore big pink earmuffs to protect them from the sound. Festivarians of all ages passed the herb openly. We danced, we laughed, we drank beer and wine, we shopped in the craft booths, we danced some more. Each day we'd walk by to check on our bikes, but we didn't even think about starting an engine.

On our second day, we decided to each go our own way and find our own adventures. I got a latte at a coffee shop in town and made my way across the street to Elks Park to listen to jamming musicians: Béla Fleck, Abigail Washburn, Chris Thile, Noah Somebody. Watching Béla reminded me of the movie he'd made three years before. *Throw Down Your Heart* portrayed him making music in Africa and showed amazing footage of marimbas and Indigenous people playing the boards over open pits. I played marimba with my band in California, and now I felt a kinship with these musicians. Respect.

When the set was over, I needed some quiet time before meeting up with Joan and Kristin again to see Yonder Mountain String Band and the Decemberists. Taking my time, I walked down the sidewalk on a quiet side street and soon heard people coming up behind me. I moved out into the empty street to let them pass, only to realize it was Béla Fleck and Abigail Washburn. Without thinking, I called out.

"Béla! Thank you for taking me to Africa!"

Looking up and seeing me smiling at him there in the street, he quickly answered. "Oh, you were no trouble at all—you were a good guest. I hardly knew you were there!"

We laughed and then had a short conversation about marking up your instrument and labeling the keys and whether or not that would be considered cheating. Béla told me that Edgar Meyer, the best bass player ever, marked his bass and got teased about it. "But he makes the best music."

After we parted ways, I walked on toward the river, where I could find a rock to sit upon. I surprised myself with the ease with which I'd talked to someone as famous as Béla Fleck and realized that I no longer idolized anyone, no matter how famous they were. That tendency—to put a famous person on a pedestal—had been extinguished when I left The Farm and Stephen.

Pulling out my little pipe and taking a toke, I thought about Béla's advice to do whatever it takes to make the best music. I thought that could be true for many endeavors: you do *whatever it takes* to make it the best you can. This was something I learned while studying to get into medical school, while still being a wife and a mother, and sitting for exams after graduating from college so many years before. My study skills may not have been what others would recommend, and some might disagree with my choices, but I did what it took to make my best effort, and it worked for me.

I studied hard for the MCAT, the grueling eight-hour Medical College Admission Test. I'd taken it a few months before, and

I did well enough to get some initial interviews with medical schools, but I hadn't been accepted anywhere. Part of that was because of my age and gender. It was 1985 and I was thirty-five, a woman, the mother of two school-age kids, and not at all like the other applicants in that very competitive and male-dominated pool.

I had taken the MCAT the first time before taking any courses in organic chemistry or physics, two subjects covered in the test. Still, I'd "double-digited," which meant I got a respectable score. Good enough to be wait-listed, just not good enough for immediate acceptance. There were plenty of reasons to give up on this ambitious dream. But I knew I could do better. I was a good test taker. And I was also wiser than many applicants, having spent the last ten years on The Farm, where I'd learned so much about getting along with other human beings. I figured that if you've lived rough in the woods with over a thousand other hippies, you could do almost anything. So I was still going for it.

Now there I was, studying to take a dreaded eight-hour exam one more time, my desk scattered with textbooks, practice exams, Triscuits, partially smoked joints, an empty Diet Dr Pepper can, and a handful of ballpoint pens. As soon as I'd get the girls off to school every morning, and as soon as Don left for work, this was my life. I didn't like the pressure of an exam, but I sure did like the learning. I often smoked cannabis to get deep into my textbooks and to fully understand the intricate workings of organs like the kidney. I'd drink Diet Dr Pepper to memorize for exams. This was a pattern that I'd follow for many years, until I got to the clinical part of my training. Then it simply became Diet Dr Pepper because I wouldn't get stoned while practicing as a physician.

One day while I was studying, the phone rang—a beige wall phone with a six-foot cord in the kitchen. No one else was home, and we didn't have voice mail, so it was up to me to go get it. As luck would have it, I was at a stopping place in my work and kind of glad for an excuse to get up and walk away from my desk. Thinking I could get something to drink while I fielded this phone call, I headed into the kitchen and opened the door to the fridge.

"Hello?"

It was the admissions office at UC Davis School of Medicine calling. "We interviewed you a few weeks ago, and I am calling to see if you would like to go to medical school."

I let the fridge door go and watched it slowly swing shut. I wasn't sure I'd heard her right. "What? Are you serious? Are you really asking me that?"

She laughed. "Yes, I am. I have called the other people ahead of you on the waiting list, and they weren't home, so you are the first I've spoken with. The spot is yours if you want it." I could hear the smile behind her words. She liked this job!

"Yes! Yes! Thank you!"

"Good. We start a week from Monday, so we will be sending out the necessary information immediately. Welcome to UC Davis, and congratulations."

I hung up the phone and stood there for a moment, digesting the news. *I am going to medical school. I am really going to be a doctor! I'll never be bored again. We'll never be hungry. I'll be able to buy a car. Any car I might want. I'll have to move to Davis—so will Don and the girls . . . oh God, there's a lot to do!*

I ran to my little study room, grabbed all my notes and

books, and threw them up in the air, whooping at the top of my lungs. "I don't have to take that damn MCAT again! I'm in!! Whoooo-hooooo!"

Then I cleaned it all up while I waited for Don to come home so I could tell him that I—we—would be moving to Davis. Everything would change.

Now here I was, twenty-six years later, a motorcycle-riding physician sitting by the San Miguel River. I was also a practicing Festivarian. As I sat there, I felt profoundly grateful for the choices I'd made, choices that had put me there by the river so many years later. The water flowed crystal clear, the mountains rose above me, and the sky was a perfect blue. Although I could see and hear the festival, it was relatively quiet where I sat, with only a few people walking by. I spent time there on a couple of rocks, letting the sound of the river be my music for a bit before I was ready to hit the Town Park again.

Day three at the bluegrass festival was a Sunday, and it all started with gospel music on the main stage. Abigail Washburn's lyrics were particularly poignant for me. "I sing because I'm happy . . . I sing because I'm free . . ." Her lilting voice made me sing along, bouncing around with happiness and joy, and it set the tone for the whole day. Even as the afternoon weather turned and the rain started to fall, we layered up and kept dancing until the rain turned to hail, and I beat it out of there.

We woke up the next morning ready to let go of bluegrass and be biker chicks again. This was the day we would ride back to Tuba City, the last day of our run. The plan was to leave early since we had over two hundred fifty miles to go—up over ten thousand feet at Lizard Head Pass to get out of Telluride, then miles through the desert to get home.

But the world outside was white.

Not only had it snowed on the surrounding peaks, but Telluride Town was covered too! "Oh, fuck!" was the general consensus. We didn't like riding in gravel, we didn't like riding in rain, and we *definitely* didn't like riding in snow!

We debated taking another route that would get us down to lower altitudes sooner but add an extra hour and a half to the trip, and then I called the local radio station. The DJ, with a good bit of humor at my lowland freak-out about this tiny dusting of snow, assured me that the pass was clear. It would be cold, but not icy. *Hmmm.* Could we believe a DJ? After all, it was our lives we were risking. The thought of ice or snow on the road under our two wheels was frightening, and so was the image of hitting that ice, slipping out of control, and flying, either into another vehicle or off the road into a canyon somewhere. No. We could not let that happen.

We were leaving no matter what, so we packed up the bikes, wiping snow off the seats, then left them parked while we walked into town for breakfast. The air started to warm up a bit and town was wild. Crowded, loud, and intense day-after-the-festival Telluride. Everyone wanted breakfast before packing up and getting out of town, and there were only three places serving. The first said there would be a forty-five-minute wait, but we had success at the next one we tried, where we fueled up on huevos rancheros.

Once on the bikes, we started out slowly as we tested the roads, and we watched for black ice in the shade as we climbed altitude. But the roads were clear, and it was smooth sailing all the way to Tuba City. We rode well, in sync, on this last day together, passing and being passed like the tight team we had become. With a mixture of sadness and relief, we arrived at Joan and Kristin's home on the reservation, where we celebrated with grilled flat sandwiches and cocktails on their back patio and agreed that, yes, we would do this again. Next year . . . California! We wondered if we could possibly plan it so it was more fun than the last time we rode my territory. Of course we could!

CHAPTER 5

CALIFORNIA ROLL, 2012

Fennel gives way to
Eucalyptus which cedes to
Cypress and sea cliffs.

One short year later, we were ready for another ride in my part of the world again, this time without the rain or the snow, given that we planned to ride in the fall, when Northern California is warm and dry. We hoped. Our route would take us north out of Sonoma County along the Pacific Coast, then inland to Gold Country and on to Yosemite National Park for a three-day layover. From there we'd make our way across the San Joaquin Valley back to the coast, passing through Santa Cruz on our way north to Sonoma County. A beautiful loop covering the high points of this area, with mountains and oceans and excellent chances for good riding weather.

After the long haul from Arizona, Joan and Kristin didn't want to even come inside my house before heading on over to Tim's to stash their truck and trailer rig for the duration of our trip. While my house was on a curve in a busy neighbor-hood, Tim had a safe place large enough to park their huge trailer, and he'd offered to help us out. So off we all went to disturb his Friday night dinner.

"Nothin' else I'd rather do!" Tim loved helping girls with big bikes.

Then back to my house for lasagna, salad, garlic bread, a bottle of Sonoma County wine, and a hot tub under the blue moon—much needed after Joan and Kristin's tiring drive from Arizona and my day of packing with great anticipation.

After meeting my new, more powerful Magdalena last year, my buddies had decided they too needed to upgrade their rides. Joan had named her new bike, a hunkered-down huge touring Yamaha, O-ren Ishii. Kristin's sleek ruby-red Victory was named Beatrix. These two gorgeous bikes were perfectly suited to their riders, and all together we felt skilled at riding huge motorcycles, brave and strong in the face of whatever the road had to offer.

We hit the road the next morning after throwing last night's leftover garlic bread in my saddlebag, anxious to make it to Sea Ranch to join the yearly gathering of friends for three straight days of good food, long walks, hot tubs under the stars, and plenty of laughter. Our first challenge was Coleman Valley Road, known for being winding, narrow, and bumpy, but also worth it for the spectacular, panoramic wide-ocean views it offered as it descended down to the Pacific Ocean. While we usually kept it easy on the first day of a ride, getting our sync together, today would change that pattern.

Once we reached the coast, we headed north on the two-lane Pacific Coast Highway. It teased us with views of the ocean, a blue vastness that one could get lost in if we had only been able to stop and stare. But every short, straight stretch that allowed a quick glance away from the road was quickly replaced by tight curves that took us into the inland woods. Our ride alternated between switchbacks in the trees and open road hugging the cliffs, and it required all our attention. When we reached Fort Ross, we finally stopped to take a breather and congratulate ourselves on making it that far. As we dismounted from our bikes, we realized we were all suffering from the same affliction: the Death Grip. On this first-day ride, the endless tight curves and sheer cliffs had already begun to take their toll, and it took some time to shake that off and uncurl our fingers.

Soon we were ready to brave the last leg. Sunny coastal Saturday traffic was intense, with some car always right behind Joan, who was riding sweep, but we would *not* be pushed into taking the curves faster just because there were cars on our tail, so we pulled over whenever we could to let them go by, working to create our safe pocket.

When we finally pulled into the party-house driveway, our girlfriends greeted us with fanfare, streaming out of the house to check out our rides. We strutted a bit to show them off, but then we were ready to put away our helmets and leathers and settle into the scene of fifteen women at a three-day party. I didn't think to unpack that garlic bread when we arrived, and when I went out the next morning to check on my bike, I found raccoon paw prints all over Magdalena. Luckily, breaking into my saddlebags was beyond their skill level, although they sure tried! Nothing a good wipe-off couldn't fix.

While the raccoons couldn't count on garlic bread for their stomachs, I had counted on that weekend with my physician girlfriends to serve as food for my soul. Medical residency training is demanding, and people's lives depended on us when we were going through that stage of our careers.

We had been so new, so inexperienced, and still so selfless. The hours were long, and the learning curve was steep. We were all training to become family medicine specialists, which meant learning to combine a broad range of scientific knowledge and practical clinical skills. There was also the expectation that we should intimately know our patients, their families, and the stressors that could affect their well-being.

In the past, some residents had broken under this load, so our hospital had developed supportive Balint groups for each of the three levels going through training. During our residency we met once a week with a trained facilitator to talk about anything that was on our minds, both in and outside of medicine, and to share our personal challenges. It was through Balint group and the long hours together taking care of patients that we forged deep friendships, sharing our fears and consistently helping each other get through the hardest times. We bonded as women do, learning life-and-death lessons together. We knew each other's strengths, weaknesses, triggers, and desires. We knew how to tell the truth and how to do so with compassion, to each other and to our patients. We knew enough to assume each other's goodwill and to laugh more than to bicker. We loved each other.

I'd turned forty as an intern and became a single mother in my second year, when Don and I divorced, exactly midway through the three-year residency. My grief, new responsibilities at home alone with two teenage daughters, and the challenges of learning to practice family medicine were almost more than I could handle during that second year of training. I brought my troubles to Balint, putting them out there so my fellow residents would know why I might look frazzled day after day, even when I was not post-call. It was during a Balint group meeting in that second year that a fellow resident, Amy, agreed to help me with my seventeen-year-old daughter, giving her a place to stay when I needed respite. Her generosity cemented a friendship that continued to grow long after residency was over, in the same way that many of our other relationships blossomed. We had created a family of choice, and this family was one I cherished. Now here we were, two decades later, still meeting up once or twice a year at Sea Ranch.

As much as I loved these women, I was an introvert and often took some time away from the constant noise of the house party to walk along the cliffs for a bit on my own. A trail stretched for ten miles right along the bluffs, and the view was never boring. Cormorants clung to the sides of cliffs, seals basked in huge clumps on rocks far from shore, and deer grazed the meadows above the cliffs without fear. The sound of the surf was a constant waxing and waning roar, and the light changed all day long as the sun rose over the hills to the east, arcing across the wide-open sky and then sinking into the ocean every night. The air smelled of seawater and salt, and it never mattered if the weather was sunny or gray—it was all beautiful. But a little alone time goes a long way, and I always found myself drawn back to the house full of friends. There was something both comforting and empowering about being with these women I'd known since my first days of training, something I discovered early in my first year of residency.

At that time, I was basking in the knowledge that I belonged in Santa Rosa, that I was finally—at forty years old—an MD with responsibilities I still hadn't fully grasped. I was roaming the halls, rounding on patients, and taking more time than usual to visit with them. I had time. I was an intern, a first-year resident physician who was pretty much going to live in that hospital for three years.

One day, I stopped by the cafeteria to get something to drink and then headed to the patio to see if any of my fellow residents were there. Cindy and Amy were perched at a table near one of the garden's pots that grew medicinal herbs. I set down my drink and went over to pick a few leaves. Just as I put them to my nose to smell the terpenes, the overhead pager blasted a call to every corner of the hospital.

"Dr. Moore to the ER, STAT. Dr. Moore to the ER, STAT."

Cindy looked at me and said, "Whoa. Guess you better go!" I still felt a thrill at hearing my still-married name broadcast with "Doctor" in front of it. *STAT! That's me! I'm needed! I'm a doctor!*

Dropping the leaves I was holding, I headed to the emergency room, where I quickly saw where the action was. A mass of people in one of the side bays with machines, trays, and beeping instruments surrounded a gurney. Barely discernible on that gurney was a human being, covered in medical paraphernalia.

The surgeon at his side looked up. "Stacey, here." I moved in close to him and saw that the patient was a man. Slightly overweight, probably in his midfifties. His chest was open. There had been no time to transfer him to the operating room, so the surgeon had made a cut and a crack to expose all that lay beneath the sternum right there in the ER. I was looking at this man's heart. And it was not beating.

"Stacey, glove up and compress the heart."

I had no time to think. Grabbing a sterile glove, I shoved my hand first into the glove and then into the man's chest. I closed my eyes and *felt*, blending the border of my hand into the muscle that was his heart. Once I felt meshed, I began to squeeze, rhythmically, steady, *squeeze, relax, squeeze, relax.*

The import of what I was doing did not escape me. My own hand, working the pump that was life. My hand, destined to save lives, was actually doing just that. My eyes were closed as I melded with this man's core. The ordered chaos of everyone else fell into my background, and it was only me and the heart, doing a percussive dance together, regaining a rhythm traumatically and momentarily forgotten.

I felt a twitch. Then another. I responded as I would on the dance floor, moving with my partner. The twitches turned into contractions, and I matched their beat, filling in when the heart faltered. Soon we were dancing in unison, and I lessened my squeeze. Gently, I was now simply supporting the heart's own beats until I realized that I was no longer needed.

My hand left this man's chest just as they wheeled him out of the ER to take him to the operating room. I did not follow. Now I *needed* to go outside and take stock of what had just happened, what my part had been in that frantic team, working on saving a man's life. A man possibly with a family, with plans and dreams of his own.

I was stunned at the presence of something bigger than myself flowing from my hand to his heart, and I knew that I had made the right choice to become a family physician. I hoped that this one patient would live to see another day because I was able to help. But the thrill went beyond my own personal gratification. I realized more than ever before that the opportunity I now had to help others was an awesome responsibility, one I could never take for granted. Even as computers and protocols and committees would take over the business of health care, I would never forget the sacred relationship between a doctor and her patient. That day was a *good* day.

Remembering that day over twenty years later, I knew it was part of why I had such good friends now. We had all been in intense situations like that and had shared our stories, and we respected each other for accepting the responsibility of our profession. Together, we had learned to handle difficult situations without losing our cool, and we'd also discovered that stress must be released somehow. Sea Ranch was the place to do it. We had lazy days with board games in the main house, food, drinks, and everyone coming and going. Long walks together south, and then north, along the cliffs—those easy walks that let us talk to our hearts' content. I baked galettes, seducing everyone with the aroma of cinnamon and baked apples.

It took some mind bending to switch from the Sea Ranch getaway into our motorcycle adventure when it was time to leave, but we were ready. Although the sun was out when we left, the coast just north of us was foggy and cold, with the added windchill bite we'd get on the bikes. We stopped so I could put on my warmer gloves and silk scarf, but the fog stuck to us until we rode inland later that afternoon. Suddenly the sun was shining through the redwoods, and when the Navarro River appeared on our right, its waters flowing back out to sea, we knew we had hit the sweet stretch of the day. Gentle curves, plenty of turnouts for passing traffic, and Navarro redwood trees adding to the magic. Whenever I enjoyed roads like this, I felt most connected to Magdalena, the two of us taking the curves together, me leaning into them while pressing with my inside hand to control the ride. We

swayed and swerved in balance with each other, and it felt
like flying . . . so smooth, gliding along through perfection.
We all wagged our tails for miles.

Coming out of the redwoods, we entered the warmth of
Anderson Valley, wine country with lush vineyards on both
sides of the road. As we rode past wineries, the strong scent
of the fall grape crush made its way through my face shield,
a fragrant reminder that there would be some excellent wine
to share down the road. We kept riding east, and in the early
afternoon arrived at Vichy Springs, a health spa where Jack
London, Teddy Roosevelt, and Robert Louis Stevenson had
come to relax and where Dustin Hoffman and Wavy Gravy
had soaked in the waters. Spanning acres of calming green
lawns, the historic resort provided a quiet sense of peace,
with its huge oak trees offering welcome shade, strategically
placed benches for spontaneous sitting, comfortable lodging,
a swimming pool and hot tub, mineral springs, and a big gate
that closed up tight at night.

After unpacking the bikes, settling into our respective
cottages, and changing into swimsuits, the three of us met up
again under one of the oak trees on the green.

"Hey!" I said. "I just had the thought that this place looks
like a psychiatric sanatorium out of an old movie, with all
these little cottages and lawns and so many benches for resting. I half expect to see someone walk by in a white coat,
coming to check on us!"

Looking around, they both burst into laughter and
agreed.

"I wonder if we'll be offered some good meds before dinner," Joan said. "Wouldn't that be great!"

When we parted for our separate lodgings that evening
after a refreshing dip in the pool, we decided that the waters

of Vichy Springs were more healing than any psych meds we could've wished for, but we still laughed at the thought that they might not let us out in the morning. Then, with psych sanatoriums on my mind, and no television in my room to distract me, my private thoughts that evening wandered to a time when I had taken my own mental health needs seriously enough to make some momentous decisions. They were life-saving choices, and even as I remembered the pain of those changes, I never regretted them.

How can I be a powerful healer, fully realizing my potential, if I don't heal myself? I had wondered this as I contemplated the deterioration of my marriage during the first year of my residency. *If my choices are always for someone else's benefit? If I give away my body for someone else's selfish use? If I hide my thoughts and feelings to avoid conflict? If I squelch much of what I think, keeping quiet so I won't rock the boat I'm in? Who am I if I don't even know myself because I'm too busy acting like someone acceptable, safe, and happy? How can I see what and who I am if I am giving myself up for the sake of peace?*

How did it get to be where what a man thinks matters more than what a woman feels?

I had walked away from my father so I could be free to find my own way. I had walked away from Stephen when he tried to control me. But my marriage was different.

My husband was a man I needed, and we laughed often and rarely argued—at least we rarely argued if I just kept agreeing with him. Just a couple of things were lacking—the things that make it all feel righteous: sexual intimacy and honesty.

He believed that the natural state for a man was to sleep

with every woman available to him. And he believed that it was okay to do this as long as I didn't know about it; most likely he considered it compassionate to keep me in the dark. Don was generally kind, and did not want to intentionally hurt me, but he continued to fuck and lie from the very beginning to the end of our twenty-year marriage. I found out about a few of the women along the way, but most of the time I was kept in the dark. Maybe I didn't want to see it, or maybe he was just that good at being discreet.

Sex was the festering abscess in our marriage. I never had more than a moment's physical pleasure in the twenty years we were together. As much as I loved sleeping in the security of a shared bed next to a warm body I could count on, that bed was not safe for me. His self-centered sex, with no regard for my response, was the price I paid to have a partner.

So for the sake of peace, I got quiet. I adapted—a skill perfected in all those years of moving from one place to another as a child. I fit in and gave up my Self for the sake of the family and the relationship. Life was calm within our family but churning inside my heart.

I let him do what he wanted, when he wanted, and however he wanted. First, I gave up my body, then I gave up my power—all to make a life that was pleasant and livable. And I told myself I was happy. I knew what I'd given up, at least in bed, but I accepted it. *My life is perfect except for one little thing . . . and that is okay. It can't all be perfect.* Don was a man to make a life with, a man who took care of us, a man I thought was my very best friend because he was the one I told my day to, every single evening. He was the one who knew me in good times and bad, and he was the one who helped me when I gave birth to both our babies. He had my back. Sure, there were problems, but doesn't everyone have problems? You've got to take the bad with the good and make a deal that works.

For years, I was a mother and a wife who kept her dreams, desires, and needs hidden while she satisfied her family's needs. Maybe I was channeling an example set by my mother, planted deeply from the day I was born. Maybe I didn't think I could find anything better or deserved anything better. It would be many years before I experienced passion with seemingly endless pleasure, and it would not be with this man. I believed in marriage, in a deep partnership with no lies. I thought we had a deep partnership. But his lies and denial were black magic, causing me to disbelieve the reality I could feel and sometimes see. His lies made me wonder what was real. I didn't consciously know about the lies until they hit me in the face, until I started getting anonymous phone calls telling me what my husband was doing out there with other women. Until he was finally forced to confess. And I was forced to face the truth.

He believed in nothing he couldn't see, hear, smell, or touch.

I believed in magic, in the unseen, in the unquantifiable. I still do.

After I became a doctor, I started taking care of others in thirty-six-hour shifts, others with life-and-death problems, others much needier than me. When I came home from work, I found little support and many demands. The balance shifted. After a while, I couldn't bring myself to go home right away, where I would have to be at my family's service helping the kids with homework, cooking dinner, and doing the laundry. This would all get done, but not right away. Instead, I would drive out to the cliffs overlooking the Pacific Ocean, throw a blanket on the ground, and sleep to the soothing sound of the surf. Home couldn't refill my heart and soul, but the waves soothed and replenished me. Then, once I was somewhat revived from an afternoon's nap, I'd go home and take care of my family.

Finally, when my patients were dying of AIDS, I had to face the facts, if only to save myself from getting HIV. I knew he did not practice safe sex. I also knew that my spirit was going to die if I had to keep giving up my power, my words, my thoughts, and my body to keep this marriage afloat.

New Year's Day, 1991. Don and I took a picnic to the coast, silently driving forty miles and setting up a blanket next to the cliffs with a bottle of wine, some cheese, a fresh loaf of crusty bread, and a few ripe pears. We sat on opposite sides of the blanket and gazed out at the Pacific Ocean.

After a bit, I broke the silence. "What's going on here? Can you talk about it?"

After a long, thoughtful moment, Don replied. "No. I can't talk about it." And then went quiet again.

I sat and stared at him. Was conversation now part of the past? Were we so disconnected that we couldn't even talk anymore? He would not look at me, instead continuing to look out at the endless ocean. And that was when I hit the Wall. The Wall that is built of unbreakable certainty.

"Okay. I'm done," I said. "I can't do this anymore. It's over." I began packing up the picnic. Suddenly, he looked over and, realizing I meant business, scrambled to help. I grabbed the now-full picnic basket, and letting him pick up the blanket, I headed for the car. I was done. No more would I try to make this marriage work. No more would I overlook the lies. No more would I share his bed.

He joined me in the car. Before he started the engine, he said, "Let's talk."

"Nope. I'm done. You wouldn't talk before, and I'm not interested in talking to you now."

Just like that, I had broken the ties that bound us together. My shift was sudden and complete, but it had taken years to get to that place. It just took that one final straw for me to set us free from the trap we had stepped into twenty years before.

What a relief to move out of our bed! How safe I felt in my own space on the pull-out couch in the family room! I never again went back into the bed we had shared for so long. Cold, hard negotiations about our divorce replaced the comfort of conversations with my husband. Fear of the future alone and anger at our failure to work it out replaced the closeness I had lived with for so many years. I missed my best friend, I missed the family we had created, and I grieved.

I had kept my awareness of Spirit, magic, and the unseen to myself when I was with Don. He would patronize me, so to avoid his ridicule I kept those thoughts mostly to myself for all those years. But now I needed to express my belief in Spirit. I needed to honor my intuition. I longed to listen to angels, to pray, and to see inside my patients' hearts. I needed to explore my own power. For me, intimacy plus sex equaled love, and I needed sex that was making love. I wanted orgasms. I could do none of those while I kept my place as the ice-queen wife of a dishonest practical hedonist. I had to start anew.

Life was not over. The next few years were some of the hardest I ever faced, full of hard times and grief, but eventually I found that the end of my marriage was really the beginning of me.

That next morning, the Vichy Springs Resort was so peaceful that we lingered over breakfast and didn't hit the road very early. As we were packing up, I picked up a wild turkey feather from the ground next to my bike and slipped it under my spider bungee cord, for luck, and also just to see how long it would last. I didn't know then that it would still be there when I pulled into my garage at the end of the trip.

As we rode east, my helmet thoughts brought me to Laura. It had been just over a year since she'd died, and this part of Northern California always made me think of her because she had lived a short drive north of Vichy Springs. I was the trustee for her estate and had spent a good amount of time during the past year taking care of business, selling her house, paying bills, and making sure Lily was covered. Somehow, doing this busyness helped me feel close to Laura after she was gone. Now, I rode Magdalena along the edge of Lake Mendocino with some of Laura's ashes in my saddlebag. Headed for Yosemite, I was on a mission to fulfill one of her last wishes.

The miles rolled on by, with Lake County turning into Colusa County as we rode through creepy, black, burned-out hills full of charred tree skeletons and dead underbrush that had been decimated by a huge fire just a week before. The beginning of seemingly endless California fire seasons had arrived. The road was hot, dry, and long, and we were sitting right on top of hot engines with no escape from that relentless metallic heat. Helmet headache—my head felt like it swelled up too big to fit. Nowhere to stop. We just had to keep going until we found someplace—*any* place—to pull over. Finally. Wheatland. *It's fucking hot. Gotta pee, wash my face and hands with cold water, get a cold drink and then another and then browse in the food mart for something—anything—to buy just to stay in the AC for a bit longer. Time for a junk-food candy bar. That's BAD.*

On to Colusa. We had it in mind to find a place to eat lunch there, but in spite of riding around town in circles, we couldn't decide where to stop. We were too tired and frazzled to make a decision as simple as a lunch stop. I finally pulled over to park my bike in some scant shade to reconnoiter—get out of my hot helmet and figure out the next move. Maybe we would find a place by walking instead of slowly cruising around on top of hot engines.

As I started rearranging my load to grab my wallet, too tired and hot to pay attention, and maybe too sweaty to hold on to the ropes, I let a bungee cord get away from me. It blasted me smack in the lip. *DAMN! Fuckin' A!* I couldn't talk, and wondered if I'd lost a tooth. This was not fun anymore. Miserable. I dug out the homeopathic arnica pellets I always carried and turned to my riding partners.

"I need ice," I mumbled through a rapidly swelling lip.

"Oh my God!" Joansie cried. "What happened?"

I pointed to the evil bungee cord, unwilling to speak another word. We were all three moving slow and struggling as we took off layers of riding gear. We were a dysfunctional group at this point, and it was time for one of us to decide, so I called it. We went for the nearest air-conditioned café. Meeting nice people behind the counter, we ordered food, and plenty of ice—that was all we needed and that's what we got. Pretty soon, with ice and some more homeopathic arnica tabs under my tongue, I was able to talk again, we were hydrated, and our cores had cooled to a normal temperature. We had learned oh-yet-another lesson: probably not a good idea to get overheated and try to make a group decision.

Group decisions are tricky at best, especially when on the road. Joan, Kristin, and I would usually figure these things out before we started riding for the day, because we knew that was the best time for clarity. We had all been in dramatic situations in the hospital when there was no time to debate, discuss, or negotiate, and these dramas had taught us well. We each knew how to take charge, and we also knew how to gracefully cede decisions to someone else when necessary. Back on the road, revived and feeling human again, my helmet thoughts brought me back to one of the first times I had been caught in a dysfunctional group of physicians, seen the need for a clear decision, and taken charge.

It was a repeat Cesarean section. Not my style—not my style at all—but that wasn't the point. This wasn't my birth. It was my patient's, and she had chosen a C-section. Her daughter had also been born by C-section three years ago, and it was what she knew.

This section was scheduled. There was something about scheduling a birth that went against my personal grain. I liked the unknown, the giving-it-up to Nature, the natural process of birth without interference. But there was always the possibility that Mother Nature might need a little help, and it was my job to be aware. To pay attention. To support Mother Nature and the birthing mother and to know when to step in with interventions. When this woman's first child was born, I had had to step in. It was necessary. There were no doubts, and we had all agreed: C-section. Now. Save the mom. Save the baby.

The day came for this baby to emerge. As the family's doctor, I usually assisted during major surgeries. I was the person who knew the patient, the physician who knew the family, the one who reassured with a familiar face and levels of trust built up through years of caring. I had assembled a team for this birth: an OB-GYN surgeon, an anesthesiologist, and the nurses to support us. All systems were go. Dad was in the room, gowned and masked, to watch his second child be born, and Mom was comfortable with an epidural, completely conscious and aware of everything going on. The OB-GYN and I scrubbed at the sink, side by side.

"I don't know how you do it, Stace," he said as he vigorously scrubbed his fingernails. "Your patients always want something out of the norm, and you seem to roll with it easier than I would!" He was referring to this dad's desire to hold his baby the instant it emerged from his wife's uterus. That just wasn't going to happen. Because it was a C-section, and because the baby wouldn't be coming through the birth canal, we would need to take it immediately to a special heated table designed for infant resuscitation. Babies who come out "through the roof" sometimes need a little extra support. They also certainly need to be dried off and examined before deemed safe and sound. Dad would just have to wait. I told him this, and with my explanation, he accepted the reality of the OR protocols.

How easily people give up their power in the face of an institution's protocols! If there weren't such a compelling reason for this, I would have bent the rules for the dad. But as a physician with the responsibility of a new life in my hands, I wanted to be sure this baby was stable before letting Dad have his first snuggle.

Fortunately, the surgery went smoothly. We worked together well, having done this particular procedure many times together. As the wet infant was lifted out of the uterus, we all looked to see that it was a boy! Cheers for a boy to follow their daughter! All was well! Until the baby boy did not take that first breath . . . did not emit that first squall that made everyone catch their own breath, without even realizing they had been holding it. We waited for the cries. They did not come.

I looked at the surgeon, and our eyes met over our masks. We silently agreed. I left him to close Mom's incision on his own and went over to join the nurse, who was attending the newborn on the resuscitation table. The baby was turning pale and blue—something had to be done and done quickly! I was all too aware of Dad hovering over my shoulder, watching with bated breath, and of Mom calling to us from behind her sterile shield.

"What's wrong? Is my baby okay?"

Stimulating this baby boy was not working. Slapping his back, rubbing his feet, talking to him . . . no breath. Floppy. Not yet here. Flaccid. Lungs simply not working.

"Call the pediatric intensive care specialist, STAT," I told the nurse. Then, because I knew it would take a few minutes to get that assist, I turned to the anesthesiologist sitting at the mom's head, managing her epidural. I asked him to please come tend to this baby. The boy needed to be intubated—a tiny tube inserted to open up his airway. That, in a newborn, is an elegant procedure, one best done by an anesthesia specialist who handles difficult airways all day long.

Leaving the mom in the capable hands of the surgeon, who was still busy closing up her abdomen, the anesthesiologist stepped a few feet over to our baby table, positioned the baby's head, and, holding a little curved plastic tube lightly in his fingertips, slipped that tube into the tiny airway. It took him a few tries, while the nurse and I stood by, ready to step in if needed. My hopeful anticipation was replaced with increasing concern because our newborn still did not breathe. Still no air movement. Still no beautiful flush of color making him pink instead of pale blue. Oxygen not making a difference. Still flaccid, no breathing, more and more blue, and it felt like we were suspended in time. Seconds . . . minutes . . . felt like an eternity.

Then, with some relief, I looked up to see the neonatologist enter the OR. He stood there, watching his colleague struggle with the situation. After a moment, he calmly gave the order.

"Pull the tube."

"No!" The anesthesiologist resisted. "It was hard getting it in there! I don't want to pull it . . . I may not be able to get it back in."

Calmly. Without anger, panic, or any other emotion, the neonatologist insisted. "Pull. The. Tube."

"No—I don't dare."

The neonatologist stood there for a moment, watching the situation in front of him: a baby not yet alive and a doctor frozen in fear. I watched these two men sort out the power play.

"Fine, then. I'll be going. It's your patient now." The neonatologist turned to leave.

That was when I became Mama Bear in the OR. I remembered one of Stephen's teachings. "You can have the presence of mind, right in the middle of a hassle, to realize the other person probably doesn't want to be in it either." Two men, neither of them wanting to be in this hassle, doing a deadly power play over a baby's life was *not* going to happen on my watch. And I was the family's doctor. These were *my* patients. Stepping forward, I released my power from the closet where I normally kept it quietly stored in that chauvinistic medical world, and I cupped my hand protectively on the baby's head.

"No. I called the neonatologist to handle this," I said to the anesthesiologist. "Please go back to the mom."

Then, I turned to the neonatologist. "You: please tend to this baby."

I had ordered them like they were residents under my authority. And they responded from deeply seated habits, formed long ago during their own days in training. The anesthesiologist lifted both his hands in surrender, backed away from the table, and with a fatalistic sigh returned to his original patient. The pediatric specialist stepped in, pulled the tiny tube out, and released a large mucus plug that had been blocking the airway. He then quickly and expertly reinserted the airway tube, and we finally saw air begin to flow. The warm glow of color replaced the paleness of cold skin, and our newborn boy began to squirm and complain about being messed with. I was never so glad to see a baby complain about his doctors!

I am a family physician and I am a woman. Those were two strikes against me when in the presence of older male specialists in the field of medicine. But in that operating room, I owned my power. I made the decision.

Making the decision to go to the nearest café with AC was nothing like deciding to save a baby's life, but both required confidence and determination in times of excessive stress. Riding hot engines in the heat took determination as well, and we did not falter. Back on our bikes, we headed farther east with the goal of reaching Placerville and the B&B we had reserved for the night. Along the way, we went through Yuba City, which was intense because, in traffic, we lost our windchill. The thermometer on the local bank showed a reading in the high nineties, and a string of stoplights and idling cars, with heat coming off the asphalt and engines, made it feel like we'd be getting blisters under our jeans. We slapped our thighs to cool them off. Stop. Burn. Slap. Stop. Burn. Slap. *Is my leg going to blister?* Go. Stop.

Finally, we made it through Yuba City and savored the view when we reached the Middle Fork of the American River. As we motored over the bridge, even the *sight* of rushing water made us feel just a little bit cooler. Then, climbing in elevation gave us hope for a break from the relentless heat, and we got it, even if the altitude and the shade were accompanied by switchbacks, including a few of those now-familiar gnarly, first-gear hairpin turns. We were good with that; we knew how to take those turns. But the heat took it out of us, and although we weren't tired due to miles traveled, we were completely wiped out when we pulled into Placerville.

The Albert Shafsky House B&B was a welcoming place to land. The shaded parking area for the bikes was easily negotiated, and our hostess greeted us with a tour of her lovely historic home. We had the whole upstairs to ourselves, so we quickly unpacked and moved in. After showers, we walked downtown for dinner and to soak up some local flavor, appreciating the community's roots stemming back to the gold rush and mining era. But the wine we had with dinner reminded us that this place now had a reputation for vineyards and fine wine, which was a welcome realization for my two wine-loving friends. The stars were out by the time we ambled back to our rooms, and as I slipped between the six-hundred-thread-count sheets, my phone got a text from the room next door: "How 'bout those sheets? Nice!" Still in sync. Very nice. Indeed.

We woke the next morning knowing that each day of this ride was pushing our limits. Switchbacks, heat, and unfamiliar roads always gave us new challenges. Today was going to be no exception. We knew we would be in Yosemite by evening, but how we got there and the logistics of bringing in supplies on the bikes for our three-night/two-day stay there was a big unknown.

The ride lived up to our lofty expectations. Edge-of-the-world cliffs, two-lane traffic, hairpin turns one right after the other, first and second gear for miles and miles. Awesome views to our right, constant traffic coming our way on the left. Death Grips on our bikes, reminding ourselves to relax . . . relax . . . relax . . . After what seemed like hours of fine riding, we pulled into Groveland and found a full parking lot at the only grocery store for miles around. Then came the decision about what to get. Three nights in Yosemite meant a lot of food and wine for three girls. I did one of my typical wander-around-the-store-in-a-daze moves for a few minutes until Kristin's most-excellent planning skills kicked in. Thank heavens for the opportunity to let someone else make decisions! After grabbing pasta, pesto, yogurt, oatmeal, coffee, salad fixings, cheese, peanut butter, and the ever-essential bottles of most-excellent wines, we also snagged a handful of sugar packets for our morning coffee on our way out the door.

Now, next dilemma: How to fit all this on those bikes? It looked doubtful we could squeeze it all in, but Kristin had big saddlebags that fit some of the food and most of the wine. Joansie found some helpful nooks and crannies in hers. And my saddlebags had an extension zipper that came in handy, offering an extra two inches on both sides. *Yosemite: here we come!*

Onward and upward, we came to a series of tunnels with light at the end, and we honked musically to each other as we rode through. The road also took us through stands of oak, pine, cedar, and fir trees, and then we finally rounded one more corner, and there it was: our first breathtaking view of the Yosemite Valley. As usual, I began to cry. Time to pull over and take it all in . . . this overwhelming, miles-wide vista of power and beauty. Together we stood and gazed at the landscape: the Merced River, appearing to be a tiny stream so far below, and the steep granite rock formations rising thousands of feet on either side of the river providing a massive presence that stole our breath away. That view was a visual prayer. It was what we had come for, and we did not rush the stop. Instead, each of us lingered as we soaked in the panoramic vista.

Back on the bikes, we slowly found our way to the address of the unknown house we'd rented for the next three nights. We all admitted to being anxious about what we might find—where to park the bikes, how to get into the house, how to haul our loads inside. All the homes we'd passed were perched high on steep hillsides with slopes that looked daunting. When we arrived, the first thing we noticed was a big, precipitous driveway in front, steeply rising to the front door. *Oh shit* . . . that looked like a challenge . . . but I made a run for it, zipping up that vertical drive to a small, somewhat level dead-end landing at the top. I was absolutely not going to haul all those groceries any farther than I had to, and I'd thought there would be enough room for all three bikes up there. But neither Joan nor Kristin liked that driveway situation one single bit. *Is there really enough room at the top? How will we turn around once up there?*

So began the hardest part of their very long day: figuring out how to safely park Beatrix and Ishii. We also needed to figure out how to get into the house and how to get our gear inside. *Fuckin' A!* It was exhausted chaos, with long discussions about bike options. Eventually, they discovered the perfect parking place just up the road in a level cul-de-sac, but after parking the bikes, they were chased away by an angry woman who yelled at them and told them they couldn't do that there. And who would want to leave their lovely girls near someone who isn't nice? So back down the hill they rode, past our house, to the first level turnout they found, a dirt patch regrettably next to the neighborhood dumpster. I started hauling in groceries and filling the fridge with food. Then came the unenviable chore of schlepping our gear up the road . . . up the driveway . . . up the two flights of stairs . . . and into the house.

We made a dent in some of the wine we had hauled in and told each other how awesome it felt to get this far. The bikes had never felt so big or hard to handle than they had that night. We were all tired, and we knew we had done well, so it was off to bed in the darkest, quietest night we had spent in many days. No need to rush in the morning . . . no need to go anywhere until we wanted to. We could breathe. And we did just that, taking our time over coffee the next morning, enjoying the house and the incredible view to the west, far across the Sierra Nevada. We even pulled the windshields off our bikes, prepared to ride "naked" down in the valley that afternoon—no bags, no windshields, just girls on bikes!

That evening, Kristin and I relaxed on the deck with a glass of red wine, watching the glorious sunset, until we heard Joan call out.

"Hey! I'm fixing food!"

With that, Kristin jumped up and called back. "Sorry, Joansie! My bad!" They had an agreement: whoever was not cooking was expected to provide sustenance for the one who was in the kitchen, which meant that Kristin needed to pour some wine for Joan, who was busy making pesto pasta and green beans. A very good agreement, I thought, taking notes for my next relationship, should there ever be one.

For a while, I had thought maybe a relationship with another woman might go better than my serial failures with men. Lisa became my girlfriend, and after a couple of years, it was so far, so good. One night, she and I were getting ready to watch a movie, tucked in together at her house out in the woods east of Santa Rosa. She was fixing dinner, and I was sitting out on the deck, watching the sun set through the trees and enjoying a rare moment of relaxation while someone else worked. I loved being out at her place, a rustic A-frame home far from town that made me feel like I was living in a treehouse. Being there at Lisa's was one of the few places I could relax and let someone else take care of me for a change.

That evening, I'd sent a woman in labor to the hospital. I assumed it would probably take hours before I was needed, and I trusted the nurses to make sure all was well and call me when it was the right time. So I felt safe being in my own personal zone. No wine that night, and no cannabis either, because I'd be working late, but a good movie with my girlfriend would be enough to make me happy while I waited. Then, the nurse called.

"Sandy is very anxious. May I give her something for anxiety? And I think if we get her mother to leave she will do better." My patient was going to be having a VBAC (vaginal birth after Cesarean), and I knew Sandy had problems with her mother. I also recognized that a laboring woman is often anxious, even without a mother to stress her. Granted, I didn't usually need to medicate someone for anxiety, and I hesitated a bit, but it still didn't raise any red flags. I didn't know about the searing pain Sandy was feeling. I didn't know that this labor was headed toward disaster. All along I was assured that the baby's heart rate was just fine.

The next call from Sandy's nurse was one I would never forget. "Stacey, you'd better get in here. I think your baby's dead."

"What? What did you say?" I had never in my life had a baby die and couldn't believe it had happened now. Last I heard, Sandy was doing better, feeling less anxious. We'd had no worries.

"Well, I sure can't find a heartbeat. I couldn't find it with the monitor so I got the portable sonogram in there and I can't find it that way either. So I think it must be dead." She was harsh. She was blunt. She was cold.

I went numb. My ears started to roar, and I heard myself ask her to call for the radiology technician immediately. Maybe a sonogram pro would find that heartbeat. When she said it was late and the tech wasn't in the hospital, I told her to get someone in from home and to call the OB-GYN surgeon in, STAT.

"I'm on my way."

I scrambled for my keys, mumbled a hasty goodbye to Lisa, and peeled out of the driveway. I raced down the hill as fast as the dark, winding road would allow. It would take me at least fifteen minutes to get there even if I drove pedal to the metal. As soon as I got off the dirt and hit the main road, I grabbed for my cell phone and called Labor and Delivery. I was relieved when my favorite nurse answered. She was supervisor that evening and was working the phones while everyone ran around getting a crew in to save this mother. I could hear the emergency activity in the background as the whole unit responded to the situation.

My teeth were chattering, and I was shivering with shock.

Above: High school graduation gift from Mom and I am oh so ready to find my own way, far from here, 1967. Below: That "Don't mess with me" look hides a vulnerability that even I can't fully appreciate in 1970.

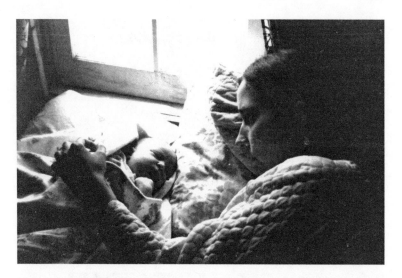

Above: Hours after Sarah Kate's birth, I am in awe at what we have done and the choices I made in 1973. Below: Our faces say it all! Sarah is brand-new and we are trying to figure out how to make ourselves into a family, 1973.

Left: Visiting California and my parents, proud and content with life as a hippie with one-year-old Sarah in 1974. Right: First-time homeowners in our self-built Dog-to-God bus, headed for Tennessee in 1974.

Born easily in the woods of Tennessee, Cara is hours old, and I am in love, 1976.

Don and me having the best of times, 1977.

Rich and active learning in our little Montessori Farm Lab School built from an abandoned trailer, 1982.

Carolyn and me, sharing youthful dreams in 1983, then age-fueled wisdom and love in 2021.

At the crossroads of a hippie becoming a healer, moving from Tennessee to Turlock and headed for premed, 1983.

Studying for Monday Morning Midterms, in my element and loving the learning, 1985.

Mutual respect at medical school graduation, where Dad and I came together as equals, 1989.

Every baby I delivered found a permanent place in my heart. They are all my babies, just like this little girl just hours old in 2001.

Above: Laura, my fellow traveler in life, sailing together under the Golden Gate Bridge and past the Marin Headlands on our way to Alaska, 2009.

Left: Tim, my motorcycle mentor, on his beloved Fat Boy. That tough-guy look hid a heart of gold, 2012.

A triumphant triad displaying our Tohelluride tats before they all peeled off, 2011.

Stripping off those heavy leathers as it warmed up in Tuolumne Meadows, Yosemite, 2012.

Tight together, celebrating the last day of the California Roll after riding over the Golden Gate Bridge, 2012.

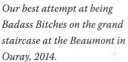

Our best attempt at being Badass Bitches on the grand staircase at the Beaumont in Ouray, 2014.

We try to take each morning's mapping and route-planning seriously, but sometimes we just crack each other up like here in Durango, 2021.

As I turned the heat in the car on high, I asked her if the specialty surgeon was on his way. I would always remember her angelic words.

"No, but we are trying his back line at home. We'll get him here for you. But Stacey, remember that we don't know anything for sure yet. The sonogram tech is on her way. You don't know your baby is dead. Don't give up. All you can do right now as you drive is pray. Pray for a miracle."

I took a deep breath and remembered my angels. The angels that attended every single birth with me. The angels that reminded me I was not alone when a new baby comes into the world. In times of stress, whenever I was responsible for saving a life and felt my own fear taking over, I had often called on angelic help. I would imagine a strong, supportive being standing behind me, with huge, white-feathered wings that draped around my shoulders, surrounding me with comfort and strength. This image would allow me to take a deep breath, slow my own heart rate, assess the critical situation, and then handle it. I had used this image many times, and tonight I needed a true miracle. So I started to pray for that miracle, and as I did, I felt a small ray of hope enter my heart, bringing with it the courage I needed. I also remembered something Stephen had once taught us. "The most important thing to understand about life force energies is that you can move them with your mind. You can do real things—healing things." Taking a deep breath, I calmed my shivering, focused my attention, and prepared myself to handle whatever I was going to find when I got to Sandy's side.

At the hospital, I ran into her room and found the radiology technician at the bedside, a wonderful woman who looked up at me with tears in her eyes and smiled.

"I just found your baby," she said. "The uterus ruptured, and baby is floating up by her liver. The heartbeat is slow, but it's alive." My angels were definitely making themselves known.

It is rare for a mother and baby to survive a uterine rupture, and we had to move fast. Sandy's husband, Bill, who had left the hospital to take his mother-in-law home, had been called to return to the hospital immediately. The OB-GYN surgeon was on his way, the anesthesiologist was getting his equipment set up, and the neonatal critical care pediatricians, and their nurse specialists, were ready to go. We wheeled Sandy's bed directly into an operating suite. With the rest of the medical team still assembling, there was nothing I could do other than keep a conscious connection with her. Somewhere in my memory, I heard people saying that when they were close to dying, it was a voice asking them to stay that kept them from leaving. Sandy was conscious but struggling to breathe; the weight of the baby up by her diaphragm and massive blood loss were compromising her lungs. I leaned close to her face and kept telling her to stay with us; we were going to save her and her baby. I said those words over and over while the world around us moved through the ordered chaos of preparing for emergency surgery.

Leaving Sandy in the capable hands of the OR nurses, I scrubbed to assist in surgery. The specialists arrived, and we got to work. Allison was born alive minutes later, giving a lusty cry that was the first herald of good news we'd had all night. We had also called in a trauma surgeon, hoping he might help save Sandy's uterus, and when that surgeon arrived, I stepped back from the table to let him in. I moved over to the infant table to check on our baby, and that was when I saw Bill standing in the corner of the operating room, eyes wide and face white as a sheet behind his mask. I went to him and briefly explained the situation as Allison cried.

"The two surgeons are working to see if they can save Sandy's uterus, and she's getting blood as fast as we can push it, Bill. I think she's going to be all right too." He remained speechless and continued to stand there in his corner of the operating room, watching the drama around his wife and child unfold. I continued to pray.

We did save Sandy and her uterus. Once everyone was stabilized, and I knew the nurses would take good care of both Mom and infant, I returned to Lisa's little house in the woods. She had been keeping dinner warm for me. It was so good to go home to someone who loved me and let me unload all the emotions the last few hours had brought. *Damn, that was close! Thank God for that nurse who reminded me to pray! And thank God we were able to save everyone. I never want to have to deal with something like that again,* I thought as I finally drifted off to sleep that night.

Allison thrived, and after a few days in the hospital, Sandy went home with her baby. She was upset that she had almost had a hysterectomy, and she had no idea at that time how close she had come to losing her life; the emotional shock that protected her from the awful truth would last for several months. A week later, she actually attended a social event at her husband's winery, one I was invited to as an honored guest. She mingled while I sat in the shade and watched her be alive and apparently well. I was close to tears more than once as I watched her work the crowd, knowing how close we had come to losing her.

. . .

After dinner on the deck in Yosemite Valley, and after the sun had given up its show, the Milky Way emerged as a vast smear across the sky, and constellations were hidden in the dense expanse of stars so crystal clear in the mountains. We all three stargazed while leaning over backward against the deck rail, a perfect ending to a restful day.

On our second day in the Park, we rode down and picnicked along Yosemite Creek, where, fulfilling one of Laura's wishes, I planned to scatter her ashes. Joan and Kristin set off to explore the creek upstream while I walked down to the edge of the water to spend some time with Laura. Standing on a big flat rock in the middle of the flow, surrounded by raging white water, I remembered playing on these rocks with her, taking photographs of the river and of each other. This had been one of her favorite spots on the planet and a place we had visited as part of her bucket list in those last years of her life. I felt close to her here. As I let her ashes go, I watched them swirl into the foam and disappear downstream with wild abandon, a release somehow fitting for the ashes of someone who loved the thrill of driving race cars. When the ashes were gone, I stayed there for a bit, just feeling her near and missing her at the same time. I wished I could talk to her once more and share my feelings about losing her, because she was the one who would understand. But that was the problem. *Who do you talk to about losing your bestie when that bestie is gone? When she is the only one who would understand what it is you need to say?*

When Joan and Kristin returned from their exploration upstream, we rode through Tuolumne Meadows and then past Tenaya Lake, where rock climbers were making their way up the sheer sides of rocks like ants. After Olmsted Point, it was a straight shot back to Crane Flat, and finally to our rented house in Yosemite West. Typical to our established patterns, I was up the hill, parked, unloaded, and into the shower before my two friends even arrived back at the house. At first, I didn't worry when they hadn't shown up, but eventually I got curious. Leaning over the railing of the front deck, I spotted them down by their bikes, watching a little bear enjoying the apples on a tree growing right in the middle of the road. A bear in Yosemite! That was worth getting dressed again and running back down the hill!

After Joan and Kristin went to go shower, I stayed with the bear, which wasn't the least bit concerned by a human watching him *snurf* and *snorf* and chomp and slobber his way through apple after apple. The tree swayed with his weight, but that didn't seem to worry him either. I started a private conversation that went something like:

> "You are a slob, you know."
> *Munch. Snarfle. Munch.*
> "Well, you're pretty much trashing that nice
>   apple tree there."
> *Crunch. Grind. Spit.*
> "Where's your mama?"
> *Grunt. Growl. Snort.*

"Well, you *are* a slob," I said, turning away to retreat back up to the house for wine, dinner, and a sunset.

The next day would prove to be the longest day of the California Roll, taking us all the way across the hot, dry Central Valley. I woke to the grind of the coffee maker at a bright and early 6:00 a.m. Our plan was to leave by eight, knowing the heat in the valley would be intense, but only after taking time to sip our coffee on the deck and watch the apple tree sway as the little bear snarfed his breakfast.

What a ride out of Yosemite! We filled our memories with one last view of El Capitan, cruised along the winding two-lane highway through forests, and rode in the shadow of sheer mountain cliffs rising up on either side of the road. When we stopped along the Merced River for a construction delay, we chatted with a group of Hells Angels who were a little lost and needed directions. Once we got going again, the sight of that whole crew riding in formation against the cliffs ahead of us was spectacular.

As we headed for Merced, a train came running alongside us. Joan pumped her fist up and down to express her joy, and the train engineer honked at us. We honked back, and soon we were making honking music together as we both flew along the landscape. Later, a trucker at a truck stop, who enthusiastically wished he was riding with us, helped us decipher some complicated directions. And still later, we encountered a lone biker who was drinking beer at the bar in a restaurant we'd stopped at before riding over the Pacheco Pass. Joan, who was always adamant against drinking while riding, said she hoped he wasn't anywhere near us when we hit the road again. But of course, he was. He came up behind us but roared on past, swerving left and right all the way.

Finally, we were on our way to the ocean and cooler air again after leaving the Sierras and crossing the rolling hills of the Diablo Range. Kristin led us through the town of Capitola, crowded on this warm and sunny Saturday with babies in strollers, young healthy college kids, surfers taking breaks from the water, and even a wedding party. It was generally a feel-good circus, and along with all the other colorful sights, we cut quite a scene as we slowly made a show of rumbling our way along the boardwalk. I felt a bit like I was in a parade. Like I should wave at everyone as we rode by. Okay—I did wave at one little boy who yelled "Vroom! Vroom!" at us.

When we arrived at the Davenport Roadhouse Inn, after bypassing the traffic in Santa Cruz proper, Joan insisted that we drop our stuff in our rooms and immediately meet in the bar for a drink. Not wine. Nope—this had been a long hot day and we needed a cocktail. Joansie often has great ideas. Afterward, we still had plenty of daylight, so we walked across the road to the beautiful Davenport Landing beach, where I gathered driftwood and feathers while Joan and Kristin explored the rocks on the edge of the water. We came back together, sitting side by side on a log, watching the sun set over the Pacific.

"Why does it feel so good to be with you two?" I had often wondered about their relationship, because it seemed so smooth and easy. I never saw them fight, or yell, or even be snarky with each other. And I'd lived with a lot of people in relationships . . . so what was different here? By now I was over twenty years out from my divorce and still wasn't sure I'd ever find anyone I wanted to be with. *What is their secret? Are they that good at hiding their fights?*

"What do you mean?" Joansie laughed. "We sure like being with each other . . . and with you!"

"Yes, but the two of you have figured it out for yourselves, and I wonder what that's about. Like, why do you always include each other in all your texts? Someone might think that was creepy-controlling . . ."

They looked at each other, confusion on their faces. "I don't know," Kristin said. "It's just what we do so we're on the same page. Seems easier." She paused for a moment to think. "We are selfish. I mean, we are not selfish people, but we are selfish with our relationship. We guard our time together, and we make sure we get plenty of it. We have date nights, and we don't break those dates. After all, we went through med school together, residency together, and we've worked together our whole careers. I guess we just really like and trust each other."

"Well, that's pretty obvious," I observed. "But what do you do when you disagree? I mean . . . everyone disagrees *sometimes*! And what about when one of you is in a bad mood? How does that work?"

There was a short silence while we watched a couple of beachcombers stroll between us and the edge of the surf.

"I don't know," Joan said. "I guess we just give each other space and then talk later. We'll go for a walk, talk, and figure out a plan to make things better. We don't really fight . . . but we're good at compromising, and we're good at laughing. That helps."

This was beginning to sound a bit surreal to me, the survivor of countless failed romantic relationships: Don, Lisa, and all those one-date men along the way. I swear, I'd go browse on Match.com just to cure myself of the wanting. Did these two friends of mine step out of a self-help book on marriage? Were they for real? But I knew they were. After four road trips together, I knew they were definitely for real.

"So you nurture the relationship, sometimes compromising for the good of your marriage," I said. "And you prevent resentments by staying on top of stuff when it comes up. And you aren't in a power struggle. I guess all that helps." I sat for a bit, watching the sun slowly sink, and wondered if I would ever find someone as sane as these two women were. As kind. As grown-up. And I knew I would never settle for less, now that I had seen it could be had. "You've given me much to think about—plenty of helmet thoughts for tomorrow," I laughed.

The next day would bring us across the Golden Gate to my home, and it was easy to wake to the sound of the ocean with a bit of relief that all we had to do was ride up the California coast and home. One more pack-it-up. It was a glorious sunny Sunday, and we shared the first miles of road with seemingly endless cyclists on a bicycle race that was also taking them north on the Pacific Coast Highway. The ocean so blue, the sky to match. Taking a neat U-turn in Pacifica, we stopped for gas and put on a few more layers; just because the sun was out didn't mean the coastal air wasn't brisk, especially with the windchill we'd get while riding.

Before setting out again, we had a big conference about going through San Francisco and then on across the Golden Gate Bridge. We were not used to riding in big cities, so we needed to prepare for heavy traffic, super-steep hills, one-way streets, and so many distractions. This was *not* the place to drop a bike! Group decision time. Agreed: we stick tight together, and if we end up having to stop on a super-steep hill in the city, we all pull to the very top of the rise with the leader on the left side. We went over the maps more than once before deciding to go for it. I had the most city experience of us three, so I was in the lead.

"You okay for that?" asked Kristin.

"Yep, I'm fine." Too bad I forgot to tell my friends that I will often mistake left for right and have absolutely no sense of direction outside a mall or off an island with clear edges.

It didn't take long to pass Daly City with all its colorful, boxy houses on the hillside and find ourselves on the Great Highway, cruising past the San Francisco Zoo, the beaches, and the Cliff House as we got closer and closer to the Presidio before hitting the Golden Gate. We rode past the site where the Family Dog had been and where Monday Night Class had attracted thousands of hippies over forty years ago. The Family Dog long since gone, I looked at the spot that had changed my life so long ago, and the seawall where I had watched the fog roll in. I gave a silent salute to those memories. All was smooth until I went left instead of right.

We ended up in a neighborhood of fine homes with the bridge behind us instead of straight ahead. Oops. But no worries; we stopped and regrouped with maps and laughter serving as excellent remedies for getting lost. Kristin took the lead, giving us some well-timed instructions on the right (or left) turns to take. Sometimes it took all three of us to navigate.

Crossing the Golden Gate Bridge felt like a ceremony of sorts, a milestone, an event to remember forever, especially for my Southwest friends. And silly us! We thought the hardest part was over.

We decided to look for a lunch stop. This ride, named California Roll, had not yet seen a single piece of sushi on the trip, and we thought for sure there would be a place to fulfill this need along the way. Since we were back in my home territory, I had agreed to once again take the lead toward Stinson Beach. We headed north on the 101, through the tunnel, and then turned off the freeway, picking up the Pacific Coast Highway toward the coast.

I will never forget riding the narrow two-lane Pacific Coast Highway from the Golden Gate Bridge to Stinson Beach. All our white-knuckle riding paid off as we handled tight turns in first gear, dodging bicycles and tourists and buses and trucks and cars. Cliffs hugged us on the right, and sheer drop-offs threatened us on the left. The good news was that the road in our direction had recently been paved, so the ride was smooth. But when we saw a huge tour bus heading toward us, and a bicycle on the shoulder on our right, simultaneously realizing that we would all converge in the middle of the next hard-core switchback . . . well, what could we do but laugh out loud in our helmets?!

The view to our left was unbelievable . . . when we dared take a second to look; the blue expanse of the Pacific Ocean stretched as far as we could see, without a speck of fog or a breath of wind. After passing Steep Ravine campground, we pulled into Stinson Beach, where we sat in the sun and ate lunch. By then, it didn't matter if it was sushi or not.

Back on the bikes—next stop: home. We rode north past Tomales Bay, grateful for the gentle curves that had replaced the gnarly switchbacks. The eucalyptus groves smelled wonderful, and we were able to cruise once again in second and third gear—a welcome relief after all those miles in first we had just completed, until we reached Marshall and discovered our last Long-and-Winding-Road of the trip inland. It went on forever. Bumps. Potholes. Twists and turns. Trucks and cars on our ass, and few places to pull over to let them pass, which we did whenever we could to create a safe pocket for riding at our own pace without having to worry about impatient drivers pushing us from behind. There was nothing we could do with all these irritating challenges but keep going and wonder if we had entered some twilight zone that would never ever end. We were all so very ready for the end of the day. The end of the ride.

That road, of course, did end. In Petaluma, where we finally beat our helmets with our fists and wilted over the gas tanks, exhausted. I briefly considered suggesting we take the

101 freeway and zip quickly home from there, instead of taking the planned scenic route across Sonoma Mountain, and it's a good thing I didn't ask, since Kristin later admitted she would've gone for that in a heartbeat. But no—we were not going to end this trip on a wimp note. We were doing it full on. So we followed our original plan and rode the gentle curves that brought us smoothly to Tim and Mary's house, where Joan and Kristin's rig waited for the two Arizona bikes.

Tim was there for us and helped load O-ren Ishii and Beatrix onto the trailer so Joan and Kristin would be ready for an early morning takeoff the next day. Only one last goal for this run: get a California roll, which we'd been unable to do in Stinson Beach. We gorged on sushi in a favorite local Japanese restaurant and then went back to my place to soak in the hot tub while listing as many Fuckin' A moments from the trip that we could remember and gazing up at Pegasus in the night sky.

We had worked hard for all of this, and the reward was more than we could have imagined. Again. We wondered how we could plan a ride that would top this one. What we didn't know was that, before the next ride, I would face another loss and would have to graduate to a new level of independence.

CHAPTER 6

JUST PASSIN' THROUGH, 2014

Watch for falling rocks.
Well that hasn't happened yet.
Let's just pass on that.
—K

"Sebastopol . . . Freestone . . . Monte Rio . . . Guerneville . . .
Forestville . . . Santa Rosa . . . fifty-six miles of redwoods and
the Russian River helps me remember that it's about the ride,
not the rig. Headed for the Great Divide!"

This was my early May Facebook post, preparing for our
next ride together. I used Facebook to share our adventures
because so many of my friends were worried about me out
there on a motorcycle, and they needed to know we were all
okay. I got so many "You be safe now!" comments that I felt
the need to reassure everyone, every single night, that we had
survived the day's ride. These friends didn't realize that the
subtext I'd hear when they said that well-meaning phrase
was *I think you're gonna die!* And I didn't need that. They

loved me, and they feared the worst, but they didn't realize that their own fears were bleeding through and landing on me. So I would communicate in the least offensive way possible, with pics and snippets of information on social media. A lighthearted way to antidote everyone else's fear.

On this next adventure, two years after the California Roll, we planned to explore Colorado together. Last year, Joan and Kristin had changed jobs within the Indian Health Service and moved to Dulce, New Mexico, to work on the Jicarilla Apache Nation Reservation. Once they were settled in their new home, Kristin texted me.

"What are you and Magdalena doing the third week of August? Wheels are turning . . ."

I texted back. "What? Did you hear me talking to you as I rode to Bodega Bay on Saturday? Sayin' how great this is, but how much greater if my best buds on two wheels were with me? I can do whatever we want in August. I'm UP for the adventure! Dreams do come true . . ."

The three of us came up with a plan: from Dulce to Creede in Colorado, then to Crested Butte, Ouray, and Durango, and then finally back to Dulce. We would visit a few favorites from previous trips, but we'd take different routes so the ride would not be a complete repeat. Most days would only be about 130 to 150 miles, but there would be lots of big-mountain riding and curves in this tour.

Kristin sent an email: "We are SO happy and SO excited to think about us all riding together again and heading out on a new adventure! The ride from Crested Butte is not too high elevation or gnarly. . . THAT will come when we leave Ouray and ride those switchbacks of the Million Dollar Highway in the opposite direction. But it will be when we are fresh and only a seventy-mile day to Durango! We and our girls will be

Spiderwomen climbing out of that canyon! I counted up the number of passes—seven in the first four days: Wolf Creek Pass, Spring Creek Pass, Slumgullion Pass, Cerro Summit, Red Mountain Pass, Molas Pass, and Coal Bank Pass. This is definitely gonna be a Colorado mountain tour."

That's when Joan spoke up. "So how 'bout 'Just Passin' Through' as a potential name for this ride?"

And this is how plans were made. Adventure named. Reservations confirmed. Trailer located, bike serviced, and Tim's agreement to help me load securely. Everything lined up for an August departure. We were definitely going to make this happen.

It was just a month later, shortly after my warm-up ride through the redwoods, when the world shifted. I came home to a voice mail asking me to call Mary, Tim's wife.

"Hi. Is Mary there?" I asked cheerfully when one of their daughters answered.

Her voice was shaky. "I guess you haven't heard."

I had a sinking feeling. "What? What haven't I heard?"

"Dad's gone. He died yesterday," she said.

"What?! Tim?! What do you mean? What happened?"

He went off the road, totaled his Harley, and died in a creek bed off Westside Road. "We're trying to figure out how to get his stuff from the CHP, and Mom needs your help."

My head started buzzing like it does when I'm in shock and can't quite integrate bad news. Part of me wanted to believe this was all a sick joke, but I knew it was real. *No amount of denial is going to bring Tim back to life, so I may as well buck up and take care of business. That lump in my throat and sick feeling in my stomach will just have to be where grief goes while I continue to function. That's what doctors do in a crisis—they function when others can't. So get to work, Stace.*

The next few days were filled with grieving and all the busywork that helps keep people sane when insane things happen to those they love. I went with Mary and her daughter to see Tim's Fat Boy where the CHP had towed it, and we picked up the saddlebags and gear that had been scattered when he crashed. They smelled like burnt metal and trauma, and I found it hard not to recoil with horror at the images that odor cooked up in my head; years in the emergency room had never managed to desensitize me to the smell of blood and hot metal. But this was about Mary. We held Mary. We helped her figure out a memorial service. We coached her on how to move on in life without her partner. And all the while I thought about Tim.

Tim was the best rider I knew. It was not like him to lose control on a curve, a curve on a road he knew from riding it countless times. Heck—we'd ridden that stretch together many times in the last couple of years! It wasn't even that sharp a curve! And Tim had, more than once, wiped out on interstate highways with grace, sliding off his bike and landing safely on the shoulder with fewer injuries than you would expect from such a move. He was *good*. I was having a hard time believing that he'd lost control.

But this was idle thought. We would never know what happened out there on Westside Road. The fact remained: Tim was gone. I felt a huge hole open up in my heart and then, to my embarrassment, had a fleeting concern. *Who would help me load my bike in August?* Feeling ashamed and guilty at my selfishness, I shoved those worries into a locked compartment in my mind and figured I'd find someone when the time came. Right now I needed to grieve for my dear friend and support his family through hard times.

Mary was kind enough to share some of Tim's ashes with

me. I found a little black leather bag, put a tablespoon of his ashes in there, and tied it to Magdalena's handlebars—right in the middle where I could see it every time I rode. I made a comforting promise to myself: Tim would ride with me every single day I rode, giving me courage when I was scared and reminding me of his strength and humor and the gentle way he taught a newbie how to ride. I would talk to him sometimes, and I could still hear his voice answering me with one of his favorite responses. *Aw, Stace! We can do* anything!

I packed away the rest of the ashes that she gifted to me in a safe place, in that same corner of my saddlebag where Laura had been packed away on our last run. I would find the right place to scatter these ashes, a place I knew Tim would want to be.

Packing for a motorcycle ride is a cross between preparing for a backpacking trip and a road trip in a car. Only so much room, but at least I didn't have to carry all my gear the whole way on my back. I've always found comfort in organizing stuff, so the packing was satisfying. Then, when it was time to load up and head for New Mexico, I called a friend to help me load Magdalena into the trailer. I still wasn't ready to do that task by myself because slow-loading a six-hundred-pound motorcycle is way different from riding that machine.

Once I headed east into big-sky country, I started to feel the excitement of our planned adventure. Big skies get me high just like mountains do. All that space opens my mind and quiets my heart. Miles and miles of big sky and endless highways.

Arriving in Dulce, it felt good to be back in the fold of Joan and Kristin's home and the welcoming energy. As I settled into their guest room that night, I thought once again about how lucky I was to have these two women as my friends.

Tim's death had hit me hard. As we all grew older, I knew we would be losing friends along the way—there was no escaping it. I thought of how my practice of medicine had joyfully included births for many years, in spite of, or maybe in opposition to, Ina May's refusal to include me in the midwife crew on The Farm. I loved the power of birth, and I loved using my talent to calm the energy every time I walked into a room full of fear and anxiety. My ability to open my heart to the family and to honestly assure them they were not alone was part of the art of healing, not just the practice of medicine. Thinking of Tim, and Laura, and others who had passed, I realized that my days of surfing the energy at birthings were moving into days of swimming in the energy of death. It was all sacred. It was where I wanted to be.

Grief is a heavy burden to carry alone. Learning how to help carry that burden was a skill I needed to practice. As I lay in bed that night thinking about Tim and Laura, I remembered the first time I joined voices with sisters to grieve. The first time I keened.

It was a moonless night, but I knew I was at the right house because all the lights were on and the driveway was full of Prius hybrids. Cheryl was a close friend from Farm days, a midwife I had also worked with during my residency in family medicine. She lived at the end of a long, winding road that followed the Russian River upstream for a few miles before it turned into a steep driveway that led to her door. I wasn't too thrilled to be driving twenty miles into the woods, all alone on a dark and icy night, but Cheryl had called, and this was a call that I couldn't refuse to answer.

Fifteen women had answered the same call.

The circle took shape as women brought their tea and

found a place in the room on one of the two couches, in an easy chair, or on the floor. The coffee table in the center of the room was arranged with candles and several photographs of a smiling young blond man with his mother, with his sister, or simply standing on his own. A large uncurtained window reflected the room back at us, but I could see that during daylight that window would offer a rare and beautiful view of the Russian River below. In front of the window, on a small table next to Cheryl's chair, was an altar. A single candle burned in front of a small, coffin-shaped box wrapped in a Tibetan prayer shawl. Several religious art objects surrounded another photograph, this one showing the same young man in glorious, good health.

I looked at the women who had gathered this night. Several nurses, a doctor, a few teachers, a retired businesswoman, a few midwives, a peace activist, and a writer. But what I really saw were women who had become sisters over thirty years earlier, when we were living together on The Farm. There, we had helped each other birth our babies, haul water and do laundry, cook meals, and commit to spiritual integrity. Many of us had also nursed each other's babies. In those days, we thought we would be strong forever.

We *were still* strong now. And we had a new awareness of what our strength was.

We were new to keening. We didn't even really know what it was, other than a primal expression of deep sorrow. We were also new to being elders and had not had much opportunity to practice grief. We knew how to ohm, but to keen? That was a new sound. So we began by listening to Cheryl talk, telling us about her son and how it was for her. As an empath, I could easily feel others' pain, and her pain filled my heart and belly until I felt swollen with unbearable emotion. We smudged the room with white sage. We lit three candles—one for maiden, one for mother, and one for crone. Cheryl's tiny granddaughter suckled noisily at her mother's breast.

And then rattles appeared out of pockets and handbags. My drum fit between my knees, and I began a pulse that the rattles echoed. Then, we began to make our sounds of grief. Other drums joined me, and somehow the rhythm of our drums helped get the keening started. We keened, and we chanted ohms, in our own voices, in our own style. After several minutes, the chant died away, and the drum slowly faded with one last rattle. The silence became full, and we all sat comfortably, feeling the natural high that filled the space when the drumming had come to an end.

After a while, we keened again, but this time without drums or rattles. This felt better to me, more direct, free. No beat to set a tone. Nothing to hide behind. Only what came from within, fully expressed and explored. I howled at a moon I could not see.

We were blessed to have each other, to be with each other, to have a history of being maidens, mothers, and now crones together. This is what really counts in life: sharing the pain and the joy, reminding each other that life is fleeting, and knowing how to be there with each other to ease the pain of intolerable times.

There had been no keening for either Laura or Tim, but just as I had honored Laura by scattering her ashes in Yosemite, I would honor Tim's passing on this adventure. Joan's name for this ride, "Just Passin' Through," now seemed particularly fitting.

Leaving Dulce that next morning, we planned on lunch

in Pagosa Springs. We wanted to take it easy on the first day out while we reestablished our synchronicity. Each time we started a trip, it took less time to fall into the smooth patterns of riding like a little flock of birds with telepathic communication. That was usually the moment I let go of anxiety and allowed myself to fully feel the joy of riding with friends. This time, we hit that sync well before lunch. Off to a smooth start in perfect weather, we were high on the excitement of new beginnings and looked forward to landing in Creede that night, where we had tickets to the infamous Creede Repertory Theatre.

On the road to Creede, we cruised to the first of seven mountain passes we planned to log on this trip. At an elevation of 10,850 feet, Wolf Creek Pass lies right on the Continental Divide, where a person can stand with one foot on the western slope of the continental United States and the other on the eastern slope. This was where I chose to scatter Tim's ashes. The three of us pulled over to take a break, to read the signs that explained what the Continental Divide is, and to give me time to be with Tim. I dug into my pack for the ashes I had carefully stashed. Carrying them with me out into a vast mountain meadow, I lined myself up with the Divide. With the wind at my back, I raised my hands as high and wide as they could go, scattering Tim to both sides, as far as I could fling. As I watched the white clouds of ash float off in both directions, I spoke aloud.

"I am sending you to both the Pacific Ocean and to those waters in the East as well, Tim, so go out there and have a great time. Ride free, my friend! Whoooo-hoooo!"

Tim was a man who loved the freedom of the ride, and releasing him to be spread across the entire continent felt like just the right thing to do. I stood there for a moment with the empty bag in my hands and said a final goodbye to his physical presence. I knew his spirit would always be with me when I rode Magdalena Pearl.

Back on the bikes again, we crossed the Rio Grande and then, following it farther north, we crossed over it again shortly before arriving in Creede for our one-night stay. The next morning, we headed for Crested Butte, taking a roundabout way that gave us the best views and the smoothest ride. This is what we rode for! We cruised over the Spring Creek Pass, up and over Slumgullion Pass, and down to where we picked up the Gunnison River, where we rode alongside those rushing waters into the town of Gunnison. It was August, and the wind we created did not counter the heat coming off our engines, but we were headed for air-conditioned lodgings.

The Elk Mountain Lodge was waiting for us in Crested Butte, another quaint and unique place to land after a day of smooth riding. Our pattern of landing, checking in, unloading, comparing each other's digs, and then settling into our individual spaces was still an easy habit. That evening, we headed out to dinner, where I decided to skip my usual cocktail and join my friends in a bottle of good red wine. They were a bit surprised, but I explained that while I usually feel "spiritual," preferring a good single-malt Scotch or some other spirit, tonight I was feeling rather grapey. They laughed with me, and that got us started on how we all developed our preferences.

"My father was Scottish, and when I tried my first sip of smooth Scotch on a visit to Edinburgh, I knew it was for me," I explained. "And while my mother was Jewish by blood, I never did develop a taste for sweet wine. But I did find it much easier to love her than my father . . . so go figure. And she loved me back with such need, it almost hurt—she wanted more of me than I was able to give."

"So was it hard on you when she died? I mean, of course it's hard when your mom dies, but you'd been independent for so long . . . were there regrets?"

"I regret that we couldn't become friends. But, in the end, I was able to guide her passage and help her die."

I had left my family home, but I did not leave my family. I didn't honor my parents as they had hoped I would; they were obviously in a different world than I, one that did not serve my own needs. But I did need family. I needed ancestral history. I stayed connected to my mom and, through her, to my father in a minimal way. She longed for me to be part of her life in an intimate way, and she was so pathetically grateful every time I visited, so *needy*. I could not force intimacy, but I could still love her from afar and tolerate Dad because she loved him.

Mom gave up everything to serve her husband, as most women did in the 1950s. She told me that she had only ever wanted to be a housewife and a mother, and I saw her enter a deep depression when mothering came to an in-your-face end. I grew up, had my own opinions, and diverged from her sphere. Mom seemed different from me, and in my youth I'd thought she was so simple. So unaware, so limited. I never had a chance to know her on a deeper level; she died before we could become true friends.

We occasionally got season tickets to Broadway musicals in the city together, and two days before her accident we went to lunch in San Francisco. It was mid-September and the weather was mild, so afterward we walked together to the

Orpheum Theater to see a Wednesday matinee performance of *Miss Saigon*.

"I thought of leaving your father," she said as we walked. "I thought of it seriously during the seventies when so many women were finding freedom. I did not leave, and I'm glad I made the choice I did. In spite of all, he provided security, and that was what I needed the most. I am grateful."

There were so many other things I wanted to know about her. So many things I wanted to say or ask.

Mom, I wanted to be friends with you. I wanted to talk about how it was for you when you were my age . . . and then my age older . . . and then again even older. Did you feel the same loneliness, the same frustration, the same joy as I do now? Could we have moved past our superficial relationship, based on the shared love of Broadway musicals? Is it even possible to be best friends with your mother? I will never know.

How did you stand living with that controlling man who was my father? I know you wanted more passion in your life, but from the looks of things, you never got it. Unless you had that affair in Japan that I've always wondered about. Now this, I really wanted to ask you about. Did you have that affair, and was it life-savingly good? Did it make you happy? Were you really learning how to arrange flowers or were you spending long, sensual hours being touched by a man who appreciated you? However did you live without closeness for so many years? You, who were such a romantic. How did you manage to survive our narcissistic family? How did you feel when you were my age?

But I never got the chance to express all my thoughts and feelings to her. She fell two days after our lunch date, sustained a massive brain bleed, and went into a coma. I got the call on Saturday morning while I was out at Lisa's; we were having coffee, and the next thing I knew I was on the highway headed for Highland Hospital in Oakland.

While Mom lay in an ICU bed, I had a hard conversation with Dad and her doctors. The head injury had caused permanent damage to her brain, and Dad had to decide whether she should be considered a "Do Not Resuscitate" patient, meaning that if her heart stopped, they would not try to revive her. Mom and Dad had been married for over fifty years, and this was not an easy decision, even for my undemonstrative, unemotional father. I let the doctors explain to Dad how she might be should she ever wake from this coma. The brain bleed had affected her speech and emotion centers, so if she lived, she might not be able to find words to express herself, or she might shout out obscenities without even realizing it. Mom would have *hated* either of those possibilities, and we both knew it. Then those kind physicians left us alone to make our decision, and I remembered one of Stephen's teachings. "You have to use all your good judgment, and all your compassion, and courage, and tact, and taste, to say heavy things to people in a way that will be valuable to them, rather than just knocking them off their own center."

"So what do you want to do, Dad?" I avoided giving in to the temptation of immediately offering my own very strong opinion.

After a few moments, he replied. "I don't care how she comes out of this coma . . . I want her to live longer and to be with me no matter what shape she is in."

I held my breath, worried that he was going to make a choice that would lead to the nightmare my mother would never want. But before I could respond to this, he continued. "But she would not want that, so I will let them know that we don't want to resuscitate her."

Even as I breathed my own sigh of relief, I felt the pro-
found grief that accompanied his decision, and my respect for
my father increased along with my own deepening heartache.

Mom died a week later. During that week, I sat by her
bed, first in the ICU and then in an isolated private room at
the end of the hall where they park patients who are simply
there to die. Day after day, I sat by her bed, taking advantage
of those hours to memorize the shape of her hands, to massage her feet so I would never forget, and to keep her safe.
In the end, I told the staff to remove the IV and the oxygen
and to pay attention to her comfort needs. I then blessed her
passing.

"Go, Mom. It's okay. I'll stick by Dad. No worries—you
can leave."

But Mom refused to pass quickly, and I wore out. Days
were spent by her bed as I called on both of my daughters
and many friends, asking them to sit there all night while I
went home to shower and recover. I was commuting an hour
each way to be there. Everything else was put on hold for this
death watch. I guarded her, keeping the doctors and nurses
from doing anything to prolong her life or to unintentionally hurt her. All this with Dad's blessing—Dad, who could
no longer bear to see her, his wife of fifty-four years. Dad,
who—the last time he did see her—commented that we treat
our pets better than this. Dad, who—once he knew her path
was inevitable—wanted it to happen as soon as possible. She
lay in that bed, tiny and fragile, only a shell of the grand and
colorful spirit we knew.

That last morning, I woke up at home and asked Lisa to
come with me to the hospital. Then, randomly picking a time,
I asked for additional help. "I will need you at 7:00 p.m. tonight, when I'll need to leave my mother's bedside. I will not

want to. I will fight you, but I cannot win. I really need you today."

Yes, Mom, Lisa was my girlfriend. I'm not really a lesbian, but I wasn't going to reject generous love when it was offered. And I'm all about exploring new experiences. Learning to make love with another woman was fun; Lisa and I had such good times together, and with her I learned things about myself I could never have learned from a man. Things only a woman could share with another woman.

Lisa got out of our bed and came with me to the hospital, and she sat with me for hours as we watched Mom, her thinking brain no longer alive. Only her brain stem was left to stimulate her breathing . . . breath after breath . . . without stopping. *How long can this go on?* Lisa got us lunch. She brought me coffee. She kept me sane.

Then, 7:00 p.m. arrived. "We must go, Stacey, now."

"No. Not yet. Just a few more minutes."

"No, now. I promised, and you must come with me now."

"First let me connect with the nurse—make sure they know she'll be alone, make sure they'll not ignore her." I did that, getting a promise from the respiratory therapist to suction her when she got full of fluid in her throat. He promised. We left.

I was driving, and we had just crossed the Bay Bridge northbound on the 101 when the call came. It had only been twenty minutes since we'd stepped away from her bedside. She was gone.

I pulled over onto the shoulder and began to cry with a confusing mixture of sadness, loss, and a large dose of guilty relief. Lisa held me while I cried. Somehow it felt right to be held by a woman I loved when my mother, who had loved

me as no other ever did or ever would again, had just left.
Forever.

A highway patrol car pulled up behind us, lights flashing,
and the large uniformed officer cautiously came to the passenger side, to Lisa's window. She rolled it down. Peering in,
he asked, "Are you two okay here?"

I couldn't even look at him. *This was all I needed, a ticket
for crying. Busted for grieving in public. Shit.*

"Her mother just died, and we had to stop for a bit," Lisa
told him.

He saw the tears streaming down my face and was surprisingly sympathetic. "I understand," he said to Lisa. "Just
. . . please move on when she can because this shoulder isn't
that safe. And ma'am, you might want to drive." And then, to
me, "I am truly sorry for your loss."

We switched seats, and Lisa started to drive us home.
*Why did Mom have to go when no one was there to hold her
hand? When I couldn't comfort her, usher her out, assure her
that we would all be okay?*

And then in a flash I knew. I had only been thinking of
me. My needs. My perception of what was right and what
was needed. My sense of right had diverged from hers when
I turned eighteen and left home. What I thought was proper
was not at all what she needed. And this was her own intimate show. Not mine.

She was a private woman who would never leave her own
party while a guest was still there. She was a proper woman
with social graces that defined most of what she did and how
she lived her life. This was her death party. She died true to
her own nature. She had been waiting for me to go—waiting
for a private time to leave, on her own, in her own style. That

was my mother. A private person who would not do something so vulnerable or vulgar as dying in front of anyone else.

I would always miss her and the talks we never had. And in spite of my desire and intentions to be holding the hands of dying loved ones, I could see that I might be the same as she was someday. I might want to die alone. Loved, but emotionally private—just as I had lived for most of my life.

As I wrapped up the story of my mom's death, I explained how it had shaped the way I counseled families in my practice when caring for the dying. "I remind family members that death is an intimate, extremely personal transition, and people's wishes need to be honored . . . if possible."

Joan and Kristin raised their wineglasses to me, and with those final sips, we toasted to my mother. In telling this story to them, and in their respectful heartfelt hearing, I felt ever closer to these two women. Later, back in my room—which I'd made my own just a few hours before, as military nomads readily learn to do—I sat on the deck with a view of Crested Butte. I gratefully let the past go, and I embraced the present moment.

Arriving in Ouray the next afternoon was an adventure in itself. We had reservations at the Beaumont Hotel. Built in 1886, it was unique, comfortable, close to town, and had plenty of character. It was also the only luxury hotel in Ouray. Trouble was, close to town in Ouray meant figuring out where to park our motorcycles so they wouldn't fall over on one of the steeply sloped streets that surrounded the hotel. We also had to figure out how and where to unload all our gear before the oncoming storm dumped its load of heavy rain on us.

We pulled into a perfectly flat retail parking lot across the street from the hotel and scouted the scene. Briefly wishing we could leave the bikes in that easy parking lot, we decided it was too far away and not really legal. So we walked the street along the side of the hotel, assessing the slope and discussing the safety of leaving the bikes there. You would have thought it was some kind of high-level engineering investigation. Deciding that parking with the kickstands on the uphill side would be safe, we made our plan of action. First, we would pull up to the front door of the hotel right on Main Street, and Joan and Kristin would unload all our gear while I'd grab a luggage cart. We'd then stash the gear inside the front door, ride and park our precious wheels sideways on the slope, and then make our way back to the hotel to claim our bags and finally check into our rooms. Teamwork! The plan worked with almost-military precision before the storm hit.

The Beaumont was all we hoped it would be, and we easily slipped into classic, old-fashioned luxury. After the storm passed, we spent the early part of the evening on the banks of the Uncompahgre River, enjoying the sound of rippling mountain water and watching the rainbows in a glorious sky with lighting unique to high mountain vistas after big storms. Later, as we paused on the landing of the massive hotel staircase, Joan voiced her hopes.

"God, I hope we sleep tonight! I haven't been able to sleep through the night for the last three nights. I guess I'm just too wound up with all the excitement of our ride."

"It's been hard," Kristin agreed. "We don't usually have any trouble sleeping, but this is getting ridiculous."

I proposed a solution. "Do you want to try some of my medicine? I travel with a flask of Kahlúa infused with CBD-rich cannabis, and I use it just for this purpose: sleeping in strange places where I might otherwise be too restless to fall into the deep sleep I need." I offered hesitantly because neither Joan nor Kristin used cannabis at all. On the other hand, I knew they'd be quite sensitive to it if they wanted to try, and perhaps a little sip would do the trick.

"Kahlúa is coffee liqueur," Joansie said. "Won't that keep us awake?"

"I know, it seems wrong, but really—it works. I wouldn't travel with it if it didn't." To my surprise, they both agreed to try some of my elixir.

I made medicine with cannabis in my kitchen in California, where it was legal. The medicine I made was for personal use only, but my professional involvement started shortly after a law was passed allowing doctors to consult with patients about cannabis as medicine. Patients soon found that I was open to these discussions. They were eager to ask questions, and my scientific curiosity led me to becoming a clinical resource as I followed the evolving research. By the time Joan and Kristin had insomnia in Ouray, I'd had several years of clinical experience with cannabis as medicine and felt safe micro-dosing them by sharing my homemade tincture.

I went to my room, dug the flask out of my travel bag, and took it out to the two of them, who were waiting for me on the landing. Telling them to take just a sip, I handed the Kahlúa first to Joan, then to Kristin. They both commented on how good it tasted and, thanking me, went off to bed. Back in my room, I took my own sip of Kahlúa and nestled into bed.

I slept deeply, as expected. Waking up refreshed, one of my first conscious thoughts was wondering how my two friends had slept. I waited until 7:00 a.m. before texting them to check in, but I heard nothing back. I waited. A half hour passed. Still no word. I texted again.

"Did you get my text?"

I started to worry a bit. I do that—I make up stories when I don't know what is going on. I have to fill the void, and I am very good at imagining wrong scenarios. I imagined I had overdosed them and they were still in a deep sleep. I imagined it hadn't worked and they hadn't gotten to sleep until 4:00 a.m. and now I was bugging them with my texts. I stopped myself short of imagining anything worse.

An hour later, I finally got a text.

"Meet for breakfast?"

I breathed a huge sigh of relief. Then, when we met up, I asked how they'd slept.

"Fantastic!" they chorused, laughing at their harmony. Kristin added that they'd slept so well that they went out for a run around six thirty that morning. "I feel great, and I'm ready for a good ride today!"

"It not only tasted good," Joan added, "but it worked really well, and I'm not at all hungover. Thanks so much!"

That was the last cannabis I shared with them because, after that, they slept well and had no need for my herb. I, on the other hand, continued to enjoy a sip of my Kahlúa occasionally when bedding down in strange places along the way.

Next on our planned route was Durango, where we would have a whole house to stay in for the next three nights. On our way there, we'd ride over Red Mountain Pass, Molas Pass, and Coal Bank Pass, and then along the Million Dollar Highway to Silverton. The Ouray-to-Silverton run would be just part of a seventy-mile day that was the gnarliest one of the entire ride.

This is the way to take a hairpin turn on two wheels: Relax. Breathe. Slow down a little before the turn, hit the throttle as you take the turn, and above all, keep your speed up enough to stay upright. Press with the inside-curve hand.

Avoid looking at the road right in front of the bike; lift your head up and look ahead at the part of the road where you want to go. Repeat as necessary.

After a while, the moves became easier as we took curve after curve together. After a while, it felt like dancing on motorcycles.

Midafternoon found us cruising the residential streets of Durango, looking for the house Joan and Kristin had found for us in a quiet neighborhood. We were glad to find quick and easy shaded street parking because we wanted to shut down our engines before we offended everyone on the block with our noise. Kristin dug the key out of its hiding place in the front garden, and we decided to explore the new digs before unloading our gear.

I liked to think that I could keep a straight face to hide my feelings when necessary. I was often wrong. Like when I walked into "my room" in this little house and realized it belonged to a little boy. The windowless room was tiny, with a bunk bed taking up most of the space. Boy toys were stacked on every surface, and the walls were covered in wallpaper with spaceships flying through the galaxy. If I carefully moved a couple of toys on a shelf near the bed, I could find a spot for my water bottle and phone, but other than that there was no room for my things.

On The Farm and during my roving hippie days, I had lived in many challenging situations, so I took a deep breath and decided to make the best of it—after all, it was only three nights, and the price was right. But when Kristin and Joan came to peek into my digs, we all stood there, silent, not sure what to say. We liked to keep things positive, but there was little that would make that room better.

"It'll be okay," I piped up. "All I'll be doing is sleeping in here, and the pillow looks clean enough."

We enjoyed our short walk that evening through this quiet residential area to find a restaurant downtown with a full bar and an open table by the window. There, we settled in to people-watch while we ordered our drinks and dinners. Children, probably of the same age as the boy whose room I was borrowing, skipped along the sidewalk.

"So, did the two of you ever consider having children?" I asked. I had wondered if the lack of children was part of the reason these two still seemed to get along so well together, as I still tried to figure out keys to their successful relationship.

"Oh, we talked about it for years," Joan replied. "But one year I'd be ready to get pregnant, and then the next Kristin would seriously consider it . . . and we never synced." She looked at Kristin for validation.

Chuckling a bit, Kristin met her eyes. "True story. What it really came down to was that we realized, if we had a kid, one of us would always have to stay with the kid while the other was out having adventures. And we didn't want to set ourselves up for that. So no. We decided not to have kids at all."

What foresight! What wisdom! So different from my own youthful, unplanned family! My face must've shown some of my thoughts, because Joan quickly asked if I thought my marriage would've lasted had we not had kids.

"Oh heavens no!" I laughed. "We would never have been married in the first place! Don didn't want to be married just as much as he didn't want to have kids! But, in spite of that, we had two, and I have absolutely no regrets about either one. They are my dreams come true."

"We know about Sarah's beginnings," Kristin said as she

topped off their wineglasses. "Was Cara unplanned as well? I mean, how did you get past Don's objections enough to have a second one?"

"Oh, we negotiated for a year or more before he finally agreed to make another baby, and then within a month I was pregnant. We lived on The Farm at that time, Sarah was two, and the community was all about pregnancy and birth. As a matter of fact, when I was pregnant with Cara, I would waddle around The Farm collecting statistics for *Spiritual Midwifery*, a book Ina May was writing at the time."

Birthing Cara on The Farm had been a high point in my life, leaving me only fond memories. Don and I were living in a little one-room cottage he had built for us there in the woods during the last two months of my pregnancy. We moved in on a Thursday. I hung curtains on Friday. And then I went into labor Saturday evening. When we knew I was truly in labor, we called the midwives and sent Sarah off to stay with friends.

The midwives came to us there in our little cottage, where I felt safe. An ambulance was on call, but I had faith it would not be needed. In my mind, birth was a natural event, and the midwives would know if something was wrong. They'd take care of it. My first birth had been easy, and I expected the same this time around. Don and I hunkered down for the duration, and the midwives left us alone, coming in periodically to check on me. I was working hard, Don was completely supportive, and there were no drugs involved—neither pain meds nor cannabis. I was too busy to even consider smoking a joint. We called contractions "energy rushes," and each time one would start coming on, I would remind myself that this was how I could open up enough to let a baby out, and I welcomed the intensity. *Bring it on! Only one way out . . . let's just DO this! Do not let fear or resistance slow this down!* These sensations were familiar to me; it felt just like it had when I birthed Sarah.

At one point, the midwives checked me and said we were making good progress. Early on, they had noted that I did much better with stronger contractions when I was left alone with Don, so they made themselves scarce each time after checking on me. The three of them stayed close, hanging out in the tent-house next to our cabin, within easy reach if needed suddenly.

"At this rate, it looks like we'll have this one around the same time Sarah was born," Don said after they'd left us alone again.

"What time would that be . . . I mean, how much longer?" I gasped after a particularly strong contraction.

"Oh, another two, three hours or so."

Fuck it. I am not doing this for another two, three hours!

And then, just as I had done with Sarah, within the next ten minutes I opened up and was ready to push that baby right on out. Don called for the midwives. The urge to push was strong. The head midwife checked me, and turning to her crew, said I was ready. "Let's get going here!"

Cara was born fifteen minutes later. Thrilled to find that we had another daughter, I looked into her face. But, unlike my first look at Sarah, who I had immediately recognized as a soul I had known forever, it seemed that Cara's face was brand-new to me. With unfamiliar features, her little frown, and reserved judgment, I guessed she wasn't sure about the world she had just entered. She took after Don's side of the family.

"Hello there, baby girl! Welcome to the world!" I said softly.

Now our family was complete. I loved giving birth, and if nine months of pregnancy wasn't so hard, and if I didn't have to raise kids for years and years, I would've had a dozen. Birth was like legal psychedelics with a grand prize at the end. In that moment I was ecstatic.

The midwives cleaned everything up and left Don, Cara, and me alone to bond. The woodstove crackled away all night long while we basked in gratitude for the miracle of this infant.

It was a good birth story, and my friends raised their glasses to me in yet another toast. We three were so very different, but mutual respect and appreciation for the choices we had all made bonded us ever closer.

Over coffee in our little house the next morning, Joan suggested we walk to town. "How 'bout we take our time and see what happens?"

"I am absolutely not tempted to get on that motorcycle out there, much less put on my boots, helmet, or any other gear," I replied. Traveling a bit on two feet rather than two wheels sounded like a good idea to all three of us. So we spent an afternoon walking around and exploring the scene, but then we decided that one day in Durango was enough. Two nights in that house was also enough. We wanted the open road, not town life, so the next morning we woke up, made coffee, and agreed: time to bail. Didn't matter that we had the house for one more night—we were free, and we wanted to move.

Motivated to get out of that little boy's room, I got on my laptop and searched lodgings for that next night in Telluride.

We liked that town but wondered if we could find a place to stay at the last minute.

"Hey!" I called out. "We got lucky. Remember that luxurious Hotel Telluride we walked past the last time we were there? They have two open rooms they're willing to give us for one night at a great price! What say?"

Later that day, while checking into the hotel with all three bikes parked together in front, I chatted up the front desk clerk, a young man in his thirties.

He gushed, "Wow—those are three big, beautiful bikes you have outside! Where'd you ride from?"

"Today? Just over from Durango. We're on a run through Colorado, our fifth ride together."

I could see him trying to make sense of this scene, three mature women riding three bikes that somehow didn't fit into his version of normal. "How'd you ever decide that this is what you wanted to do?" he asked as he took my credit card and clicked keys on his computer.

"Well, we met through our work in medicine," I answered.

He reacted as I'd expected. "Oh! Are you all nurses?"

I replied out of long habit. "Nope, we're all doctors."

Clearly showing his embarrassment, he apologized for his sexist assumption and quickly handed me the key to my room on the third floor of the hotel.

It was good to be back in Telluride, if only for an evening and one more morning. That small town in the pocket canyon with so many good memories was a perfect one-night stopover. With no expectations, we took our time. I enjoyed the luxury of my room with a view and the space I had lacked in my Durango digs. Soon after we had all settled, Joan and Kristin joined me for a walk downtown and a late lunch.

"Ever since our talk in Davenport, I've been thinking

about relationships," I said as they bit into their huge sand-wiches. "I go back and forth between wanting a partner more than anything else in the world, and not wanting to try—yet again—to make a relationship work. Seems I've spent my life yearning for something I can't manifest."

My two friends stayed silent, listening and clearly ready for whatever came next.

"So last year," I continued, "I realized that, as time passes, I'm getting wiser. I am better at being me, through and through. One day I realized that I don't want to live a life of wanting. Longing. Feeling incomplete because I have no partner. I can be my own partner and find strength in that relationship. So I decided to marry myself."

I paused to see if I was getting through to Joan and Kristin. They'd put down their sandwiches and sat there watching me, waiting for the rest of the story. They were all but holding their breath.

"I am my perfect spouse. After all, I know exactly how I like my coffee." I laughed. "This was a clear choice, so very different from when I married Don because the state of Missouri said we had to. The more I thought about it, the more this felt like a powerful gift to myself. I took my mom's wedding and engagement rings to a jeweler and had him re-move the diamonds, and then together we designed a ring that would be my own—see?" I held out my hand to show them my left ring finger, where I wore the ring of white gold with three of my mother's diamonds beautifully set in a swirl pattern. "The day I put it on my finger I sat out in my garden alone and made a commitment to myself: to love myself, not in spite of my flaws but *because* I was flawed and still trying. I vowed to take care of Stacey, to be kind to her when she is sad, and to love her as fiercely as I would love a soulmate. I admit, it felt a bit silly, but it was me being honest and making a promise that I would keep." I twirled the ring on my finger. "I thought about what you two told me about your relationship and vowed to treat myself as well as you two treat each other."

"That's a beautiful ring, Stace," Kristin said, as I imagined her trying to relate to what I said as best she could.

Joan nodded her agreement, and I could tell that she was also taking some time to integrate my news, maybe even wondering if it was some sort of hippie nonsense.

"I know . . . I know . . . it sounds weird. And I wasn't into any public ceremony or big announcement; this was for me and me alone. And it did make a difference, really quite a few differences, changes I couldn't have anticipated. For example, that very evening I looked in the mirror and automatically went, "Ewww," when I saw the parts of me I wished were different. Then I caught myself. *Wait. Would I feel and say that if the person in the mirror was the one I loved unconditionally? My lover who was perfect, endearing flaws and all? My sweetheart, whose flaws made my own acceptable? Absolutely not!* Immediately, I did a little twisty dance to shake off the bad vibes, took another look in the mirror, and saw myself through the eyes of love. That's when magic happened. There was the person I loved with all my heart, looking like my mother, muffin top and all. Love makes all the difference."

Joan was starting to get it, and Kristin was already grinning with joy and acceptance. I decided to settle an obvious question before they could ask it. "Don't get me wrong! It's an open marriage. I'm still open to someone else coming into my life and giving me the chance to love with all my passion. But I now see that if I give up my own self to disappear into a relationship again, the love will not last and neither will I. I see that I can be strong and be *me* while fully loving someone else. It's the only way. And I'm done yearning."

Kristin picked up her sandwich again, and in between bites, offered her support. "I think that's so cool that you looked in the mirror and did that little . . . what'd you call it? A twisty dance?"

"Oh, but that's not the whole of it!" I added. "You know, I look a lot like my mother. Always have. But these days, when I look in the mirror and see her face, it is shocking to me. Not so much that I look like her, but I look like her at a point in our lives when I had so little regard or respect for her. When I thought she was so simple. I look in the mirror, and seeing her face, I automatically feel the disrespect I felt when I was young and arrogant. But now that judgment is aimed at my own reflection in the mirror and I am ashamed. So here's a word of warning: do not judge the relative that you favor too harshly. It may matter later when that face is your own." We laughed, but there was a note of seriousness in all of this. Life lessons from someone over ten years older than either Joan or Kristin. Food for helmet thoughts.

After finishing our Telluride lunch, we walked around town, leaving the bikes parked until the next morning when it would be time to ride on home to Dulce and, from there, to haul Magdalena, my trailer, and myself all the way back to California.

As I drove home with my trailer in tow, I wondered how long it would be before we'd ride together again. However long it was, I would spend that time learning more fully what it meant to be my own spouse; I would learn to care for myself as if I were my own loving partner. This would be new to me and would take some adjustment. It would also bring changes—more changes than I could have ever expected.

CHAPTER 7

CALL OF THE CANYONS, 2017

Thoughts in my helmet
sort themselves out to the roar
of Magdalena.

It had been three years since our last ride, and we were ready to ride the Southwest again. In those three years I'd been busy traveling. I'd accepted a position as medical director for a cannabis dispensary on the Big Island of Hawaii. In this role, I hoped I'd be able to study what types of cannabis helped with specific conditions and be able to educate patients in the safe and appropriate use of the medicine. I'd also get business-paid trips to Hawaii. My youngest daughter, Cara, lived on Maui, and I'd graduated from high school when Dad was stationed on Oahu, so I had some roots in the Islands. Visiting family in Hawaii on my way to speaking gigs was a dream come true, and I was excited about the opportunity to learn new ways to help patients. But three years in that role did not dampen my enthusiasm for another ride with Joan and Kristin.

Call of the Canyons would take us through at least six canyons in Colorado and Arizona. We planned a relaxed layover at the South Rim of the Grand Canyon, where Joan and Kristin were going to splurge, celebrating their anniversary in a luxury suite at the El Tovar Hotel with a balcony overlooking the canyon. This was going to be a good run; we had learned how to plan for what we wanted and how to roll with the inevitable uncontrollable surprises. At least we thought we had.

The three-day haul I'd made to New Mexico for Just Passin' Through had not been much fun, so we decided to meet somewhere in the middle, somewhere it would only take me two days, and them one day, to reach—a place that would serve as a good starting point for all of us. We made the most-excellent choice of the La Posada Hotel in Winslow, Arizona.

Road trips can be all about the food that keeps you awake. From my home in Sonoma County, heading east across the coastal range over to the I-5 that would take me south to Barstow, I ate. Drive and eat cherry tomatoes, picked yesterday in my garden. Eat some Babybel cheese. More cherry tomatoes. Taco Bell seven-layer burrito from a surly server and back on the road. I broke down and bought a small bag of chewy chocolate chip cookies at a Love's truck stop and devoured them as guilty road food. And here came Barstow. It was 5:45 p.m., and I'd been driving for nine hours. This place was nothing but an intersection in the middle of the desert, but my motel reservation was waiting for me, and I was so happy I could've just laid down flat and groaned.

Ahhh. A big bed. AC. Veggies and Orange Chicken from Panda Express. A fortune cookie. My cannabis vape pen. All was well.

I texted with Joan and Kristin to let them know I'd gotten this far, and Joansie said they had another day of work before they loaded up and headed south. *WTF?* I thought they were arriving in Winslow tomorrow, same as me! I had a few moments of disorientation, wondered about my own sanity, and thought perhaps, if I made scheduling mistakes like this, I may be too old to have adventures like this. Then I adjusted, remembering that mistakes do happen; they don't necessarily mean I'm losing my mind, and maybe it was Joan and Kristin who had made a mistake. Didn't matter who caused the mix-up—I was going to need an extra night in Winslow. So I called La Posada, and lucky for me, the Betty Grable room was available! *Bonus!*

After a seven-hour drive the next day, I reached Winslow, a tiny little roadside town on the railroad tracks along old Route 66—and a welcome sight for me and my rig. I found a gravel lot next to the hotel to park the rig and went in to register at the front desk. After lugging an overnight bag into my room, I headed back out to explore the hotel and stretch my legs. I ordered a cocktail at the bar in the Turquoise Room and took it out to the covered patio, where I sat sipping and watching the trains go by while a light rain fell, the water quickly soaking into the desert sand. I was so glad to have an extra day in this town, familiar from a classic 1972 song by the Eagles but brand-new to me as a visitor. I never figured out why the Eagles made it famous, but I had time to take it easy, and explore.

Next morning, I headed out to check the rig, brought in the rest of my gear, got coffee in the lobby, and then went back to my room and put everything I brought with me on the bed. I sorted for what I'd really need to carry with me on the bike for the next ten days.

I wanted Magdalena off the trailer. But I couldn't do it by myself. I imagined flagging down and asking one of the many motorcycle dudes endlessly cruising through town for help, but I couldn't bring myself to do it. So I decided that the least I could do was go out, cut the zip ties on the back gate of the trailer, and be ready for help if it should happen to come by. Soon, a white pickup truck pulled up next to me, and the driver called out to me through his open window.

"Hey! That's a beautiful bike you have there!" Big grin.

"Thanks! You ride?"

"Nope, but I'd like to . . . someday . . ."

I got brave with this friendly man. "Well, you think you could help me unload this beauty? I can't do it by myself and was looking for some help."

The man was both strong and willing. So we decided to check it out together.

"Just yesterday, one of my workers taught me how to undo these kinds of straps," he said as he happily practiced his new skill. Together we took the ratchet straps completely off the bike, he with strong hands and me sitting on the bike to stabilize it. He dropped the back gate of the trailer, and I was glad to see that he was very can-do about it all.

"I'd like to switch places now," I said, "and have you back it down the ramp. I've never done it before, and I don't know if I can without getting off balance." There was a brief moment of shock, and his face went pale.

"Hey—I'm sorry, but I can't do that for you. I've never ridden a motorcycle and I'm not up to trying that with yours . . . can't you do it with me spotting you?" *So okay. Deep breath. I'm going to have to do this part myself. Another deep breath. If I drop it, he's strong and I won't be alone. I can do this.* With him behind me, and without starting the engine, I backed it slowly, inch by inch, off the trailer, using the brake to control. He was supporting/guiding me with all his strength, holding on to the back of the bike with both hands. And we did it! I unloaded my own motorcycle for the first time ever!

He was as excited as I was. "What now?"

As he ran back to close the trailer gate, I started the engine. Magdalena roared to life, and I rode her over to nearby pavement, getting her off the gravel. When I stopped and turned around, my helper was beaming.

"You look so good on that bike! I wish I had a camera! You look *great*! With your platinum hair—that's so cool!"

His compliments were like a drink of clear water for me on this warm day, completely cooling any leftover stress I felt from the fear of unloading. Getting off the bike, I hugged him, he hugged me back, and then off he went. I was proud because we had unloaded safely, and proud because I had been able to ask a stranger for help. Two wins. All these new beginnings. And more to come.

Joan and Kristin arrived late that afternoon, and the Unloading of the Bikes was such an event that I was glad I'd done mine before they came. Kristin's bravery and long legs, combined with Joansie's steady support and guiding directions, were once again a winning combination, and soon all three motorcycles were beautifully lined up in front of La Posada Hotel. We made plans for later, after they'd hauled their gear up into their room, and the first order of business was to go stand on the corner in Winslow, Arizona.

That evening, my friends found me in the Turquoise Room enjoying a Rusty Nail (Scotch and Drambuie) while chatting up the barkeep and learning about Tetanus Shots (brandy, peach schnapps, and whiskey cream). We three doctors initially agreed that it would be wise to chase exposure to a Rusty Nail with a Tetanus Shot, but on second thought, one cocktail for me was plenty. So they each ordered a drink, and then we leisurely explored the hotel as we reconnected after our three-year hiatus.

Breakfast the next morning was full of discussing our first day's ride together. We were headed for the Canyon de Chelly.

"So, are we staying right in the Canyon de Shellie?" I asked.

Joan laughed. "Yes, but it's Canyon de *Shay*, not Shellie!"

I practiced saying that, trying to figure out how those two *l*'s got lost when pronouncing that word correctly. This was confusing. But properly educated, I continued. "I have to say, I am so grateful that you know where we're going, how to get there, and how to say the names . . . it makes it so easy for me! And honestly, I hope you don't feel like you're carrying too much of the load."

"Absolutely not," Kristin said. "You drive twice as long to get to us, and you carry plenty of the load. It's all good." With that, we left the breakfast table and started packing our saddlebags and other riding gear onto the bikes. Hotel gear went into our cars, which would stay there, secure in the parking lot, for a week while we rode.

We headed north, arriving at the rim of the Canyon de Chelly midafternoon. We had not found a single place to stop for food, and we were feeling it. Parking the bikes on the edge of a vista viewpoint, we checked in with each other. Yes, the view was fantastic—massive red rock formations stretching all the way to the horizon, ancient cliff dwellings visible at the base of some buttes, and the spectacular blue Arizona sky overhead. But all of this was hard to appreciate when hungry. This was an unusual instance of bad planning: no snacks prepared for this first day out, and we all knew that Kristin got exceptionally hangry when her blood sugar dropped. I wasn't seeing Kristin as especially ornery yet, but I believed Joan when she said it was coming. So, what to do?

With a good amount of smugness, I dug down into my saddlebag and handed Kristin a box of ripe Sungold cherry tomatoes. My constant road snacking had not finished all the cherry tomatoes I'd grown in my garden back in California, and I'd brought the leftovers with me. It was a show of joy and ecstasy when she and Joansie bit into some of the sweetest little nuggets that grow in a summer garden.

"Those Sungolds saved our lives," they both agreed. It may not have saved us from starvation, but certainly from irritable moods.

Fortified for a bit, we were ready to ride to our digs for the night in Chinle, the gateway to Canyon de Chelly. Knowing there was food there, we were motivated to move quickly. I had been looking forward to visiting the heart of Navajo country and sleeping in that sacred place that had provided Indigenous people food, water, and shelter for almost five thousand years. As we rode under wide-open skies, without a hint of storm on the horizon and no obstacles in our way, my heart swelled with gratitude for being together again with my riding buddies.

The Thunderbird Lodge, set in among the trees, was built in 1896. This was the site of an old trading post, and my room was in a stone building that may have been one of the originals. It looked like it on the outside, but I wasn't complaining. A shower, a comfortable bed, and AC was all I required. The fact that the lodge had a cafeteria that was open all day long was a bonus.

With nightfall, I relaxed into a light sleep and opened

myself to the energy of this sacred Indigenous site. As I drifted off, I had a dream that was really a memory. Sometimes they blend together, and in my dream state, it felt like I was there again, in that room on the northern coast of California many years ago.

She was a psychic reading tarot cards—part of the fun we were having at a coastal house party sometime in the early 1990s. Sitting calmly in the living room, the psychic made a tarot spread on the low table between us, and gazed at what the cards revealed. She then looked at me with a strange, somewhat confused expression.

"You were born into the wrong family. It was a mistake. And the angels feel really bad about it, so they've been with you since you were born, trying to help out and smooth your way the best they can." *What?* I always thought mistakes like that don't really happen, but somehow this information made sense to me. I had never felt whole in my rootless family, and I knew those angels. They were helpers with Spirit; I ran into them all the time, always grateful when I felt my guardian spirits near.

The more I looked for angels, the more angels I saw. The angel I called on when delivering a difficult baby, conjured up by my need but real enough to be of service. Real people, often perfect strangers, who take on angelic missions. Anyone can be an angel; all they have to do is step up and help out. I call that *doing sacred work*, and that is the work of angels. The dream faded, and I slept deeply in that place teeming, I felt, with the spirits of ancient Navajo elders.

The next day's ride would take us to the little town of Snowflake, Arizona, once again traveling through canyon-lands with plenty of vista pull-offs to explore red rocks off the beaten path. The day warmed up, as it will in Arizona, and after a while, with temperatures in the high nineties as we sat on top of piping-hot engines, it was hard to remember we were headed for a town named Snowflake. Later, I learned that the town had been named for its two founders, Erastus Snow and William Jordan Flake, so it had nothing to do with cold weather. On the other hand, thinking of snowflakes while I burned was a nice diversion.

The heat really sapped our energy, but there was nothing to do but keep riding until we got to a cooler destination. Finally pulling into town, we found the tree-shaded Heritage Inn, a B&B with rooms ready for three hot motorcycle mamas. I immediately spied a hammock under two big leafy trees, and before checking in or unloading gear, I was in that sling completely relaxed and enjoying a cool breeze coming off the fountain nearby. Joansie lurked discreetly until I finally climbed out, and before I could turn around, she was in the hammock cooling off while watching hummingbirds in the branches above.

Gear unloaded, refreshed by cool showers, the three of us decided to go out and find a place to get a drink. Google Maps said there was a bar within walking distance, and the late afternoon temperatures had cooled a few degrees, so we set out to find this place. It would only be a fifteen-minute walk, which seemed quite doable, even in the lingering heat. So we trudged along on the shoulder of a highway and across a bridge until we found what looked to be a saloon. Dented pickups parked in front. Tiny, barred windows. Definitely a dive. We walked up and peeked through the dirty panes, checking out the scene before we went inside.

"Well, we could try it out . . . They have a full bar," I said. "And I'm pretty thirsty."

My two buddies looked at me like I was from another

planet. "You're kidding, right, Stace? You really want to go in there? I don't think so!" Joansie replied.

I was thirsty. I thought they were being wimps. Where was their sense of adventure? But taking one more look through the small window, and seeing a row of exposed hairy butt cracks on stools at the long bar, I swallowed my desire for a cold one and agreed to hike back to town. They were both relieved, if a little shocked that I'd even considered going inside that seedy joint. Back in the center of town, we found a Mexican restaurant with agave margaritas that was right across the street from our B&B, so we settled for dinner there and then moved to a lounge outside our inn on the beautiful patio where the fountains made music.

The ride had been going smoothly—no emergencies, no thunderstorms, no unexpected challenges—and we were getting spoiled. The next day would change all that. We easily rode through the White Mountain Apache Tribal Lands and Salt River Canyon, where a lightning storm didn't dump water on us, so we were still feeling blessed. Not hit by lightning and didn't get wet. So far so good. Then somewhere between Snowflake and Globe, Arizona, Kristin's check-engine light came on.

We were not mechanics, and we were fearful of mechanical breakdowns in the middle of nowhere because that was a situation we might be powerless to fix. And doctors do not like situations in which they are powerless to diagnose and fix whatever is wrong. So when the check-engine light came on, we took it seriously.

Stopping by the side of the highway, we gathered to confer. "It doesn't feel like I'm losing power," Kristin said, "but what if the engine blows up because I didn't pay attention to the warning?" She was clearly rattled by this situation . . . and it was rare to see Kristin rattled. Unusually serious and very worried. I wondered if this situation would finally let me see these two working it out and maybe even using some tense, harsh words. But it turned out they just didn't bother to waste energy on stressful arguments. No time for that—let's just problem solve.

Joansie offered some thoughts. "The turnoff to our digs is just two miles ahead, but town is on down the road another five miles or so. Should we go straight to the inn or forge ahead into Globe, where we might find a mechanic? Do we even need a mechanic? What would make you feel more secure, Kristin?"

I piped up then with my two-cent summary suggestion. "Let's ride on into Globe. We can get supplies for dinner to fix in our kitchenettes this evening, and you can call your mechanic back home while we're there in town. Getting more information about your bike, and what this might mean, would be really helpful. Knowledge is power, and that's what we need most, right?"

We all decided that the safest choice, with the least amount of angst, was to ride on to Globe and see what we could find. It was another super-hot day, and for me, the thought of an iced latte was a definite pull in the direction of town. We cautiously rode ahead, with Kristin taking the lead super slow with a tension I'd rarely seen her carry in her shoulders and back, worried that her motorcycle was going to fall apart on her at any moment. We found a grocery store with a Starbucks inside, and the minute we got off the bikes, she got on her phone and started calling her mechanic in Santa Fe.

Meanwhile, Joansie and I headed for the air-conditioned store and ordered three iced coffees, trying to stay positive about that pesky check-engine light. A half hour later, Kristin joined us and said she had some clues to work with.

"The problem might have something to do with my battery connectors."

Whew! This meant it wasn't the engine, and her motorcycle probably wasn't going to blow up. Stocked up on food and wine to take back with us to the Dream Manor Inn, we headed back the way we'd come, feeling cooler after our break and iced coffees, and riding that last little leg of our day's journey with ease.

The inn stood on the edge of the Mogollon Rim, with a spectacular view of the red rock vista that stretched for miles in all directions until the desert met the endless sky. We settled into our rooms, jumped in the shower to wash off the road and the sweat, and then met outside where Joansie worked on Kristin's bike, checking the suspicious connections and finding something she could fix with her handy-dandy pocketknife tool.

We all had our special skills, and Joan was much more mechanical than Kristin or me, so we trusted her to find and fix the problem. We watched, handed her tools, cheered her on, and congratulated her when the loose connection was found and tightened. *Yippee!* No more worries! Disaster averted! Kisses all around!

The days were long, and we still had light, so we brought a bottle of chilled chardonnay outside, where we could sit and sip while enjoying the sunset. The Mogollon Rim is actually the southwestern edge of the Colorado Plateau. It opens out to a vast, sage-studded desert with mountain peaks rising in the far distance, and that evening's stillness was broken only by the occasional lonely screech of a hawk. This view, with all the sunset colors of orange red and pink, with remnants of blue, was the reason we had chosen to stay on the edge. We were not disappointed.

Raising our glasses to celebrate our successful recovery from a nerve-racking mechanical problem, we indulged in some worst-case scenarios we had narrowly escaped. Kristin's bike could've been dead, and then what would we have done? Stranded on that highway, no cell service, heat turning to dark desert cold, coyotes howling, alone and at the mercy of strangers! It could've been *so* much worse! Then, we began telling stories about other, more personal challenges we'd faced in our past, each of us trying to outdo the other. Joan and Kristin were a few years behind me in residency, so they had never heard about me being the first grandmother to graduate the program, and by now I felt comfortable enough with them to share a time in my life I really was not proud of.

I'd survived my year of internship right out of med school and I'd celebrated my fortieth birthday that fall, but I was challenged more than I'd ever been. I'd endured a major depression during my second year of training, when Don and I split and I became the single mother of two teenage girls. Now, I was in my final year of training, a senior resident with life-and-death responsibilities, and I was also anticipating the birth of my first grandchild. A grandmother resident? No one had ever expected this! I was in over my head and treading water as fast and hard as I could.

Eight months before, Sarah had informed me that she was pregnant, the father no longer in the picture. It would be an understatement to say I did not take this news well. Already overwhelmed, this was more than I could imagine. My unconditional-loving self knew I should support her in any way possible, but my realistic emotionally exhausted self knew I could not. Besides, this was triggering memories of my own unexpected and unsupported pregnancy so many years before. I was horrified, terrified, and devastated.

"I cannot raise this child with you," I told her. "You shouldn't be a parent . . . not without more support than you have, and I can't give it to you." Later, I would regret having to say those words. If only things had been different. If only I had been able to support her. If only I'd had the resources to be the ever-supportive mom I wanted to be. If only.

We fought. We were both passionate, and the stakes were high, so it was loud. It was ugly. When the fight was over, she ran out of the house to find her own way forward, and I was on the floor of the hallway sobbing with pain and grief, not sure when I'd see her again. It was a new low. It was my hit-bottom moment. It was Hell.

Fast-forward eight months. By then, my daughter and I had made a sort of peace, and she had agreed to stay at my house those nights when I had to work at the hospital. That way her younger sister, Cara, who was still in high school, would not be alone while I was gone. At the time, I was chief of Obstetrics, responsible for teaching a team of junior residents all I knew about labor and delivery, and supervising their work.

One afternoon, I came home from a thirty-hour shift at the hospital, tired and needing a shower and sleep. I walked in and found Sarah sitting on the couch in the living room with a confused look on her face.

"Hi! What's going on?" I asked.

"I think I'm in labor," she replied. "I've been having pains for a few hours, but I don't know what they're supposed to feel like, so I don't know." Just looking at her I knew she was right. I knew what a woman in labor looked like, and we had to get her to the hospital. No sleep for me. Shower, yes. Then a change of clothes and back to Labor and Delivery.

By the time we headed to the hospital, I was in function-mode. I had slipped right back from being a mom when I'd walked in the door, into my doctor-self as we'd walked back out. I spent the rest of the day flip-flopping back and forth, trying to balance doctoring with mothering. Our relationship was still so fragile, but she needed me.

We got her checked in, the nurses put fetal monitors around her pregnant belly, and her midwives were called. My daughter had made all her own choices for care, and I was glad that the midwives she had chosen were well known to me and trusted.

The fetal monitor showed the baby's heart rate going a worrisome 180 beats per minute without variability. It was supposed to be around 120 bpm with lots of ups and downs, showing resilience and the ability to survive. Rapid and flat is a very bad thing, indicating severe fetal distress and the need for prompt intervention. But the midwife had not yet arrived . . . so when I saw that heart rate, I went to an attending physician who was sitting at the nurse's station writing in a chart. He was my superior, with more experience than me, and I thought he might be of help.

"I'm concerned with this fetal heart rate. Shouldn't we do something?"

He looked up at me and smiled indulgently. "Aw, Stace . . . you're just going to be a worried grandmother here all day, aren't you." Then he chuckled a bit at his own joke and went back to his charting. This patronizing physician hadn't even looked at the monitor, and he had no idea we could be losing a baby and maybe even a mother.

"Well, the heart rate is 180 and flat," I persisted, but he

still didn't take me seriously. He only smiled and shook his head, like I was just a silly woman. I felt powerless. I honestly don't know what I would've done had the midwife not arrived just a few minutes later.

Seeing the heart rate tracing and the fetal distress it signaled, the midwife turned to me.

"Oh Stacey, I'm sorry but we have to rupture her membranes." She thought I'd be upset at this intervention, knowing that I prefer as few interventions as possible at a birth.

But I quickly replied. "*Yes!* Do it now!"

Then, to preserve my daughter's privacy, and breathing a sigh of relief because the midwife had the situation well in hand, I left Labor and Delivery to go get a cup of coffee in the hopes it would help me handle this marathon. As I walked into the cafeteria, I heard the hospital's overhead pager call out with urgency: "Dr. Dunn to L&D, STAT! Dr. Dunn to L&D, STAT!"

In protective denial, I idly wondered what was going on. I hadn't seen any other impending dramas there, and it just did not occur to me that it was my very own daughter who had turned into a crisis, one step short of a full-on code.

When I returned to L&D just a few minutes later, I could see the nursing staff in crisis mode. Dr. Dunn was not in the hospital, so Dr. Parker had been called. I slipped into my daughter's room, and the midwife turned to me with a pasty white face.

"Stacey—I broke her waters and blood poured out. She has an abrupted placenta—the placenta has torn away from the uterus, and she has been bleeding into the amniotic fluid. We have to do an emergency C-section as fast as we can."

In that moment my doctor-self almost completely took over from my mother-self. It was *my* team that needed to mobilize. We had a primary surgeon. We had the nurses. A pediatric intensive care specialist was already there, ready to resuscitate the baby. It takes two surgeons to do a C-section, and my team needed to provide a surgeon to assist Dr. Parker. The resident had been called and had not responded to her pager, so we called her backup and we waited. This was not the time to be waiting on anyone, but there we stood, watching my daughter on the operating table, everyone waiting to start the operation that would save her life.

I would always vividly remember being in the OR, standing on one side of my daughter, with Dr. Parker on the other. The anesthesiologist stood by, ready to put her under general anesthesia because there was no time for an epidural. Still, no assistant surgeon had answered the STAT page. We could not wait any longer. Lives were in the balance.

So, I looked over my mask at Dr. Parker. "Can I start?"

I was deeply grateful that he considered my offer before replying. "No, not this time, Stace. Not this time."

We looked at each other, a whole conversation in our eyes, both of us knowing the gravity of the situation. That was when the neonatologist stepped over and offered to assist until the resident could be found. There would be hell to pay on my team when this was over.

Within minutes, a baby boy was delivered and quickly carried to a resuscitation table. I stood to the side, held by the two midwives, two angels who had realized that once the surgeons took over, they needed to support me. As my tiny grandson flew across the OR in the secure hands of the neonatologist, I watched an arc of dark red urine spray the nurses. Because the placenta had broken free and blood had flowed into the uterus, he had been swimming in thick blood instead of nourishing amniotic fluid.

The backup resident arrived right then and stepped in where the neonatologist had been just moments before. Together, she and Dr. Parker stopped my daughter's bleeding, closed her up, and saved her life. I remained standing in the corner, held together by the midwives and watching my peers work on my own family.

The next morning, we had rounds with our team's attending physician—an older, experienced obstetrician, wiser than the one who had blown me off by calling me a "worried grandmother" during labor. This doctor had seen it all. Without any explanation, I handed him the printed fetal heart-monitor strip.

"This was what we had to deal with yesterday."

He looked at the strip's tracing, running it through his hands from one end to the other and seeing that flat 180 bpm heart rate. "Hmph. Did anyone survive?"

I was still numb from it all, but I remained calm. "Yes. That's my daughter and grandson there."

The embarrassed shock on his face matched his apology for appearing so callous. He hadn't known.

My grandson went to the pediatric ICU. He recovered from his traumatic birth, his kidneys cleared up, his lungs worked well, and he thrived. My daughter, a strong eighteen-year-old with resilience, also recovered, and they left the hospital together three days later.

I remained an emotional, physical, and professional wreck. There was no way I could continue as chief of Obstetrics the next day, but my dear friend Laura was able to step in, taking over my duties for a week so I could be a mother and a grandmother without professional demands.

I had struggled through all those months after Don left. I was challenged by all the demands of my residency. Don wanted nothing to do with me or our daughters at a time when Sarah was just coming into her own, which meant she didn't have a stable launch pad. She made choices that truly scared me, but over which I had no control, culminating in her surprising pregnancy. And then came the horrifying experience of her labor and delivery. I was alone during this time, without a partner for the first time in almost twenty years and with more responsibility than I could handle, while also grieving the loss of my marriage and holding on for dear life. There was no way to make it pretty.

But I did survive. We all survived, and with time Sarah and I found our peace together again. It took years, but we did it. I loved her and had since the moment I first saw her newborn face.

I'd been gazing out at the desert while I told this story, and I ended by saying there weren't many parts of my life I'd change if I could, except for this. "Sarah and I lost so many years when we were estranged and could have been closer. God, I love her! If I had only been stronger . . . less overwhelmed . . . able to be more supportive to my daughter. If only I'd had the support I needed to help her. At least I can be grateful that she ultimately grew into a kind, smart, funny, strong woman who makes me proud every single day. And the amazing son she raised is a credit to her hard work and loving intentions."

The sun had long since gone below the horizon, and the last of the light was fading. I knew these two did not judge me, and if anyone knew the challenges of residency, it would be my fellow physicians. We sat for a moment in respectful silence; words were not necessary.

Afterward, we went to Joan and Kristin's suite because my AC wasn't working, and there we ate scrumptious salads they had lovingly prepared while I looked for a movie we could watch to end a stressful day with something that felt comforting and normal. By the time the movie was over, the night had cooled enough for me to go back to my room, where I opened all the windows to the desert night air and fell into a deep sleep, exhausted from the day's worrisome adventure and from the heat that had finally, after a stunning sunset, given up its punishing force.

We rode through the Prescott National Forest the next day, on our way into Sedona, an Arizona city surrounded by green trees and red sandstone cliffs that glow as the sun rises and sets. We had rented a house for our one-night stay and wanted to get there early so we'd have time to relax a bit before dinner. Cruising with our engines rumbling slowly through the town, we found our Airbnb house set back from the street, surrounded by trees, with a lovely large driveway perfect for three big bikes. There was plenty of room inside for all of us to settle in comfort, and we were soon at home in our new digs.

Dinner was within walking distance because we simply did not get back on the bikes once they were parked. That was a hard-and-fast agreement on these rides, especially because we wanted to be able to have a glass of wine at dinner and would not ride after wine or cocktails. Or after, in my case, toking a bit on my pipe. So we set out through the neighborhood, and, within fifteen minutes, we were at Dahl & Di Luca Ristorante. Kristin is Italian, and this suited her just fine. That meal left us feeling fat and happy, and we all decided to go to bed early so we'd have time the next morning to explore the energy of Sedona.

After breakfast and coffee, we headed out to find the Amitabha Stupa, a spiritual center at the base of Thunder

Mountain, within walking distance of our house. Sedona is known for vortexes—high-energy centers that can be life changing—and I was looking forward to meditating in a sacred space. As we climbed an easy trail through the scrub and trees and neared the clearing at the top, both the air and our conversation grew quieter and quieter. We could feel the energy, similar to what I had felt every time I walked into a grove of towering redwoods in my home territory. God's church. No religion. Just Spirit.

The three of us explored the stupa, with all the altars, prayer flags, and prayer notes scattered everywhere. Joan and Kristin decided to go on farther and hike up into the red rocks above the stupa, while I chose to stay and spend that time meditating. It was a relief to sit and to simply be quiet. I let the noise of the motorcycles fade from my memory. I let my thoughts and challenges become irrelevant. I opened my heart to that sacred space. The whisper of the wind and the occasional cry of a bird kept me grounded, and I felt more at peace than I had for many days.

In a place steeped in Spirit like the stupa in Sedona, I was able to easily slip into a meditative state. I firmly believe in a reality that humans cannot perceive with our limited senses, and I believe it is arrogant to assume otherwise. While Joan and Kristin went for a hike, I opened myself to the unseen, to the source of miracles. I allowed my scientific mind to meld with my spiritual soul.

My mother was the one who brought the awareness of Spirit into our family. Dad never talked about much of anything, certainly not his feelings or an awareness of spiritual matters. Mom found God in nature and passed that on to me. When I was very young, I was baptized and taken to Presbyterian churches because it was expected as a part of good parenting, and for a while I believed all I was told there at church. I even hoped, when I was a naïve twelve-year-old, that I'd get to be the next mother of the Messiah . . . when he came again. But soon that belief system lost its allure, and I found it difficult to believe in those stories from thousands of years ago, stories edited in rewrites by countless opinionated editors. I realized that I felt closer to God when I was in nature than I did in any church pew. I found it much easier to believe in an all-pervasive Energy that was the same for all the major religions, in the karma of good and bad deeds, and in the miracles I saw in the natural world. Just like my mother.

She kept her own beliefs to herself, but I could see them reflected in her art and in the things that brought her joy. She would gasp at the colors of the sunset, the sound of raging waterfalls, and the beauty of the mountains. Between her love of nature and my own need for comfort, I developed a personal spiritual practice. Without emotional support from my family, I relied on invisible angels who taught me how to comfort myself. There in Sedona, I felt grateful for my awareness of unseen spirits, angels that felt so close to me there.

Looking up from my reverie, I saw Joan and Kristin returning from their hike, huge grins on their faces. They were energetic, but I was not, being a bit disoriented while I slowly came out of my deep meditation. Their liveliness and our walk back to the house brought me back to clear focus, a state of mind I would need for the afternoon because, together, we would pack it all up and head out for a short afternoon's ride over to Flagstaff to spend the night on our way to the South Rim of the Grand Canyon, the last stop on this adventure.

Arriving at the South Rim, we drove up to the front of the El Tovar Hotel, got off the bikes, and pulled off our helmets, revealing to the crowd of visitors that we were three women on three huge motorcycles and causing a bit of a scene. A German tourist asked me if he could take my picture next to Magdalena. I posed for him, grinning ear to ear and thinking of all his European contacts who would see that, in the USA, women with white hair ride Harleys. We were riding high, literally, on the edge of the Grand Canyon.

I relaxed alone in my room at the Kachina Lodge, having flopped horizontally on the flat, soft surface of my bed as I looked out to the rim and the canyon beyond. I watched the endless parade of people walking the path along the rim, while giant elk grazed on the lawn below my window. Later, I walked over to Joan and Kristin's hotel and spotted their huge patio balcony. There they were, sitting in chaise lounges and watching the late afternoon sun create a light show on the walls of the canyon. I called up to them.

"Hey there! You're looking mighty happy up there!"

"We are!!" Joansie called down. "It's beautiful!"

I pretended I didn't know them, since everyone else in the tourist crowd around me was watching. "I'd sure like to be up there with you! I bet it's pretty cool!"

Joan called back. "Come on up! We'll fix you a drink!"

Giving them a thumbs-up, I headed for the elevator, and a man standing nearby smiled.

"Think I'd be welcome too?"

I had to let him know it was a private party.

He laughed. "I thought so, but it didn't hurt to ask!"

We would stay at the Grand Canyon for two nights, giving us a full, unpressured layover day without riding the bikes. That first morning Joan and Kristin hiked down just a bit into the canyon, and I walked among the artists' easels at a plein air painting event along the canyon rim. Then, saturated with people and paintings, I found a rock big enough to comfortably sit on, one that was somewhat secluded from the constant traffic on the Rim Trail. From there, I could quietly appreciate the panorama of the Grand Canyon, the light always changing on the far-side cliffs, and the satisfying sense of freedom and peace that views like this, with so much open space, always gave me. I could easily imagine being a large bird of prey, soaring over the canyon, the wind supporting me as I spread my wings and flew on the currents. It was so natural to soar free like that—I could almost feel the wings that would grow out of my shoulder blades, so instinctively a strong part of me. I shrugged my shoulders as I imagined them catching wind.

Freedom, independence, and the ability to soar were fundamental values for me. I learned how important they were the hard way; I had once been jailed, and it could never happen again. I had been foolish then and had learned some valuable lessons, lessons that had come at a great and painful cost.

It was 2009. This felt good. I mean, this felt really, *really* good. Frustrated for years in my desire and inability to learn the art of spiritual midwifery, I had broken free of the controlling cult at The Farm, and I had found joy in being a family physician delivering babies and then caring for the whole family's medical needs while those babies grew up. Cradle to grave, I was there to be a part of the families I cared for. My dream was being realized in spite of the obstacles I had pushed against while living on The Farm.

Although I delivered babies in the local hospital, I honored the empowerment style of spiritual births, a practice that kept unnecessary hospital interventions and protocols out of the room. I only brought out the heavy-handed hospital management style as a last resort and with the full, conscious agreement of my patients and their families. I also collected stories, interviewing families and writing down, in their own words, their birth stories so those tales could be shared with other women. This was a way to empower women during one of the most intense life transitions they would ever face. Birth and child-raising require strength and support, and my collection of stories would illustrate how to encourage that in today's environment. Years ago, I'd helped with Ina May's book *Spiritual Midwifery*, but her birth stories were dated and difficult to relate to if you were a woman giving birth today.

I got an agent. We found a publisher. My book, *Homebirth in the Hospital*, was published, and I was asked to hit the road to promote it. I set up a national speaking tour, bought a cart for hauling my boxes of books around, and made plans to fly coast to coast, from birth conference to birth conference, speaking my truth and selling my books. I celebrated the day Ina May agreed to write a blurb for my book. My, how we'd grown up!

I was in Fort Worth, Texas, staying in a suite at a luxury hotel and enjoying the recognition I was getting as a physician, an author, and a keynote speaker. Several hundred fans listened to my every word, and books flew out of the box onto the table, where I sold them as fast as I could sign them. My dreams were realized. I was a respected physician with a book, an agent, and a publisher. I had surpassed my own expectations and dreams that had first germinated in the woods of Tennessee. I was riding high.

But how quickly everything can change, and later, whenever I would reflect back on this time, I would be hit with painful emotional whiplash.

After Fort Worth, I planned to catch a short hopper flight to San Antonio, where I had cousins to visit. I couldn't get that close without flying down to see them! I decided to pack a bit differently for this trip and rearranged my gear. Toiletries . . . best to keep them at hand in my carry-on luggage. Cash from book sales . . . best to keep it all close and in my backpack on my person. Boxes of books . . . strapped onto the cart, I'd check the whole load through to San Antonio. Main suitcase . . . also checked through. A quick scan of the hotel room to make sure nothing was being left behind and one more gaze out the window at that priceless view of the city's skyline, and then I schlepped out with all my gear to catch an airport shuttle.

We were all still getting used to the TSA searches. Even though it had been eight years since the 9/11 tragedy, TSA was still a gauntlet to run. But I was brave, and after all, I was also a respected physician author who knew her way around the professional world. I was not afraid.

Until the TSA agent discovered my toiletry kit in my carry-on. The kit was a zippered pack with many pockets for things like my toothbrush, my razor, my shampoo products, my makeup, and my medications. I had forgotten about the three-ounce rule and soon realized that she was going to take apart my whole kit as she ferreted out illegal liquids. Which would not have been a problem had I not put my Special Medication in along with my supply of shampoo, Sudafed, and Advil. I tried to think of a way to rewind the last five minutes, to escape the TSA search spot, to repack my gear.

There was no way out. I stood there in a cold sweat while she relentlessly plundered my bag.

She found the tiny pipe and asked if I had anything to go with it.

Knowing there was no way around it, I told the truth. "Yes," I said, pointing to the little film canister that had a single tiny bud of cannabis tucked inside, which was supposed to be on its way to my girlfriend in Missouri—my girlfriend with breast cancer, going through chemotherapy, who needed the relief that this single bud could bring. But this was Texas, and the agent's gleeful smile reminded me that I was in a state with strict laws against my innocent flower bud. In that very moment, I lost my freedom. I lost my pride. I lost my professional high. I lost my self-respect because I had been stupid.

"Why are you carrying a controlled substance?" the TSA agent asked loudly as she held up my bud and my tiny pipe.

"I live in California, and I use this to help me sleep when I cross time zones. It's my medicine," I replied, unwilling to expose myself to a charge of trafficking.

She left for a few minutes while I was guarded by another TSA agent, and when she returned, she said that my reason for carrying that substance wasn't good enough.

"What—I need to have cancer to be legal here?" I snarked.

She sneered. "Texas is a zero-tolerance state." She nodded to the other agent and gathered up my gear. Then, pulling out a pair of handcuffs, she ordered me to put my hands behind my back, and she cuffed my wrists together.

I was escorted through the terminal, flanked by two agents with guns on their hips as people stared. I prayed that no one who'd applauded me last night could see me now. *On the other hand, maybe my book will be worth more now that I'm in trouble. Don't they say any publicity is good publicity?* Nope. I wasn't buying it. Instead, I was flash-frozen cold in disbelief and fear.

After being escorted to a small windowless room furnished with a conference table and a few chairs, I was parked with the cuffs on. I watched as six police officers rifled through my possessions piece by piece, and I felt violated. When they found my Sudafed and Advil, they asked me to identify the drugs, and I could tell they didn't quite believe me when I explained that I get sinus headaches when I fly. That was way too innocent for their high expectations. *This is the most fun and the most action they have seen in months! They've nabbed a California doctor with a controlled substance!*

Bringing in a test kit, they gloved up and got to work testing my flower. I had already told them it was marijuana, but they did a special chemical test anyway—double-gloving and treating it as if touching it with bare hands would cause great harm. I watched in further levels of disbelief. The chemical turned my little bud into a positive-cannabis blue. Then they weighed it: 1.92 grams of marijuana, just under the 2-gram limit of some Texas state law.

There was a young Black policeman in the room. He had been watching me watch them. He sidled over. "You've never been arrested before, have you?"

"No, I have not." In some small way, I was grateful that someone was seeing me clearly in my shocked naivete.

"Well, you're lucky because they'll take you to the airport facility, and they have a special cell for women there."

Oh joy. Oh lucky me. A women's cell! Special! This trying-to-be-helpful news was not encouraging. I didn't want to be in a cell anywhere! And now I would miss my flight to San

Antonio, although my luggage had gone on ahead. And my cousin was going to wonder where I was. I had moved from frozen in fright to wishing I could move on to panicked flight. That was exactly what they were not going to let me do.

The cash I was carrying also caused quite a bit of excitement. Counting it all out in front of me, to avoid any question later about the amount, they documented $746.90 in cash and checks. They were certain it was drug money, even though I told them I was an author and had sold books. They didn't believe me, but there was nothing they could do about it.

Next, I was searched. Grateful that I didn't have to remove all my clothes, I still felt invaded by the thorough search of my body. The policewoman's hands slid up my abdomen and invaded the space inside my underwire bra. They slid down the back of my jeans, stopping just short of the crack in my ass. I felt dirty, and I had to tolerate all this without comment. I had no voice. This hurt. Every part of me was shut down tight, holding on and refusing to feel anything but unavoidable shame. *Not yet. Not safe to feel right now.*

Once they had all the information they needed from their searches and chemical tests, I was again escorted by gun-toting agents through the terminal to the pickup zone out front. Once again, I prayed that no one who knew me could see my humiliation. They placed me in the back seat of a patrol car, and I perched on the edge of the seat. Hard plastic to protect it from vomit and other bodily fluids—I found it slippery and unstable. My hands, cuffed behind my back, prevented me from sitting up straight, and I leaned forward so my forehead could rest on the divider in front of me. It stabilized me, and as I looked down, it created a tiny space that felt private. In that moment, when no one could see my face, I finally realized what I had done wrong. I had not packed with care. I had spaced out. I had put liquids in my carry-on, which were now in the hands of the cops. This was all my fault, and now I was in big, big Texas trouble. *Fuck fuck fuck.*

This refrain haunted me all the way to the airport jail facility just over two miles away. There, I was unloaded and escorted into the intake area, where my handcuffs were finally removed. I was photographed and fingerprinted. I was told to witness yet another inspection of all my personal belongings and yet another counting of the money. I was subjected to yet another body search, even more thorough than the last, going higher under my bra and lower down my pants. This may have been the worst humiliation I'd ever experienced—worse than when Don argued during our marriage vows, worse than when Ina May told me to rub his ass, worse than being told I was a tripper. My one victory was when they asked me to remove my shoelaces, supposedly to protect me from harming myself, and they found that my travel shoes, Keen hikers, had shoelaces that weren't removable. They let me keep my shoes. This victory wasn't enough to restore feeling to any part of my body, however, and I was still frozen in shock, going through the motions, and scared out of my mind.

I had never been arrested. I had always been careful to slide under the eyes of the law, only breaking rules that hurt no one else in their breakage. *I am discreet. I don't get caught.* I privately used cannabis so no one noticed. I exceeded the speed limit when I was sure it was safe to do so and there were no cops nearby with radar. Now, I didn't know how to do this dance and found that I didn't do well when I lost my freedom.

My cell, next to the intake desk, was a windowless steel enclosure measuring eight-by-eight feet with two steel bunk beds attached to the wall, each with a grated platform and no pad. A stained metal toilet hung on the wall next to the cell door. There was a pay phone on the opposite wall, but it required coins, and all my coins were taken away from me. Besides the clothes on my body and my precious shoes, the only other thing I had was a piece of paper they gave me listing all the bail bondsmen in the Dallas/Fort Worth area. I needed to arrange bail, and I had never done that before.

Having tasks to do is helpful; I was always better at finding solutions when I felt like I had a bit of control. First, I needed to call my cousin. I asked for a coin or a phone.

"I do get one phone call, right?" I knew this from watching countless *Law & Order* episodes.

They brought me my cell phone so I could find Stuart's number and call him.

"Stuart, don't go to the airport to pick me up. I've been delayed."

In his thick Texas accent, Stuart replied, "What's going on, Stace? You okay there?"

"No, I'm not, but I will be." This was my standard answer for whenever I was drowning in Shit Creek but unwilling to admit it. "Just . . . I'll let you know when I reschedule my flight there, and in the meantime, please find me a lawyer."

There was a short silence while he integrated this news. "Okay. You keep yourself safe, and I'll be there when you arrive. We'll figure this out."

I was the renegade in our family. Well, not so much the renegade as the maverick. The one who always refused to play by the rules, who embraced adventures no one else in my family would dream of, the one who entertained everyone with her wild and unexpected life choices. Like joining a hippie commune, like going to med school in my midthirties, like riding motorcycles. My family watched me with a bit of awe, a lot of respect, and a good dose of appreciative humor. Right now, though, I was not laughing.

My next call needed to be to a bail bondsman, selected from the list they gave me. *How to choose? Does it matter? What's the protocol for this?* I'd never had to get myself bailed out, so I had no clue. I focused on a name halfway down the page: Doc's Bail Bonds. I figured it was a sign, because I was a doc. I knew I'd need my credit card to pay the bail, so I called for the guard to bring me my wallet. He was quick, bringing me my purse, and he stood outside my cell while I gave the information to Doc's Bail Bonds. Then, there was nothing else to do but wait. I had no idea how long.

Finally I began to feel again. I lay down on the lower bunk's cold metal platform, and using the paper with the bondsmen list on it as a head rest, I started to cry. In my life, I had not cried easily. I was a stoic who only shed scant tears of joy. Tears of sadness brought little relief, and sinus headaches. But this was all too much. I was bereft. I had fallen from grace about as far as I could fall, and I didn't know how to make my way back. *Will I go to a Texas prison? Will I lose my medical license? How much is this whole thing going to cost me? How stupid can I be?! I'm fucked.* Here I thought I was a mighty motorcycle mama, and now this.

Suddenly, I heard a door open and another woman being brought into the intake area. If nothing else, I was grateful for the interruption in my own sob story and the possible distraction provided by someone else's. From the sounds of it out there, it seemed like this new prisoner knew the ropes and wasn't going to cause trouble. After a few minutes, my cell door opened and the guard brought her, a young agile brunette, in to join me.

"Here, you can get to know Dr. Kerr for a bit," he said to her. I was pissed that he outed me as a physician, with a tone suggesting I was the best catch of the season. *Fuck him.*

Now acclimated to jail, I used easy-access anger to manage my situation and maintain some sense of control. I was ready to protect my claimed space. *This bottom bunk is MINE. You climb to the top one, bitch. I own this cell and you can be here and be safe at my discretion.* How quickly I'd become the tough jailbird bitch I needed to be. Yes, I was angry, and I let myself be that way, because, even privately, it was the only power I had there. Of course, I didn't actually say these things; I didn't need to pick a fight.

My cellmate climbed up to the top bunk. Cheerfully, she asked what I was in for.

"Cannabis. I packed my bags wrong."

"Whoa. You're *my* kinda doctor!"

"Hmm. What are you here for?"

"Bunch of parking tickets I was running away from." She was obviously not traumatized by being here in a cell, and her aplomb helped settle me a bit. Things weren't quite as surreal with her matter-of-fact point of view as part of the mix. We chatted for a while.

"Hey—how about we be Thelma and Louise?" She asked when we had become a bit friendlier.

"Good idea," I said, willing to take on the persona of an outlaw if I was going to be treated as one. I couldn't help but think of Joan and Kristin's motorcycles.

"Just . . . I just don't want to be the one who gets beat up, and I can't remember which one that was," she said.

"I don't know either, but I'm willing to be that one." This wasn't real, so I didn't mind. We decided I would be Thelma and she would be Louise, and she wouldn't get beat up even if we had it backward. We lay on our bunks trying on our new identities.

Our social time was suddenly cut short by the appearance of a guard at the cell door.

"Both of you have posted bail, so Dr. Kerr, you are first. Come with me."

I walked out to the intake room, where once again my cash was counted out in front of me and once again I explained that the $746.90 was from book sales. *Yeah, right.* This guard didn't seem to believe me any more than the others had. No matter. I was going to get out of there anyway. As I clutched my possessions in my arms for the first time in eight nightmarish hours, I was led to the back door of the facility and told to wait on the curb for a taxi to pull up. It was night, and if I missed my cab, I would have to walk the two miles back to the airport. They would not help me. I stood on the curb, staring into the empty darkness, searching for headlights.

The cab arrived, and I thankfully got in the back seat on my own power. This seat was not hard plastic, and there was no barrier between me and the driver. This driver was nice to me, asking me how I was.

"I'm having the worst night of my life. I'm from California, and TSA busted me for a tiny flower of cannabis. I've missed my flight to San Antonio, I have no luggage, and I'm fried."

The cabbie took pity on me and didn't charge me for the ride back to the airport's departure terminal. By now, it was 11:00 p.m. and the airport was deserted, only an occasional janitor pushing a mop to break the empty space. I walked the cavernous halls, pulling my little carry-on behind me and wondering what I was supposed to do now. I was still frozen with fear, but now that I was able to move freely, I began working toward the flight stage of my trauma response. Trouble was, no flights were going out at 11:00 p.m. from Dallas/Fort Worth.

It was difficult to walk and cry at the same time. *I have to stop this fear!* Suddenly I thought of Willie Nelson, a Texan through and through. He'd been busted for marijuana so many times I'd lost count, and he'd never let that bum him out. He took it all in stride and continued to inhale vast quantities of that thick illegal smoke. More than I could ever tolerate. Willie was my hero, so I stumbled through the airport, reminding myself of his strength. *Willie gets through this all the time. Willie can do it. So can I.* I tried to banish thoughts of Willie's huge support crew that helps him when he needs it, because I was alone and had no crew. But I *was* brave, and Willie helped me find my courage.

I knew I couldn't sleep on a chair in the airport; I needed a safe place to be. A safe place to spend a bit of time putting myself back together. A safe place to plan a life that now included me going to jail, at least in my worst-case scenario. Looking out the windows of the terminal, I spotted a luxury hotel tower looming on the other side of a football-field-size parking lot. With a deep sigh and a firm resolve, I dragged my carry-on bag across the parking lot. My face, when I arrived at the front desk, must have said it all.

"Are you a distressed traveler, dear?" the front desk lady asked.

You have no idea! "Oh yes. Quite distressed."

They had a special rate for travelers like me, which was how I found myself ensconced in another luxury hotel suite with a king-size bed, wondering what the fuck just happened.

I felt filthy. I had no clean clothes; they were all in San Antonio by then. But I had to take a shower. I ran the water as hot as possible and scalded the day off my body. I washed off the TSA agent's hands. I washed off the guard's hands. I washed off the steel platform and the stale air in the jail. I also washed off as much shame as I could but was still left with a thick layer that would remain for a very long time.

I slept fitfully for a couple of hours that night. When morning came, I was anxious to get the hell out of Dallas and out of Fort Worth, where I never ever, *ever, EVER* wanted to return. After a night in San Antonio with Stuart, who kindly recommended an attorney to me, I left for Missouri, sad that I no longer had the cannabis I'd intended for my friend to use during chemo. Once there, I couldn't stop crying for two days.

"I've held your hand through many hardships—your divorce, the death of your parents, and the death of Laura. I have never seen you cry like this," my friend said.

It would be many months before I could tell my story to even my closest friends back home, feeling so ashamed from having been stupid. But before that time came, I had to resolve my legal issues.

My attorney's first suggestion was to settle the matter with what he thought was a simple solution. "All you'll have to do is attend drug rehab and do some community service, and you'll be clear."

I replied without hesitation. "That's not going to happen. I am not a drug addict, and I will not be attending drug rehab. I am a professional physician in my community, and I will not be seen out on the highway picking up trash. Figure out a better way." I had found my voice again, the frozen-flight fear having turned into deeply entrenched and pure cold anger.

He did find another way. I paid money to the police on

top of the money I paid for his legal services and the fees to expunge my record.

Although I continued my book tour, leaving Missouri and heading east to buy a fifth of whiskey along the way in Richmond, Virginia—a less effective but legal replacement for my sleep-aiding cannabis, I continued to process the connection between loss of freedom and shame. I was ashamed of my pride that went before the fall. I was ashamed of being a space cadet who forgot how to pack when traveling as an outlaw. I was ashamed of being treated as a dangerous criminal.

Using cannabis should not have been a cause for shame. The herb had benefited me many times in my life even as it changed the course of events dramatically over and over again: My eviction from my parents' house. My marriage. My career. It was a gentle herb that, unlike other drugs, could never cause a fatal overdose. It hardly seemed all that trouble over a weed was worth it. Eventually, my shame lessened enough to make space for more clarity, and I found myself able to look at that night in Dallas and ask myself why it had really hurt so much.

Why can others go to jail for a few hours and be none the worse for wear? Why was I so traumatized? What was the big deal? I had felt abused, but that wasn't the core of my pain. I had felt persecuted, but being angry at laws that make no sense was futile.

More to the point, more to the core of the matter, was that I realized I would always be intolerant of being caged, controlled, and without the ability to be independent. I decided I would need to dig in and work on getting smarter. I must be allowed to make my own choices. I must be allowed to soar.

. . .

The light had changed over the canyon, and my butt was sore from sitting on the rock. I was ready to let go of Dallas and focus on the present, ready to join the constant flow of tourists along the Rim Trail and to be with Joan and Kristin. There was more here to explore.

We walked the Trail of Time, where each meter we walked represented one million years of the Grand Canyon's history. Even with the clear comparison and all the explanatory signs, it was hard to fathom such a long time, hard to envision the changes in geology that had created this natural wonder. We tried to wrap our minds around it all and then gave up, preferring to experience the now instead of trying to understand eons past.

The next day we rode along the East Rim of the canyon, passed through the Navajo Nation, and headed for Winslow, all feeling the familiar sadness we did at the end of each ride. That evening, at dinner back in the La Posada, we envisioned our transitions from being biker chicks on the road to being physicians in our regular lives. I asked how long they'd have before they had to go back to work, knowing that these changes can be difficult.

"No problem," Kristin said. "We'll have a day to get the dog back from camp and do laundry and then slip right back into doctoring. We're pretty adaptable."

"I wish you had someone to greet you when you got home, Stace," Joansie added. "I think you'd like that, and it's easier to reenter when there's someone to help you ground."

Oh gawd. I *did* have a boyfriend, but I really wasn't sure about sharing. I didn't want to jinx anything by talking about him. I didn't trust relationships, but this one had stuck around for a long time now, and it might just be going somewhere. If there was anyone safe to talk to, it was Joan and Kristin, so taking a deep breath, I decided to share.

"Well, yes, I actually do have someone. My open marriage is really open, and this man is worth it. I don't know . . . we are going slow . . . we have been friends for over twenty-five years and now we are lovers. And let me tell you . . . I do like making love with a man. No. I take that back. I like making love with *this particular* man.

"He is kind, and he thanks his Spirit guides for bringing us together. He's a big man who flies helicopters, drives a huge truck, loves tools, and gets totally excited about heavy machinery. He is also a man who grows plants, and when he strokes the leaves, I see gentle, nurturing energy flowing from his fingers, nurturing that I get to feel every time he touches me. He sees me more deeply than anyone I've ever known. It feels so good, and we love each other. We are passionate together. Oh, that passion! I am finally getting the touch I've wanted for my whole life. I have realized that making love with him is like drinking from the Fountain of Youth."

At this, I know I must've blushed, but both Joan and Kristin lit up with big grins, because they'd wanted this for me.

"I feel young when we're together. I don't know where this is going, and I am not ever going to divorce myself, but I am hopeful. It took me all these years to realize that I don't have to give up my Self and disappear into a relationship. It took me even more years to know that I am enough even if I am on my own forever. That growth is what gave me the clarity to make room for this man's love. But I don't know yet if I can adjust to the chaos of a relationship. Wish me luck . . . I might just get what I've always wanted, warts and all. And even if it doesn't work out for the long run, at least I've had passion. At least I've had loving touch in this lifetime. At least I've made love."

I fell silent, unwilling—or unable—to tell them more. This was all still too new, and I was feeling vulnerable.

"Talk about burying the lead! You waited until the last day of our ride to tell us this?" Joansie cried. "Dang, girl! You've been holding out on us!"

I tried to cover my embarrassment by pouring wine into our three glasses, my hand shaking a bit after my big reveal, thinking maybe I had already said too much.

"Well, we are glad you are stepping out again," Kristin said. "We both hope this works out for you because you really deserve it."

I smiled back at her, grateful for her understanding. We toasted to this with the last of our wine and called it a night.

When we pulled away from La Posada the next morning, we did not know that it would be four long years before we'd be able to ride together again. So much would happen and so much would get in our way. There would be a pandemic, and as physicians and humans, each of us would be affected. I would delve deeper into a relationship with a man I loved and would begin to trust again.

But we *would* ride again. There was no doubt.

CHAPTER 8

POST-PANDEMIC PANDEMONIUM RIDE, 2021

Cruise control is set.
Extreme yin is changing to
Extreme yang. Right now.

We had this all planned out for 2020. Then, like so many millions of others with plans that summer, we COVID-canceled. When the vaccine started making the world a safer place, we went back to planning and made all our reservations. I started gearing up for another three-day haul to New Mexico, where Joan and Kristin were now living in their forever home in Arroyo Seco. In the four years since our last adventure, they had retired from the Indian Health Service and taken on new pre-retirement part-time jobs near their casita outside of Taos. Joan was practicing telehealth addiction medicine, and Kristin was seeing patients in a local clinic. These girls were red-rock women through and through. The desert does that to many people—takes them in and keeps them there.

This time I had plenty of help with my trailer and all the work that goes into prepping and loading. My strong and capable lover, now much more a part of my life, loaded Magdalena Pearl onto the trailer and locked everything down more securely than I ever would have. This, which I thought was overkill at first, would turn out to be an unexpected blessing. My sweetheart was the first angel to help me on this trip, one of many who would be there when needed.

The several months leading up to this ride had been unusually worrisome. COVID had filled everyone with fear, and I was getting well-meaning warnings every single day from almost everyone I knew. It seemed like everyone was fearing the worst, and I had to antidote their fear each time they wished me well. I had to remember they said these things because they cared—and remember that I was being careful and had skills. I also had to consciously refuse to give in to anxiety. I wasn't worried about COVID so much; after all, a full-face helmet is a pretty good face mask, but after a while, I inevitably felt myself being more fearful than usual. *Was I taking on too much? I'm four years older . . . over seventy now, but most days I don't feel older than sixty . . . am I being foolish? Am I going to crash and burn? Worse yet, am I going to crash and end up disabled for the rest of my remaining life? Am I really up to this?*

My boyfriend was worried. "It's a strange position to be in, Stacey," he told me one evening. "It's weird for me to be worried about a woman I love going out on a dangerous adventure and not being able to protect her . . . I haven't had to do that before."

I laughed at him. Not because he worried, because I knew that was a way of caring. But I replied, "You? You who loves taking risks? You who flies helicopters with long lines hanging out two hundred feet while you lean out to guide them? Well, it's about time for you to feel the other side of the coin here."

He understood. Worrying excessively about someone is kind of like casting a bad spell, almost encouraging something bad to happen. If you are aware of the power of your thoughts, you try not to put those worrisome ones out there in words. He never voiced his fear to me again, but he was right there to support me and make sure my rig was as safe as he could make it.

Still, I knew I had more anxiety about this adventure than I had ever felt before. Whether it was because of the scared soup we were all floating in, seasoned with COVID fears and vaccine fears and climate worries and mental/emotional health worries . . . I didn't know. I just knew that I was scared and finding it difficult to overcome the fear. There were many *What the fuck do I think I'm doing?* thoughts running around in my head during those weeks leading up to the ride.

Fear did not stop me, though. It rarely did. *As long as I am able, I will face fear head-on and attempt to banish it by succeeding anyway.* That was my plan for the Post-Pandemic Pandemonium Ride. Move forward, be as smart as possible, and don't be stupid. Fear would not win.

An easy drive from Sonoma County to Barstow lulled me into thinking this was going to continue to be easy. I'd forgotten that three days with a trailer is a long haul, but that first day went by without a single problem. Before hitting the road on the second-day haul, which would take me to Gallup, I went to the nearest Starbucks to load up with banana bread and a soy latte.

The desert was endless. I had a book on tape with plenty of suspense to keep me hooked, and folk-rock music I could sing along to, but nothing kept my attention very long. I ate to stay awake. Gas stations were few and far between there in the middle of the Mojave, and my gas tank was running on fumes the last few miles before finding fuel.

Then the check-engine light in my SUV came on.

Then road work stopped traffic. I mean *stopped.*

At least this gave me time to use my phone to look up a service dealer in Flagstaff. I made my way there, and glory be, the manager moved mountains to take care of me. An angel in a suit, he got his busy crew to diagnose the engine problem and said it was probably okay to keep going and get it fixed when I got back home—that it may even be under warranty. *Maintenance Required* was still lit up on my dash, but at least I quit worrying about the engine blowing up in the middle of nowhere. Back on the road, I wrote a haiku for the occasion.

Check-engine light on.
Challenges bring in angels
Coming to my aid.

After two eight-hour days of driving and one two-hour visit to the service department in Flagstaff, I finally found my hotel in Gallup, New Mexico, right next to the freeway. I pulled into the parking lot. That was the moment I realized that this place broke *Rule #1 of hauling a trailer when you are me: Never set up a situation where you have to back up your rig. Always find a pull-through.* Now, sitting there in the driver's seat and contemplating my options, I knew I was trapped. I was stuck in a dead-end parking lot full of cars with no way out other than backing up the rig somehow to turn it around. All I wanted to do was get out of the driver's seat. *This is not going to work. I can't do this now. Not tonight. Tomorrow morning. Tomorrow I will face that task.*

Leaving my rig at the end of a long row of parked cars, I rummaged in the back seat for food. Two gas-station packs of cookies . . . pistachios . . . turkey jerky . . . banana bread . . . banana . . . mandarin . . . trail mix . . . diet Dr Pepper. *Who could eat more?* Taking my found treasures, I headed into the motel, checked in, and made sure it would be okay to park my rig where I'd left it.

I was going to drink some twelve-year-old Glenlivet and vape my pen to see if they would change my point of view. At least I was in for the night, and I reminded myself it could have been worse. Much worse. I prayed for smooth sailing from there.

Prayers were in vain, however. I did drink that mini of Scotch. I did vape. And lying on the bed while watching a *Blue Bloods* marathon that I didn't have to pay attention to, I started to fall into a deep, exhausted sleep. Just as I was going down into that lovely place where you are still conscious enough to appreciate the falling, I heard a knock on my door. I thought it couldn't be, but then it came again. I considered ignoring it, but I realized I wouldn't get away with that, so I jumped up, stark naked, and grabbed for my long sweatshirt. Peeking through the peephole and half expecting, in my late-night-strange-hotel paranoia, to see a threatening figure out there, I discovered the woman from the front desk. I opened the door with the security latch still in place.

"Are you the owner of the white SUV and the trailer with the motorcycle?"

"Yes, that's me."

"You're going to have to move it. I know I told you that you could leave it there where it is, but we've had complaints from other guests. You'll have to move it. Now."

"It's 10:00 p.m. I can't move it now," I said, thinking of all the sleep substances I had just ingested. Thinking about how I was almost deep asleep a few moments ago. Thinking that I probably couldn't even do that job in the morning when well rested.

"You have to," she said and walked off.

I squelched my panic and went into that reserve place I found whenever I was a resident physician charged with the seemingly impossible. I steeled myself, shoving my fear and inadequacy into a locked compartment somewhere inside. Putting on some short leggings, I grabbed my keys and stumbled out the door, muttering *I can do this* thoughts to myself. I made my way to the rig, got in, and backed up—hoping to back into an open lane between parked cars, then turn and pull out the other way. But it was dark. There were cars parked everywhere I looked, and I couldn't tell if I was going to hit one of them. And the car and the trailer kept going in different directions. Without a spotter, this plan was not going to work. So I pulled forward, went around into the next lane, and tried to back and fill and turn my way out of that damn parking trap. I went forward, then back, then forward, then back—over and over—but never enough to free myself and get the hell out of there.

I could not stop trying; the woman had told me I had to move it. Finally, after almost an hour of trying, I sat there, my head resting against the steering wheel, and wondered how I was going to get out of this hell. I wanted to cry but I was too tired to find my tears. The least they could've done was to have someone come spot me . . . but no. I was out there all alone trying to do something I could not do.

Then a man came out of the darkness, asked me how I was doing, and offered to turn it around for me. I was only too grateful to let him take over, and in one smooth move, he had my rig turned around and headed in the *out* direction. He made it look so easy, and had I not been so grateful, I would have been mortified. I told him he was my angel, jumped in the driver's seat, and headed for the Hobby Lobby parking lot behind the hotel. That was where I had been told to park my rig. Not a great option, but it was now 11:00 p.m. in Gallup and I had no choice.

I drove out onto the street, around the corner, and into a completely empty parking lot as big as two football fields. I hated leaving my rig out there. Parking it under a light, next to a fire hydrant, I checked all the locks—once again thanking my honey for all his locking/safety/over-doing-it moves. Then I started hiking back over to the hotel, trying to find the back way onto the grounds so I could get back to my room and into bed. I was alone out there, feeling vulnerable as I walked along a fence line that separated three different looming hotels from one huge shopping center. This was a business park right off the I-40, absolutely deserted that time of night. It was surreal. Just when I thought I'd have to walk back out to the street and around to the front door, I heard a gentle voice in the dark.

"The gate is right here, ma'am."

I smelled cigarette smoke, and peering into the darkness, I saw the angel who had helped me turn my rig around. As it turned out, he was the security guard. "Oh! It's you again! Oh thankyousomuch!" I cried in one long, relieved breath, making my way through the little, almost invisible, gate and back into the hotel.

Inside my room again, I was wide awake. I needed to sleep, but after the last hour and a half of fear and frustration, sleep was not going to come easily. *Was I really up to this task of hauling Magdalena thousands of miles after a four-year hiatus?* This day had made me wonder. *Then actually riding her thousands of miles? Am I in over my head, but too far into it to back out now?* I knew that middle-of-the-night fear is almost always blown out of proportion. I knew I had to calm down the stress hormones, take some deep breaths, and talk to myself as my supportive spouse. *Now you just calm down, Stace. The rig is safe where it is, you are safe where you are, and you can do this. And . . . your angels still have your back. How 'bout that helpful dude? Pretty special . . . and you've been in worse situations . . . this is going to be okay.*

I finally closed my eyes, slept fitfully, woke early, and got the hell out of Gallup. I was back on my way to Joan and Kristin.

There they were at the end of their driveway, in the middle of the piedmont that is Arroyo Seco, waving me in. The sight of my two best biker buddies was just the tonic I needed at the end of that long haul. The hard part was over. I was with my crew, and now someone had my back. I was safe. We sat outside that night, eating a Greek salad picked fresh from their garden, looking out at the mountains that surrounded the beautiful plateau. They described how they'd found this new place, their forever home.

"It has the perfect house for us," Kristin said, "and a little casita guest house that is yours right now. And all sorts of outbuildings for our gear, including an art studio for Joansie's projects. We are feeling incredibly lucky."

I commented how far away they were from the Sea Ranch crowd and asked if they ever got lonely. Their answer was a resounding no. Then they asked if I still had the boyfriend I'd told them about at La Posada.

I was feeling at home and pretty comfortable by now as

the desert's evening sky deepened. "Yes, I do still have that man. And I am finally, completely, madly in love."

That got their attention. "Madly in love? Really, Stacey?" Kristin seemed to be searching my face for certainty.

"Yep, truly madly," I replied. I pulled out my phone and showed them photos of my sweetheart. They congratulated me on having someone in my life.

"So what does he think of you on this trip?" Joansie asked.

"He has accepted it, but I gotta tell you . . . *I've* been especially afraid of this trip, this time," I admitted.

They quickly agreed—they too had had reservations.

"I don't know why, but the anxiety has been more than before any of our other adventures . . ."

"We feel it too . . . and we can still back out," Joansie said. "We can spend this week here, do some local rides, and have a great time."

"That's true. We have options," I said.

But then we looked at each other, and with a big grin and putting out her hand flat and floating above the table, Kristin said she was still in. "Let's do this!"

I slapped mine on top of hers, and Joansie put hers on mine, and the three of us agreed. "We are *on* for the Post-Pandemic Pandemonium Ride!"

Nothing but big sky.
We ride straight into the clouds
Fleeing desert heat.

"Today we get to ride to Georgia O'Keeffe country," Kristin said over breakfast the next morning. "The house where she lived and painted is in Abiquiu; the light and colors of the desert there are going to be gorgeous." It was only about seventy-five miles to the Abiquiu Inn, and we had planned this first day to be short and easy. A warm-up day.

But it was a hot one, and the heat was intense—July in New Mexico. Fires were burning throughout the state, and the smoke made the mountains, which stretched in all directions, a soft blur. This was not the dramatic crystal-clear panorama I had anticipated. When we reached the Abiquiu Inn and realized we were early for check-in, we relaxed in the sculpture garden behind the main lobby and talked about angels. I told them the story of my trailer trials in Gallup, and Kristin said that wasn't the best place to layover.

"Well, you could've told me!" I replied. "Why'd you let me do that?"

"Aww, your reservations were made, and we figured you knew what you were doing," Joan said.

This had often been a common problem for me. I'd be so good at coming across with clear intent that sometimes even good friends couldn't see how open I might be to another point of view.

"It's okay that I stayed there. After all, I've had more than one angel already helping me on this adventure, and that's the stuff of magic that keeps me going."

After all these years, they were getting used to my talk of Spirit and angels and such.

"I consider my sweetheart an angel for helping me set that rig up safe and sound. And the man in the dark at the hotel in Gallup. And the service manager in Flagstaff who moved mountains to help me get back on the road . . . did you know he called me yesterday to make sure I'd made it to Arroyo Seco safely? That's a real angel!"

Joan and Kristin agreed that, if you look at it the right way, angels *are* present.

My room was so perfect for that first night out on the road that I laughed out loud as I entered it. The walls were a calming off-white with a burnt-sienna feature wall behind the glorious big bed. There were weathered wood accents, tile floors, a large open shower in the roomy bathroom, a fireplace shaped from cream-colored adobe opposite the bed, and a back door out to a shared courtyard with a fountain pouring cool water over its edge into a clear shallow pool. And on the wall above the bed hung an angel made of soft desert wood and carved with a gentle, benevolent face that seemed to be blessing whoever slept in that place. How right it all was! Chalk up another score for the angels! And when Joan and Kristin stopped by later, and saw the angel above my bed, they were definitely on board with me that angels just might have to be the theme of the ride.

The other magical component of this ride, I realized as we explored town that evening, was the permeating presence of Georgia O'Keeffe, who had always been dear to my heart. Yes, I liked her art. But one of her quotes had been hanging in my office for many years as an inspiration: "I've been absolutely *terrified* every moment of my life—and I've never let it keep me from doing a single thing I wanted to do." I read it almost every day, and it reminded me to keep going, to keep moving forward. As we walked past her home and witnessed the views of the mountains and the light that had inspired her so many years ago, I felt close to that woman and her spirit.

That second day, a route that would take us into Durango where Carolyn would be meeting us for dinner, turned out to be killer hot. The heat of the desert, the heat of our engines, and the heat coming up off the asphalt were all enough to fry my brain. I got a pipe burn on my right leg, right through my jeans, but I hardly noticed it since the air was as hot as the burn. It was a message to sharpen up in spite of the six-thousand-foot altitude and the temperature in the nineties. *Stay safe. Don't forget to drink water.*

That evening, I met up with Carolyn, and when I saw her walk in the door of the lobby, I felt love and joy rising in my chest as it did every time I saw this dear friend. Joan and Kristin soon joined us with a bottle of wine to share, and the four of us sat in the lobby of the hotel, easily starting up where we had left off the last time.

Later, as I lay in bed listening to the sounds of the street below my window, I knew I was a bit homesick. I missed my honey. I wanted to be in my lover's arms. I was also tired and hot and challenged—all expected, but oh boy, I could already have used a day off. After the long COVID year, I was out of shape and longed for some cooler temps and less challenge. But this was only the second day on the road, and this was the name of the game: we must rise to the challenges. My worries were right on schedule—the initial thrill of getting this far was gone, and now I waited for the thrill of future moments to take over. *I will rise to it,* I affirmed. *I know this place. I've been here every time we ride. I will make peace with the heat. I can do this.*

The next two days, we rode first to Ridgway, then to Basalt, and the heat remained intense. It seemed like every ten miles we would see a sign saying Road Construction Ahead, often making us stop on the hot asphalt while we waited for our turn to go. Engines off, helmets on, we would get off the bikes and take that time to check in with each other. We'd share the haiku we were all composing inside our helmets as we rode.

Two lessons learned on the road to Basalt: First, when it is so hot you can't take it anymore, lean forward into the bike for a few miles. Then, when you straighten up again, the sweat that you made in your fat rolls turns into instant air conditioning! You can do this over and over and it works every time.

And second: Kristin has a way of riding that is perfect for the leader. I know she is freaking out as much as I am, that she is as hot or cold, wet, scared, whatever as I am—but to look at her back as I ride behind her, all I see is contentment, and casual easy riding. She sits up straight, her slender form at ease in the saddle, sometimes putting her left hand down in her lap, looking around her as we pass interesting things. She exudes *I'm totally comfortable up here—no drama, no worries.* This is what I count on over and over as I follow her lead.

As on previous rides, we preened and checked ourselves out as we passed through small towns with countless reflective store windows. On open stretches of highway, we revved our engines and passed trucks and slow cars in the mountains, one by one, always coming back together in our tight threesome formation. When we finally arrived in Basalt, we used teamwork to park at the Frying Pan River Lodge, with heat, exhaustion, and gravel parking lots challenging the end of that day's ride.

A two-night layover in a beautiful little house right on the Fryingpan River was the perfect place to land. While Joan and Kristin celebrated their twenty-fifth anniversary with adventures that took them back out into the heat, I stayed by the river and basked in the luxury of my own time and my own thoughts. I found a large rock to perch on, right next to the water, and listened to the roar of the rapids. The heavy surrounding greenery was like a balm to my eyes after riding through miles of desert the last few days.

One evening, Joan and I were sitting out on the front porch in the warm night air with a bottle of good white wine, when Kristin came out to join us. As she set down a plate of cheese and fresh fruit, she said she'd been inside talking to her mother on the phone.

"My mom is doing pretty well, but I worry about her sometimes. It's hard to take care of family when we live so far apart." Both she and Joansie were at that age when we watch our parents get older . . . when they need more support . . . when we begin to face the inevitable.

"How long did your dad live after your mom died" Joan asked me. "Were you the only family he had left?"

Hers was almost an idle question, but my answer was not. My father's death was a momentous change in my own life, and as much as I'd struggled with that man, he was my father, and I knew I had a safety net as long as he was alive. With his passing, I grew up as a woman, as a doctor, and as the matriarch of my remaining family. Sitting there by the river in the long afternoon light, I told them about my father's dying, but I had to start by letting them know our relationship was never easy.

I spent a lifetime making peace with my father. He was a man who loved but did not know how to physically show it. He showed very little emotion, which may have been an asset in his profession as a naval intelligence officer—an intelligent man who played his cards so close that you didn't even know he was in the game. A spy. I longed for warmth. I longed for touch. He could not offer it.

Dad provided well, though. I was that special asset that was cherished, valued, and cared for like an expensive car. All maintenance done on time and no expense spared to keep it functioning well enough to perform up to its full potential. Excellent educational opportunities, timely health care, high performance expectations—all part of the maintenance package.

I once told a therapist about this experience. "It just makes me totally irritated when I do something as simple as ask him how he is! He says, 'Fine,' with that stupid smile and it doesn't mean a thing. It's hollow. I just want to *goose* him to get something *real* out of him! So frustrating!"

She leveled her eyes at me. "Don't ask him that. He obviously can't answer you, so Just. Quit. Asking."

That was the best advice given to me by one of many therapists I had seen over the years. She was so right. *Why hadn't I thought of this before?* I quit asking. I quit being so very angry with him. Instead, I accepted his limitations. He and I settled into a superficial yet significant relationship that had limits, set by his own inability to be honest or close with anyone. I wondered how my mother had survived a lifetime with this man and thought that maybe he was different with her. I would never know.

Now, Dad was dying. It was 2003, three years before I'd get my first motorcycle, which was good because me on a Harley might've stress-killed him right then. He'd been given amiodarone, a medication for his heart that destroyed his lungs, and after just a few months there was no way to reverse the damage. I had tended my mother when she passed five years before, and now it was Dad's turn. *Had I become a doctor/healer just to usher my own parents out of this world?* I was the one to honor him, and I knew I must be his daughter, a doctor, and a healer for him. This triple role was where my path had led.

One day, he made an unexpected request. "Stacey, I want you to kill me like you did your mother."

What? "I didn't kill Mother, Dad!"

"Well, it looked like you did," he replied, almost with a pout. Dad had not been at my mother's bedside during those final days, unable to handle anything as raw and honest as the death of a loved one. All he knew was that I was there, and I had allowed her to leave.

"Dad, I did not kill Mom. But I am here with you now and won't leave you alone. I promise." Unlike my mother, Dad wanted attendance, not privacy.

The day Dad finally died, I was in my office seeing a full day's schedule of patients. Between patients, I was on the phone searching for an extended-care facility where Dad could be cared for in comfort until he died. His lungs were destroyed, there was no chance of recovery, and setting him up in a five-star facility was the best I could do. The doctors had given him three months.

My cell phone rang, my boyfriend calling me from his work out of state. "Hey, Lady! How are you? What's going on?"

"My Dad is dying and I'm trying to run a business, see patients, and care for him. But it's so good to hear your voice . . . your timing is excellent. I miss you!"

"Well, then, I'm glad I listened to my Spirit guides, because I'm on my way to you. I'll be there tonight."

I breathed a sigh of relief. The thought of being held in his comforting arms right now was just what this doctor ordered.

The phone rang again. The hospital.

"Hello?" I answered.

"Dr. Kerr?" Dad's nurse. "Your father asked me to call. He says he's going to die today and wanted you to be here."

Now, to anyone who didn't know my father, this might have sounded like a wish, or maybe an attempt to gain sympathy. But my father spent his life controlling everything he touched, and his death was no different. I believed him. He had given the order. He would die today. Forget the care facility and get right on with the dying.

I answered the nurse with professional efficiency matching my father's request. "I'll be there within the hour."

After telling my staff to cancel the rest of the day, and the rest of the week, for that matter, I packed up and left my office to go to Dad's bedside. The hospital was just across town. As I drove, I called my daughter Sarah and my best friend to let them know this was the Day, and they both agreed to meet me there at his bedside. Cara lived a few states away, so she'd have to be with us in spirit only. We all arrived at the same time, walking into the private room to find Dad comfortable in a clean bed and glad to see us.

"I am ready to die," he said. "I see no reason to stick around in this condition when I can't even move my bowels anymore, so please help me."

This statement was a brave one for him to make—this man who had never acknowledged bodily functions in any way. This was a man desperate for a way out. The Captain was asking, but I took it as a direct order.

"Let me talk to your nurse, and I'll see what we can do. I'm working on this, Dad. We'll figure something out, okay?"

He smiled and gazed at me with a gleam of love in his eyes. "Your mother and I did a couple of good things in our life together. You were the best thing we did."

I did not know how to take this deeply felt sentiment he had laid at my feet. I was honored and knew it was the highest compliment he was able to give. I also was aware that I was still, even on his deathbed, a Thing. An asset. It was the only way he knew to look at his world.

Twenty minutes later, the nurse came into the room and gave Dad the first of what would be countless sips of oral morphine. Every ten minutes, for the next seven hours, she would come in. "Ed? Are you in pain?" Then, she'd look over at me.

I would nod. "Yes, it looks like he is in pain for sure."

And she would dose him again.

In between doses of morphine, we spoon-fed him Häagen-Dazs butter pecan ice cream. It was his favorite, and he had not been able to eat it for many years since he had been diagnosed as diabetic. The Captain was disciplined. But now sugar didn't matter, and the look of sublime pleasure on his face every time we chased the morphine with ice cream was priceless. Morphine and ice cream. Not a bad way to go.

The nurse promised to stay past her shift if necessary. That was the first warning I got of the conflict going on outside our room, outside this bubble of holy transition we had created. I told her I was grateful, even as I worriedly considered the battle that could loom if anyone chose to fight it.

We were well into the day of dying, and the afternoon sun was streaming through the window, when the door opened and a large, elderly woman energetically barged in, holding a flowering plant and a get-well card. Introducing herself as a friend from Dad's apartment complex, she was clearly unaware of the energy in the room.

"Ed! How are you?" she asked with robust cheerfulness.

It was surreal. We were in an altered state, in our own

intense reality of imminent death, and her cheerful presence
was jarring. I knew she had good intentions, but she had no
idea what was going on here. I switched roles—becoming
Mama Bear, or rather, protective Daughter Bear and assertive
physician all in one.

"Oh, thank you so very much," I said, placing the plant on
the windowsill. "Dad is sleeping right now." It was true. His
eyes remained closed.

She stood there for a moment, and I could tell she wanted
to wake him up so they could talk. She had driven for over an
hour to come visit and she wanted her say. But Dad was busy.
Dying.

I smiled a welcome at her while thinking frantically of
a way to get out of this without offense. My experience at
that time was more with birth than death, but the energy is
very much the same. I had asked people to leave a birth when
they were being obstructive, and I knew how to do it without
anger or shame. But this was different.

Quickly, I pulled a line out of an old movie. "I'm so glad
you were able to come. And now I would really like a bit of
time alone with my father. I have some things to say to him."

She bought my line as I knew she would, assuming she'd
watched plenty of old movies. Flustered, she looked down at
Dad's face resting peacefully, said her goodbyes, and, still a
bit unwillingly, left the room.

Everyone else left along with her. I had not expected
that, in spite of my manipulative line, but there I was. Alone
with my father. Expected to say some final important things.
Sacred space.

I did not know what to do. The words "You were the best
father I could've had, Dad," would not come. It wasn't true,
and I would not stoop to lying while he was on his deathbed.

He may have been a professional liar, but my spiritual practice was truth. I could not speak to the emotional neglect, to
the cold and controlling military expectations, to his rejection, or to the constant lies and secrets that came with his
work in military intelligence. What could I say that would be
true? What would be worth this momentous moment I had
manipulated?

Perched there on the edge of his bed, I searched for what
my father had done that was good in my life. I knew he loved
me. He had taught me discipline and skills such as how to
balance a checkbook and how to present a proposal. He had
funded my first college education. He had always made sure
our family had food, shelter, and basic needs. I sat there looking down at the face that had frustrated me for so many years,
and I said simply, "Thank you, Dad."

"Stacey. There's something wrong," he said, opening his
eyes with a dissatisfied frown.

"What is it, Dad?" I asked. I knew he had one foot on the
other side. "Do you see Mother?"

He scowled. "No," he said with clear disgust at my strange
assumption. "I am supposed to be *dead*."

The Captain to the end, he still expected orders to be carried out forthwith.

I quickly recovered my military persona. "You're doing it,
Dad. You're doing fine . . . just keep it up and you'll get there.
It takes a bit of time." I heard myself saying words usually
reserved for birthings.

He closed his eyes and said not another word.

Two hours later, after what seemed like endless doses of
morphine, our angel-nurse came in. "I know I told you I'd
stay even after my shift ended, but my sister just went into
labor and I have to go."

There we were—birth and death tangled into a knot—and who would help us with the dying now? The fight was on. The nurses on duty refused to help us. We had to find a team that would honor my father's wishes. We all sat there, waiting for resolution. Waiting for angels.

After an hour, the IV team leader came into the room. "I'm going to start an IV in your father," he said, and without another word to any of us he placed the IV in my father's arm. The tension and judgment in the room was palpable. He was followed by the nursing supervisor, who came in, agreeing to give Dad one single dose of IV morphine. No more. Only for pain. I was ready to take whatever we could get.

The IV morphine, slowly flowing into Dad's vein and chasing all the morphine already in his system, did the trick. The nurse left the room. Five minutes later, Dad stopped breathing. Forever.

I sat again on the edge of the bed, looking at the man who had shaped my life in ways I would still discover for years to come. I was not sad. I was moved, as transitions in life have always moved me. I was now an orphan. Nothing between the pearly gates and me. I was next in line. That weight settled on my shoulders.

Becoming the doctor that had made him proud, I pulled my stethoscope out of my pocket and placed it on his chest. One last time, I embraced him the only way he would allow, and I heard no sounds.

I went to his chart to write in it, to officially pronounce him dead. It was the most honorable thing I could do. My father's legacy was as alive as ever, and he died as he desired. I could do no more.

That night, when my boyfriend arrived, he held me long into the night. When he put his arms around me, I thought my heart would burst with love and gratitude. I had never felt this emotionally safe or cared for, and it was almost more than I could take. This angel, this kind and loving man, was holding me, when the first man I loved, my father, was never able to do that. For the first time, I was being held by someone who held my heart as well as my body, and I think that's when I fell deeply in love.

I took the last piece of cheese off the plate. "Dad's was a righteous death, and we had no regrets. After all, if you can't honor someone's choice at the inevitable end, then you aren't that honorable."

Kristin nodded in agreement, and then asked, with a twinkle in her eyes, whether that boyfriend who held me then was the one I was madly in love with now.

I laughed. "Yep. The very same. He still holds my heart."

I had finished my tale, the light had faded into dark, the wine bottle had been emptied. It was time to go inside, leaving the roar of the Fryingpan River and the gentle breeze behind. Content and at ease, we settled in for a good night's sleep and the promise of getting back on the bikes, on the road, tomorrow. We did not know that the next three days would give us challenges of a lifetime and miles of hard riding we could never have anticipated.

A hundred and fifty miles took us to Buena Vista the next day, and I had to admit the ride wasn't much fun. It was all about perseverance and fortitude. The weather turned from brutal heat to cold and wet. I had started the day with my leather jacket but soon had to stop to put on my rainsuit and a warm neck scarf. We rode through driving rain, getting pelted by trucks and semis going the other direction. My gloves got wet, and my fingers turned to ice. My rain pants were too short, and I melted them on Magdalena's hot pipes. I knew that was a risk, but frankly—with everything else to deal with—that was the least of my concerns. My boots also filled with water, soaking my socks and turning my toes icy. I changed to my heavy gloves. *Better.* Although not really warm, they at least allowed function to return to my fingers.

It was hard to see out of the helmet with water pouring down my face. I had to trust the road, trust Magdalena, trust Kristin and Joansie. My whole day ran on trust.

In spite of the challenges, we rode well. We passed excavators and slow-moving trucks, and we kept right on going through construction zones. We lived. We got to the hotel, where there was unlimited hot water. Thank you, angels.

If the road to Buena Vista seemed difficult, it turned out that riding from Cimarron to the Casa del Gavilan, two days later, was the ride of all rides. Deemed the Hardest Day of All Riding Days Ever. There was no doubt in my mind: med school was way easier than this!

Let me just start by saying that, for years, we would absolutely not ride on anything that wasn't paved. No gravel or dirt for us on our beautiful highway bikes! And it wasn't the cosmetics as much as it was our dubious ability to handle big highway bikes without a smooth surface under our wheels.

And let me add that I had always been a fair-weather rider. At home, Los Locks–style—if it was too hot or too cold, or if it looked like it could rain, I would choose not to ride. But out there, we had to take what came along and deal with it. That was part of the adventure. We'd outrun many a storm by seeing when and where it was coming and racing to shelter. Today, while riding to Casa del Gavilan, all that good fortune would catch up with us. We would be tested on those skills that we had been developing for the last fourteen years.

We knew it was risky when we left Cimarron. The sky was full of huge black thunderclouds to the west—the very direction we were headed. We hustled, and I layered on my leather chaps and rain jacket over my heavy leather armored jacket. After burning that hole in my rain pants, I decided not to put them on over my jeans and under my chaps. Too much trouble.

But, by putting all that other gear on my body, I was able to make room in my saddlebags for the burritos and chips we'd bought from a little burrito shack in Cimarron. Kathleen, the owner, was a vivacious blonde who built amazing custom burritos for a long line of hungry patrons, all while dancing to the music she played on her portable speakers and challenging her customers to name that song, which Joansie did every single time. Kathleen also packed a huge pistol on her right hip and a long-sheathed knife on her left. We hit it off with her right away and were happy to stock up on her burritos to take for dinner later that night at our hotel, just another five miles down the road. Taking one last look at the clear sky behind us, we jumped on the bikes and headed into the darkness with hopes of outracing one more storm. It was not to be.

I rode in the middle, behind Kristin. She was her usual assured self ahead of me, riding smoothly and giving me confidence through her riding style. Ahead of us, a huge black thundercloud loomed, and even without much knowledge of weather in the high desert of New Mexico, I knew this was a colossal threat. Looking in my rearview mirrors, I saw Joansie hunkered down on her bike, way back behind me on the long, straight, two-laned highway, her handlebar tassels flying. Behind her, the magnificent and massive New Mexico sky was filled with billowing white storm clouds against a vivid blue. I fervently wished my rearview mirrors had a camera function, but I could only take a picture for my memory. It was the last beautiful memory of that afternoon.

Joan is so tiny
Thunderclouds and sky so big
We are in for it.

The next thing I knew, rain started hitting my helmet and bike, making a racket like a whole set of drums. It turned into a fierce downpour, violent huge drops coming down fast and hard, hitting me with a force I'd never felt before. Each massive drop was like a strong finger poking at me, making me think I was doing something very wrong. Poke, poke. *Pay attention! What the fuck do you think you're doing out here in this kind of weather? You should be smarter than this!*

The deluge made it hard to see Kristin up ahead, and all I could do was keep moving forward at a slower speed, hoping all was clear ahead and no sudden moves would be needed. I wasn't comfortable with this, but I did have faith. In fact, I was running completely on faith right then—faith that Kristin knew what she was doing, that the road would not disappear completely, that Magdalena was up to this kind of ride, and that Joan was okay back there behind me. Faith that I could do this. Faith that there were angels watching out for us. I could no longer look to Kristin for confidence; I could barely see her through the downpour.

There was no other traffic on this two-lane highway; it seemed that everyone else had been smart enough to stay out of the storm. The road quickly flooded with the massive amounts of water coming out of that black cloud, which was now directly over our heads, and then the hail mixed in.

Where I had seen black pavement, now I only saw rushing water and a road that had become a river. My chaps were letting the rain in through my crotch, and soon my legs were soaked with cold water which I could also feel trickling down my neck and back. I was cold and wet all over in spite of my gear.

Okay, Stace, underneath the soaked leather chaps, under the jacket and the jeans and the boots and the sopping-wet silk liners, I am still me. I am a human being encased in skin, and inside that skin, I am warm and intact. The world may be a fucking wet mess, but I am okay. Or at least I will be when I get somewhere out of the weather.

The wind and the rain and the buffeting of the motorcycle made a roar inside my helmet that drowned out the roar of the thunder. It was a miracle we were not hit by lightning—it was all around us—we could smell it. Still, we kept on. Nothing else to do. There was no place to shelter, just empty fields on either side of the highway.

Finally, the barely marked entrance to Casa del Gavilan came up on the right. In the torrential rain, I got a glimpse of the sign, but we all missed the turn-in and rode on past. Sticking together, we kept riding into the downpour, looking for a place wide enough to turn around. It was another mile or so down the highway before we found a little gravel pull-off that would give us enough room to turn our massively loaded bikes around. Even that was a challenge—each of us maneuvering our bike alone, backing and filling, feet slipping on the wet gravelly pavement, no spotters. But we did it, and soon all three of us were facing back in the other direction.

Kristin gave me a hand signal: "Come up here next to me!"

I pulled up, leaned toward her, raised my face shield,

and heard her yelling at me through the rain. "I have no idea where that drive is! Did you see it?"

Seeing her confused, scared face right then, I knew that I had a chance of finding it on the way back since I did get a glimpse, so I took the lead. We set off again, and yep, there it was on the left now, the small sign facing us this time, so I was certain. I slowed, and grateful for the lack of traffic on this two-lane highway, turned left—only to find more challenges.

We now faced a four-foot-wide cattle guard with massive amounts of muddy water churning up out of it like brown vomit, and then, about ten feet in, a closed locked gate. Behind that locked gate was a very long dirt/hardpan/rocky road. A road being washed out by the violent storm. I didn't need ears to hear all three of us, inside our helmets, yell *"Fuck!"*

What could we do? Nothing other than forge ahead. We each rode slowly over the overflowing cattle guard and then stopped between that gushing flow and the locked gate. Kristin was closest to the gate control box, so she punched the contact button. Nothing happened. We had no code, and even if someone did answer our buzz, we couldn't have heard them. The pounding rain, the roar of our engines, and our helmets would have blocked any voice that might have tried to come out of that tiny speaker. We turned off our engines, and, with no place to go, we sat there in the rain, unsure what to do next. I mean, we'd always risen to challenges, but what would have been the right move for this one? We looked at each other, heavy helmeted heads nodding and bobbing, expressing WTF emotions without any answers. *I am numb. I am only able to keep Magdalena upright in place, and not at all feeling like I can problem solve in this moment.*

Then, looking up the drive, we saw headlights coming

our way. Through the dark rainstorm, someone was driving out toward the gate, toward us! As the vehicle came closer, we identified it as a FedEx truck. Joan, who had already left her bike to go help Kristin at the control box, walked over to a little side gate, unlatched the chain, and made her way around to connect with the driver. She looked like a little walking wet Jack in the Box with her helmet still on and her head nodding as she talked with FedEx. After a quick conversation, the main gate automatically opened for the truck, and he pulled over far enough to let us pass. *Good. FedEx angel lets us in the gate.* I silently chalked up one more save to angels.

Joan quickly got back to her bike, mounted, and started her engine to follow us through. Oops—she needed to put it in gear, and by the time she had the bike revved and ready, the gate had already started slowly closing. *Shit!* But the FedEx driver saw the same thing and moved his truck back and forth to trigger a reopening. Grateful for his awareness and help, Joan finally made her way through.

Now the really hard part started. Our bikes were made for highways, and this was definitely off-road riding. The drive was flooded with muddy rainwater, and what wasn't a lake was a slippery surface of sand and fine gravel that created a slurry. It was like riding through warm peanut butter. The rain continued to pour down as hard as ever, and we kept looking for the high-dry sides, but there were none. Kristin, ahead of me, veered off the drive to ride on the grass, but that looked even more slippery than the slurry. I didn't even try to follow her lead there.

I eventually lost sight of her and could only focus on the surface directly in front of me. *Got to keep going at a speed good enough to keep me upright.* Crops of rocks the size of grapefruits started showing up, and there was nothing to do but ride right over them, every bone in my body and every part of my bike rattling with the force. The rocks threw Magdalena off balance and we caught air, coming down to one side or another, grabbing traction when we could. *Keep moving forward. Because forward drive is all we have to keep us upright.* I simply had to keep gunning the engine to get past the next lake, the next slurry, the next rock outcropping.

At one point, I felt Magdalena shimmy out of control. Her front end was moving in one direction, shimmying to the left, while the back end moved in another, and the whole motorcycle started to tip over to the left, ready to fall into the mud and water. Images raced through my head of my beautiful bike lying in the rain. All my belongings soaked and muddy and ruined for the rest of our trip. And me, standing next to my downed Magdalena, drenched while waiting for a rescue that could take hours to come. Pissed at the situation we'd gotten ourselves into, I angrily gunned the engine to catch some traction, and we were again upright, still moving forward. In my early days of riding, this had been really hard to do—to gun the engine when feeling unstable—but slowing down was exactly what I didn't want to do now because then I would have fallen over. *Stay upright. Keep the power up in spite of fear.* Best lesson of the ride.

I didn't know how long it took us to make that run. Five minutes . . . ten minutes . . . a half mile . . . a mile or more. I would later find out that we rode 1.2 miles through that slick to get from the gate to the Casa, but it seemed like a lifetime. We all, finally, did make it to the front of the inn in one piece, arriving like drowned, shocked, traumatized rats. As we stood under the shelter of the inn's portico, I knew that I never wanted to do that again. I was also proud of us for being able to handle it, and I felt as tightly bonded with

Magdalena Pearl as you can be to a motorcycle. She and I had survived hard times together, and I loved her for it. And I wasn't ashamed of loving a machine. Not at all.

How to stay upright
Just keep going and don't stop
Works on bikes and life.

That was the perfect challenge at the perfect time, and the Casa del Gavilan, a serene, healing space, was exactly what we needed for the last night of this adventure where we could recover and dry out, and where angels were present at every turn.

I was restless in my sleep that night and woke at two thirty in the morning. Taking advantage of the dark desert sky, I ran outside to look at all I could see. There I stood beneath the clear sky in the middle of the night, all alone, in my nightie and hoodie sweatshirt, studying zillions of stars and constellations. Scorpius. The Big Dipper. And another amazingly bright star—planet?—in the southeast. The next morning, I ran back outside again, this time to see the sunrise, forgetting to put on my shoes. Didn't matter. It was beautiful. Alone at sunrise, one more morning to enjoy before we parked the bikes for who knew how long.

The next day we white-knuckled the ride back to the highway, through the slurry that had dried up a little overnight, and once we were on pavement, I breathed a sigh of relief that could've been heard coast to coast. From there, we rode along the Red River, over Bobcat Pass, and back to Arroyo Seco. This time, we beat the weather, skirting huge thunderstorms on the surrounding horizon. I thought that our dues had been paid and then some; we had credit in that bank. We were resilient. We rode with joy. We wrote more helmet haiku.

Must pass slow RV
Pronghorn leaps across the road
We are all okay.
—J

Our final night together, back at Joan and Kristin's place just outside Taos, was bittersweet. They helped me load Magdalena back on her trailer and we tied her down as tightly as possible. Probably not as good a job as my sweetheart had done, but I figured it was good enough to get me safely home. Then, because all three of us were craving it, we ordered sushi to-go, which Joan would pick up on her way back from retrieving Macy, their beloved dog, from the dog-sitter. We chowed down together one more time, but I could tell that Joan and Kristin were quickly moving back into the pattern of their lives there on the mesa, and I needed to pack for my drive northwest. I wanted to go home to my love.

Even as tired as I was, I still had to run outside in the dark early morning hours for my last chance to see that glorious New Mexico sky full of stars—a darkness undiluted by the lights of the city, unobstructed by clouds—a view that opens my heart and mind to the mysteries of the Universe. Arroyo Seco was on the Taos Plateau, a huge, open volcanic field along the Rio Grande Rift, and so very different from the coastal redwood forests of my own home territory. Standing one more time out in the gentle, warm breezes of the night, I felt close to the Source. I felt nurtured as I had in Zion, in the Grand Canyon, in Arches, in Cimarron, along the Rogue River in Oregon, and in so many other places we had visited together on our adventures. I felt gratitude for my ability to go on adventures like this one with Joan and Kristin.

This last ride had pieces and reminders of all the other rides we had done together. The red rocks in Georgia O'Keeffe country reminded us of Red Rock Roar. When it rained, we remembered the rain of Redwood Rogue (Rain) Run. Stopping at Lizard Head Pass gave us echoes of time spent on the Tohelluride Tour, and riding through high-desert thunderstorms took us back to Call of the Canyons. This, our seventh ride, had elements that pulled all the others together in a thread, tying them into one long chain of challenges and magnificent adventures. Challenges we had met and escapades we would never forget. We did not know if we would do another ride. For now, basking in the memories just made, and congratulating myself on yet another successful run, I would be content.

I am not done with challenges. I have more adventures ahead, and I don't plan to stop anytime soon. I will continue to look for the angels that have been there for me as long as I can remember. My mother's spirit, her creativity, and her sense of adventure have played out in my life as they were never able to do in hers. For that I am grateful. I may have been born into the wrong family, but she was the right mother for me. Even so, back when I realized she was cooking three meals a day every single day of our lives, I sat down and did the math. I must have been twelve or thirteen at the time. I figured if I lived to be eighty years old, and got married when I was twenty, that would mean sixty years of cooking three meals a day. That's 65,700 meals. And while I honor those who can live that kind of life, that may have been the day I decided to do my own life differently. In time I'd grow up, become a hippie, and join a commune. I'd rather roll a foot-tall stack of tortillas once a week, without access to running water or electricity, than serve three balanced meals a day for a lifetime. I'd rather deliver a baby or give comfort to the dying than continually clean my house or go shopping. I'd rather ride Magdalena Pearl all afternoon than stay home and cook dinner. I'd rather make wild passionate love with my lover while married to myself than settle into a marriage of need or convenience.

I will keep riding. I will keep the throttle on and stay upright as long as I can. I will be passionate in love and righteous in work, and I will continue to do what I can to make this world a better place. I will live by my own rules, and I will remain free. I will live this one life I've been given to the fullest of my abilities, leaving nothing on the table when I go. No regrets. Full throttle.

ACKNOWLEDGMENTS

This book is a labor of love, and much of that love came from some very special people. I would never have written the first draft had it not been for Tanya Taylor Rubinstein, who, in her magical mentoring and her gentle wisdom, allowed me to find my way into telling this story with truth and spirit. Lennie Dean, my dear friend and acting coach, opened my heart to feeling again. By telling me the truth at every step of the way, she allowed me to open my heart to you, the reader. Sarah Kate was kind enough to let me tell some of her own story, and I thank her from the depths of my heart. Joan and Kristin—so generous on the road—this book would not have been possible without their support and deep friendship. And Tim. Tim who taught me to be brave on two wheels, who opened doors to adventures I had never imagined would come true.

Stacey Marie Kerr, MD, has practiced family medicine, including obstetrics and surgery, in Sonoma County for over thirty years. Dr. Kerr is an educator, a physician, a mother, a grandmother, and an adventurer. She has published essays in *FringeWare Review*, the *Sun*, and *JAMA*. For five years she wrote a medical column in the *Santa Rosa Press Democrat*, and she has written on the safe and appropriate use of cannabis as medicine for the blog *Hawaiian Ethos*.

Dr. Kerr has combined her experience with homebirths on The Farm with a passion for preserving a woman's power when giving birth in the hospital. This philosophy became the basis for her first book, *Homebirth in the Hospital*, where, through dramatic birth stories, Dr. Kerr encourages women's self-empowerment in their birthing experience, no matter where that birth occurs. Dr. Kerr has lectured across the continental US on birth empowerment.